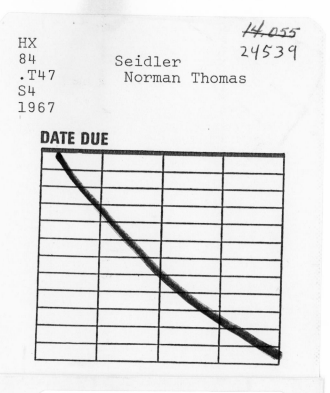

DATE DUE

NORMAN THOMAS

Respectable Rebel

Men and Movements

Men and Movements

The Technocrats, Prophets of Automation
HENRY ELSNER, JR., 1967

Vito Marcantonio, Radical in Congress
ALAN SCHAFFER, 1966

Father Coughlin and the New Deal
CHARLES J. TULL, 1965

Eugene V. Debs, Socialist for President
H. WAYNE MORGAN, 1962

Conscience in Politics: Adlai E. Stevenson
in the 1950's
STUART GERRY BROWN, 1961

Gifford Pinchot, Bull Moose Progressive
MARTIN L. FAUSOLD, 1961

Henry A. Wallace: Quixotic Crusade 1948
KARL M. SCHMIDT, 1960

Oswald Garrison Villard, Liberal of the 1920's
D. JOY HUMES, 1960

NORMAN THOMAS
Respectable Rebel

+++

Murray B. Seidler

SYRACUSE UNIVERSITY PRESS

In memory of my father,
who greatly admired the subject of this book

Murray B. Seidler, who received a D.S.S. degree from Syracuse University, is Associate Professor of Political Science in Wayne State University.

Preface

AT THE TIME the first edition of this book was written, no other extended published treatment of the leadership of Norman Thomas existed. Now, in its second edition, this book remains unique in its attempt to interweave the development of the political career of Norman Thomas with the history of the Socialist party in America. While retaining and updating the material in the first edition, this volume adds a chapter focused on the role Mr. Thomas plays in contemporary American society; here his attitudes and activities in the 1960's are discussed. The bibliographical section of the book has also been updated to include the recent publications by and about Mr. Thomas that were used in research for the second edition. In addition to examining the recent published literature, I have reviewed recent deposits to the Norman Thomas Papers in the Manuscript Division of the New York Public Library and have had the pleasure of interviewing Mr. Thomas while preparing the second edition of this book.

The publication of this book is not difficult to justify. By any standard, Mr. Thomas is one of the most important public leaders of our time. A more personal motivation, which should be revealed at the outset, is that I have long held a deep personal affection and admiration for Mr. Thomas. I have known him since my childhood, when he first became my hero, and confess that throughout the preparation of this work I have felt like a pygmy writing about a giant.

Yet let it be crystal clear that this is in no sense an official account of Norman Thomas. In countless ways, Mr. Thomas has been unfailingly and graciously helpful, as is more specifically acknowledged in later pages, but he did not suggest that I write this book, nor did he read it prior to publication.

The problem of achieving objectivity concerning the career of a contemporary figure, who has devoted himself to unpopular causes, is in itself overwhelming. And it must be admitted that my personal attachment to Norman Thomas has made a difficult problem more difficult. Yet it must also be said that I have attempted at every turn to guard against my personal bias. About my success, the reader will have to judge for himself. If my personal relationship with Mr. Thomas complicates the problem of attaining objectivity, it also carries with it the possibility of understanding him more completely.

This study emphasizes the public rather than the private life of Norman Thomas. I have concerned myself with his private affairs only insofar as they seemed relevant to his role as a political leader. I have not attempted to write a biography in any orthodox sense.

There is no final answer as to what should be emphasized in a study of political leadership. Many authors have written about leaders largely in terms of personality traits. While these traits are obviously important, it should be remembered that there is no personality make-up which functions equally well in all situations. Different social groups require and develop different kinds of leadership. Essentially, the careers of political leaders have to be comprehended in terms of the reciprocal relationships that exist between them and their followers. No leader—not even the most dictatorial—is a free agent. Every leader must constantly make adjustments to the expectancies of the group he attempts to lead.

Thus I have examined Mr. Thomas' behavior in terms of the major situations that have confronted him as the foremost leader of the Socialist party. The culture of American socialism—the shared attitudes and traditions of its participants—constituted an ever-present situation in terms of which Mr. Thomas had to behave. A basic frame of reference for this study has been that the American socialist culture is unique and set apart from the general American culture. The socialist culture is discussed implicitly throughout the entire book and explicitly in Chapter IX. The other situations that provide the framework for this study are somewhat more tangible in nature. They are: fascism, communism, the New Deal, the upsurgence of labor, the outbreak of World War II, and the quest for peace in a nuclear era.

Other acknowledgments may be found in the sources for this book, but I should like to point out here that my father, the late Emanuel Seidler, to whom this book is dedicated, contributed greatly to my understanding of American socialism in the course of our long and frequent conversations about politics. I am also very grateful to my wife, Judith, for help with some of the basic research tasks, and to my mother, Ida Seidler, who made many admirable suggestions for improving the style of this book. I should like to thank also the Wayne State University Research Committee and the American Council of Learned Societies for generous financial assistance, which furthered the development of this study in important ways. I am also indebted to the secretarial staff of the Political Science Department of Wayne State University for much assistance far beyond the call of duty. For errors in fact or judgment I, of course, am exclusively responsible.

MURRAY B. SEIDLER

Detroit, Michigan
December, 1966

Contents

Preface vii

I. A Christian Road to Socialism 1

II. Setting the Stage 30

III. A Leader Emerges 69

IV. The Roots of Factionalism 104

V. Fratricidal Warfare 125

VI. The All-Inclusive Party 171

VII. From War to Peace? 212

VIII. Plenty, Peace, and Freedom 251

IX. "Successful Failure" 294

X. Epilogue 318

Chapter References 343

Sources 360

Index 385

NORMAN THOMAS

Respectable Rebel

Chapter I

A Christian Road
to Socialism

THE PLACE was the Starlight Room of the Waldorf-Astoria; the date, November 18, 1959; the occasion, the celebration of a seventy-fifth birthday. Some eight hundred people were in attendance. Eleanor Roosevelt and Norman Cousins headed the long list of sponsors, which read like a Who's Who of the political and intellectual elite of America. The list abounded with names of persons who were at the very top of their respective fields. It included past and present United States senators, congressmen, governors, university presidents, journalists, poets, novelists, editors, publishers, union presidents, industrialists, and distinguished scholars from virtually every field.

The guest of honor rose to address this large audience of admirers. It was hard to find a taller man in the room. His striking height; his aristocratic bearing; his long, thin, sensitive face; his lively blue eyes; his sparse, snow-white hair—every feature, every move seemed to give the correct impression that here was an elder statesman. He looked the part of a leader, an overpowering personality, the center of any group.

His commanding voice matched his commanding presence. Obviously, he was deeply moved, but in no sense was he flustered. The experience of facing thousands of varied audiences and the reputation for being one of America's most brilliant orators had given him a supreme platform self-confidence. He spoke, eloquently and earnestly, indeed passionately, on "A World without War," the subject which had been closest to the heart and mind of Norman Thomas for almost half a century. He received a standing ovation.

To the audience he was addressing and to millions of his fellow countrymen Thomas has become America's "Mr. Socialist." The dubious distinction of having run, unsuccessfully, six times for the Presidency of the United States, more often than any other man in American history, belongs to him. Yet, had he been willing to make the necessary compromises and joined one of the major parties, election to high political office might well have been his. Considering his great personal magnetism, plus his outstanding physical, intellectual, oratorical, and literary powers, even the Presidency was not beyond the realm of possibility.

Though he never occupied the White House, from time to time he called on presidents, invariably in an attempt to right some wrong. In 1935 he met with Franklin Delano Roosevelt in order to impress upon him the inadequacy of the New Deal's Agricultural Adjustment Act in meeting the problems of the poverty-stricken sharecroppers. On this score, the President did not defend his administration with any great vigor but said, "Norman, I'm a damn sight better politician than you." Thomas retorted, "Certainly, Mr. President, you're on that side of the desk and I'm on this." [1]

In his biography of Grover Cleveland, Allan Nevins, the eminent biographer, has suggestively written of two types of political leaders. The one is the person of average talents who makes outstanding use of the capacities that he possesses; the other is the unique individual who brings to his leadership role striking gifts and brilliance. In his own career Norman Thomas has displayed qualities and powers of personality so original that he has undoubtedly earned a lasting place in the latter category.

A Minister's Son

No observer of Thomas as a child, or even as a young adult, could have predicted the political role that he would one day play; yet to fathom America's leading Socialist, one must take into account his formative years. The mold for these years was fundamentalist Protestantism, from which he has long been estranged, but apart from which he cannot be understood. For better or for worse, his was a Christian road to socialism.

Thus he "was not born or reared a socialist." [2] In most ways his boyhood experiences were typically those of a Protestant minister's son who was brought up in a small midwestern community during the closing years of the nineteenth century. Born on November 20, 1884, at Marion, Ohio, he was the eldest of the six children of Emma Mattoon and Welling E. Thomas. Until his graduation from Marion High School in 1901, he continued to live in the city of his birth.

Marion has no particular claim to fame except that it was the home of Warren Gamaliel Harding. In Thomas' memory it was no less a typical small town than Muncie, Indiana, upon which Robert and Helen Lynd based *Middletown,* their classic work of sociological investigation. During the seventeen years that Thomas lived there Marion's population expanded from approximately 6,000 to 12,000. It was something of a farming, railroad, and factory center, with some reputation for the production of steam shovels. Thomas recalls Marion with no great fondness but as a youth was a "loyal Marionite." [3]

In many ways his youth typified that of the all-American boy. He was the president and outstanding student of his high-school graduating class. He loved animals and was very much interested in athletics. He even sold newspapers for the Marion *Star,* which at that time was owned by Harding. But the latter never commanded the admiration of this younger Marionite, who was also destined to fame. "It was his misfortune," concluded Thomas, in later years, "and his country's, that, especially after his wife and Harry Daugherty persuaded him to go to a good tailor, he looked like the American ideal of a statesman." [4]

The atmosphere of the home of his childhood was distinctly middle-class and fundamentalist Protestant. His father and both grandfathers were Presbyterian ministers. His paternal ancestors arrived in America during the 1860's, and his maternal ancestors arrived here during the seventeenth century. The Thomas family lived a frugal life, but they never knew desperate poverty. Perhaps the family's most important possession was an adequate library, though Norman was to remember it as being "too long on old-fashioned theological books." [5] Nevertheless, in a home where books were treasured, he established a lifelong habit of omnivorous reading.

He remembers himself "as a rather bookish type, too tall, too awkward, somewhat self-conscious, probably tending to compensate by an interest in studies." [6] One of his brothers recollects that "everyone was always telling you how bright he was." [7] He looked so painfully thin and appeared so ill that some neighbors told his mother, in his presence, that they doubted he would survive childhood. This sense of being a sick child marred the happiness of his early years, but, when he was of high-school age, he was healthier and happier.

There is no evidence that would support the kind of theory —so often advanced in interpretations of radicalism—that Norman Thomas was drawn to social-reform politics as a way of easing neurotic conflicts arising from his home situation. There was no marked revolt against the authority of his father or mother. Indeed, his parents enjoyed an unusually harmonious relationship with each other and their children. His early recollections are not only devoid of bitterness but are those of one who "adored" his family.[8] To an unusual degree he felt love, respect, and admiration for his parents.

As has already been said, Welling E. Thomas and Emma Mattoon were both the children of ministers. Grandfather Thomas was born in Wales but came to the United States as a child. After graduating from Lafayette College, he was a minister for long years in Bradford County, Pennsylvania. According to his grandson, he was "a man of few words, of simple devotion to a stern Calvinistic creed, . . . and father to a whole countryside." [9] Norman was thrilled when this old patriarch, not given easily to praise, sent him a congratulatory note. The occasion was the defeat of Harvard by the Princeton debating team of which the grandson was a member.

Emma's father, the Reverend Stephen Mattoon, enjoyed a more illustrious life than grandfather Thomas. He spent his youth in Jefferson County, New York. Via teaching, he worked his way through Union College at Schenectady, New York and the Princeton Theological Seminary. For twenty years Reverend Mattoon and his wife pioneered as Presbyterian missionaries in Siam. The Mattoons are favorably alluded to in *Anna and the King of Siam*. After returning from Siam, Stephen Mattoon was for several years attached to the Presbyterian church

in Balston Spa, New York. His greatest achievement, however, from the viewpoint of his crusading grandson, was that
he was founder and president of Biddle University (now Johnson Smith University), a Presbyterian Negro college at Char-
lotte, North Carolina. A graduate of that institution once told
Norman Thomas that he had held the Mattoons in high esteem
but added that the most dreaded mode of discipline on the
campus was to have "Mrs. Mattoon pray over us." [10]

Rigid puritanism was probably more pervasive in the homes
of both sets of Norman's grandparents than in his own boyhood
home. Yet his parents, the Reverend Welling Thomas and his
wife, did not depart in any significant way from the religious
orthodoxies that they had learned as children.

A graduate of Lafayette College and the Princeton Theological Seminary, Norman's father carried on God's work during
most of his career in the religiously conventional settings of
Marion, Ohio and Lewisburg, Pennsylvania. Certainly, the religious and political heresies that his eldest child was one day
to embrace bore no direct relationship to his pattern of belief.
He was a fundamentalist in religion and a Republican in
politics. A competent minister, a highly literate and scholarly
person, an effective if not a brilliant speaker, he was a much-
respected member of the communities in which he lived.

Emma Thomas was the dominant figure in the family, and
her husband was quite willing that it should be so. She was not
bossy but used love—not always wisely—as a way of controlling
her offspring. She did not exert this control directly. Her usual
way of getting her children to hew to the puritan line was her
insistence that "father wasn't to be hurt." [11] In the eyes of
Norman she was a more remarkable and more intelligent
person than her mate. She played a very important role in the
actual administration of her husband's church. Emma Thomas

was a graduate of Elmira College. Alone, the fact that she was a college graduate must have set her somewhat apart from the women of her day.

Both parents were deeply immersed in community affairs and gave serious thought to the great world issues and problems of their time. They were also concerned about problems of a lesser magnitude. Their stern puritan code would not permit dancing, card playing, or Sunday frivolity. But, according to their eldest son, they had "a fund of kindness and tolerance for the departure of people in general from their orthodox moral and theological creed that they did not expect to need for their own children." [12]

Emma was inclined to be more liberal in her theology than her husband; yet, rather paradoxically, she was later more concerned at Norman's changing religious outlook than was her husband. The probable explanation is that she feared that she might be carried along in her son's direction; whereas Welling, who was more secure in his orthodoxy, felt no such apprehension. Her son's abandonment of orthodoxy in religion doubtless concerned her more than his embracing of socialism. She could understand abiding by a principle, but the acceptance of card playing was beyond the limits of her tolerance.

The Thomas family had no real perception of the fact that Norman would one day become so prominent. His brother Evan put it this way: "We weren't supposed to become famous; we were brought up to be good. Success was not a goal in our family." [13]

Princeton and Woodrow Wilson

Just after Norman's graduation from Marion High, the Thomas family moved to Lewisburg, Pennsylvania, where

Norman enrolled at Bucknell University. In him Bucknell gained no booster; he found that "its standards were low, most of its extracurricular activities poor, and its cultural atmosphere almost nonexistent." [14] But he concedes that it has improved greatly since his time.

It had long been his dream to attend Princeton, America's most important Presbyterian institution of higher learning, where both of his grandfathers and his father had attended seminary. A four-hundred-dollar subsidy from a prosperous uncle by marriage enabled him to spend his last three college years at Princeton. This financial aid did not cover the costs of even his first year; but, by working diligently at tutoring and part-time summer jobs, and by practicing rigid economy, Norman managed to scrape his way through without any further subsidization. The generosity of the same uncle also made it possible for the three younger Thomas brothers to attend Princeton.

Insofar as scholastic standards were concerned, Norman was only slightly more impressed by Princeton than by Bucknell. Nevertheless, he fell in love with the place, and his fondness for it has remained unabated through the years. He was a remarkably brilliant student, placing in the "first group"—the equivalent of an all "A" record—in every subject that he took during his Princeton years—a record which his children always viewed with some discomfort. He graduated as the valedictorian of the class of 1905. His extracurricular involvements included debating, orchestra, and singing.

Raymond B. Fosdick, later to be president of the Rockefeller Foundation, was among Thomas' close college friends. Both boys were members of the varsity debating team, and their mutual enthusiasm for forensic contests drew them together.

On occasion they even debated against one another, especially
when monetary prizes were awarded, for Fosdick also faced
a financial struggle to get through his Princeton years. They
were pretty well matched as debaters and doubtless represented
the best that Princeton had. They both recall, however, a dismal verbal contest known as the French Medal Debate. Apparently, the ground rules were that the subject would be some
aspect of French life and politics and that the actual topic
would not be announced until the day before the debate. Both
young men were totally ignorant of things French, and their
quick excursions to the library did not enlighten them very
much. Fosdick was granted the prize, as his performance was
slightly less bad than Thomas', but only after it was announced
that in the "considered opinion of the judges it was the worst
debate that they had ever listened to." [15]

In *Chronicle of a Generation,* Fosdick recalls Norman
Thomas, who was the outstanding student of their Princeton
class, as being fundamentally more conservative on practically
all questions than he. "Theologically," reports the man who
was to manage millions of Rockefeller dollars, "I was far more
radical than he, and it never occurred to me in those days that
a time might come when his position on anything would be
further to the left than mine. I remember trying, without too
much success, to get him interested in Frank Norris' two novels,
The Octopus and *The Pit.* . . . As I look back on our college
lives together, I am amazed at the limited interest Norman and
I had in economic questions. . . . The consciousness of aroused
social forces, of new conceptions of justice that were struggling
to be born, had not penetrated the academic seclusion in which
we lived. The impact of these fresh ideas on the eager mind of
Norman Thomas had to wait for a later period and for a more

hospitable climate than the Princeton of our day." [16] "Why Socialism Ain't So," is Thomas' summary of one of his economics courses at Princeton.[17]

Though he does "not consider in retrospect that the educational standards were too good," he feels a debt of gratitude to his alma mater.[18] He writes and talks of Princeton with much more feeling than of Marion or any other place. "Princeton," he admits, "meant very much to me. It opened doors and I was a very loyal Princetonian. I still think of it with a great deal of kindness. It opened doors in spite of the fact that I don't think that some of the door keepers were too good. It opened doors intellectually, though less than I could have wished; my education was somewhat of a delayed reaction." [19]

Lack of notable economic or social-class credentials proved to be no particular handicap in developing relationships with his college classmates. To his "surprise," he discovered that "Princeton boys were just like other folks only at that period worse dressed in corduroys and jersey often stiff enough with dirt to stand alone." [20] Princeton's Philadelphian Society—a YMCA club—was one of his basic avenues of extracurricular expression. To his great and unexpected pleasure—as he has candidly confessed—he was also elected to the more exclusive Colonial Club during his last year at the institution. "It didn't make a snob out of me," he insists, "but it did in later years give me a curious confidence that if I espoused unpopular causes it wasn't some personal incapacity for ordinary social success which drove me to them." [21] It can be said, emphatically, that Thomas did not decide to remake the world because nobody would dance with him.

Any account of Norman Thomas at Princeton would be incomplete without mention of his political science professor-who was destined to become president of the United States. "No man made a deeper impression upon my youth than Woodrow Wilson," writes Thomas. "I was his admiring pupil at Princeton. I even tried, unsuccessfully, to model my public speaking on his." [22] But even as a student he was not an uncritical admirer of his "favorite professor," and his appraisal of Wilson eventually became rather negative. Yet he continues to delight in reminiscing about Wilson as teacher and President. "When looking back on a wide experience with orators," Thomas recalls the late President as "the speaker I most liked to hear. Now when I read over some of his speeches I wonder that he or they could have moved me as they once did. But I have heard him . . . address a predominantly hostile audience of students and alumni and move them to enthusiastic cheers. I must add that in most cases the conversion was impermanent. But that is a common experience with orators." [23]

Thomas found in Wilson, the professor, intellectual and personality shortcomings which later proved to be deficiencies in Wilson, the President. He feels that his Princeton mentor's political theory, interests, and knowledge were too narrowly confined to the British parliamentary system. "His masters were Burke and Bagehot. He had little to say about Jefferson or Hamilton and nothing about Marx. . . . His illustrations were rarely drawn from countries east of the English Channel and never east of the Rhine." [24] In Thomas' view, moreover, Wilson's understanding of the historical process was seriously limited because he did not sufficiently recognize the impact of economic forces.

Thomas also questions whether his professor was temperamentally fit for high political office in a democratic society. "To disagree with Wilson was to take a great risk." [25] "All his public life he was inclined to take strong opposition or criticism as a sin against the Holy Ghost. He was sorely hurt by it." [26]

Minister to the Poor

Upon graduation from Princeton, Norman followed in the tradition of his family and became involved in church work, as was to be expected. His ultimate goal was ordination in the Presbyterian ministry. First, however, he went to New York and took a job at the Spring Street Presbyterian Church and Settlement House, which was located in a very poor and tough neighborhood. "Poverty was very great," he recollects, "strong liquor the chief escape, and much of the neighborhood was lost in a kind of sodden apathy to which drunken quarrels brought release." [27] His association with the Spring Street Settlement House marked the beginning of more than a decade of ministering to men's bodies and souls in poverty-stricken areas of New York. During these years Norman Thomas became certainly as much social worker as minister.

Firsthand experience with urban poverty apparently had a tremendous impact upon this sensitive and extraordinarily intelligent young man. Much of what he saw seemed far removed from the theories that he had been taught by his Princeton professors of politics and economics. But he did not immediately abandon their teachings and for a while was considering writing "a book refuting socialism in favor of capitalism." [28] But ultimately his social-work experiences convinced him that "our various reform efforts were, in the words of the familiar simile, like bailing out the tub while we kept the faucet running." [29]

His horizons were also broadening in other ways. In 1907 Thomas accompanied the director of the Spring Street Settlement House on a trip around the world, during which most of their time was spent in Asia. Before going abroad, Thomas was inclined to accept a view of empire not unlike that popularized by Rudyard Kipling, but he developed in Asia a distaste for colonialism that was to be part of him for the rest of his life. He developed a special affection for the Chinese and was revolted by the signs in the parks of Shanghai which read: "Dogs and Chinese not allowed." While on a streetcar in Calcutta, he saw a Britisher who, to show his dissatisfaction at a dusty seat, struck the Indian conductor. Thomas was profoundly disturbed by the experience but also enlightened by it. "The blow was light," he writes, "the affront grave, and I began to understand that men could more easily forgive injuries than insults born of arrogance." [30]

After returning to America, he continued with his settlement work but now worked as an assistant to the pastor of the Christ Church on West Thirty-sixth Street. The poverty in this area was real but, even though it bordered on the famous Hell's Kitchen section, not quite so dire as that which he encountered in his Spring Street work. It was through Christ Church, which was closely affiliated with the more fashionable Brick Presbyterian Church of Fifth Avenue, that Norman Thomas met Frances Violet Stewart in the spring of 1908. Miss Stewart, who apparently devoted a good deal of her time to Christian social service, founded and secured financial support for New York's first class in the home care of victims of tuberculosis. Her grandfather was John A. Stewart, a real pillar of the New York community and a confidant of presidents from Lincoln to Coolidge. In association with John Jacob Astor, he founded the United States Trust Company.

Norman and Violet (as he always called her) were married on September 1, 1910. Although Emma Thomas had misgivings about her son's marriage—seeming to distrust wealthy New Yorkers—her premonitions were not well founded. According to every report, her son and daughter-in-law had an ideal marriage.

During the early period of his courtship and marriage, Thomas was enrolled at the rather heterodox Union Theological Seminary in New York. His parents would have preferred him to attend a more conservative institution, but they raised no vigorous objection to his choice.

During the first decade of the twentieth century, suggest two students of American social reform, "the theological seminaries seethed with unrest and social criticism inspired largely by Dr. Walter Rauschenbusch and Dr. Harry F. Ward."[31] Just prior to World War I, Rauschenbusch, in particular, was bringing the message of Social Christianity to large numbers of Protestant theological students. During his many years as a teacher at the Rochester Theological Seminary, Rauschenbusch was actively engaged in the attempt to socialize American Protestantism. He argued that the teachings of Jesus Christ could not be reconciled with the materialism of capitalism. Thomas was very familiar with the writings of Rauschenbusch and was increasingly impressed by the arguments of the Christian Socialists. "Insofar as any one man or any one book, or series of books made me a Socialist," he has written, "it was probably Walter Rauschenbusch and his writings."[32] Though Thomas did not actually embrace socialism during his seminary training, he was being influenced in that direction.

By the time of his ordination in 1911, there was already some indication that he was destined to take an unconventional path, at any rate in church matters. Indeed, his answers to the church examiners were so unusual that they made the New York City papers. "There was a great deal of debate as to whether so frankly an unorthodox young man should receive the official sanction of the Presbyterian Church," reports historian W. E. Woodward.[33]

Once ordained, Thomas was in a mood to think about long-run vocational plans. He decided to leave Christ Church, and he also gave up his post as associate minister of the very swank Brick Presbyterian Church. He was looking for greater challenges, and in his new positions he was to find them. From 1911 to 1918 he was pastor of New York's East Harlem Presbyterian Church and chairman of the American Parish. The latter was, in effect, a federation of a group of Presbyterian churches and social agencies which were located in immigrant neighborhoods. In this district, which he nostalgically recalls as his "little League of Nations," he worked with Italians, Poles, Hungarians, and Russian Jews.[34]

The inhabitants of the American Parish were desperately poor, and they fell prey to every conceivable social problem. The area which it encompassed was reputed to have had New York City's highest homicide rate. Intergroup relations, it would seem, were extremely tense. Soon after assuming his new job, Thomas wrote a letter to a fellow minister protesting anti-Italian sentiment in the latter's congregation—a letter which reflected his developing sensitivity to social injustice. After making a plea for more tolerance, he declared that "the Christian Church faces no more burning question than the problem of making brotherhood real, . . . concrete kindness to the Italians will do more for the church at large and for community neighborliness than scores of sermons." [35]

World War I: A Break-Through of New Ideals

When World War I began in the summer of 1914, Norman Thomas received a letter from his minister father. "This will

mean hard times," wrote W. E. Thomas, "for all kinds of
Christian work and all benevolences. It is a time that will test
our faith as it is seldom tested. But it is a comfort to know that
God is over all and that he can make the wrath to praise him." [36]
And these were "hard times" for the young Reverend Thomas.
World events and the social conditions that he observed on a
day-to-day basis were forcing him to crystallize his thinking
about the world around him. World War I was the crucible,
so to speak, in which his radical social philosophy became more
clearly formulated. His careful reading of Robert Hunter's
Poverty (1904), Henry Noel Brailsford's *War of Steel and
Gold* (1915), and the famous debates on socialism between
Father John A. Ryan and Morris Hillquit which appeared in
the pages of *Everybody's Magazine* in 1913 tended to push him
farther in the direction of Christian pacifism and socialism.

The trend of his thought is clearly revealed in his correspondence during the months just prior to the United States'
entry into World War I. In a letter of August, 1916 to a fellow
clergyman, he points to the relationship between effective
church work and general social health:

> As you know, I am more and more convinced as time goes
> on that there is no such thing as creating the type of church
> life we desire in New York either among the very rich or
> among the poor (or for that matter among the middle class)
> so long as unchristian conditions characterize industry, hous-
> ing, and amusements. These unchristian conditions will not
> be conquered simply by a general feeling of good will but
> require definite and well thought out plans of action by
> which good will may be made to work.[37]

To another colleague in October, 1916 he writes of the dangers
inherent in an arms race:

Every nation in the world has said that it was only preparing to defend itself and no nation believes the others. If America utilizes this opportunity to become one of the strongest military powers it will awaken suspicion, force the exhausted powers to keep up a race in armaments and delay the establishment of a righteous peace.[38]

Reverend Norman Thomas appeared to be quite cognizant of the fact that his developing thought and his sphere of activity were carrying him rather far from the world of the average Princeton graduate of 1905. Some eleven years after leaving Princeton he wrote a letter to an alumni group in which he attempted to summarize the kind of living and thinking that he had been doing in the outside world:

My own life has gone on quietly; yet I have been privileged to touch a most absorbing drama of life here among these people of many races who have made their homes, or what must pass for homes, here in our city. Tragedy and comedy, sordid misery and discouragement, and high hope, brave living and real success are strangely mingled. I have become, I suppose, in these years what someone has called "the worst of provincials, a confirmed New Yorker," yet the New York I know best is not the New York most familiar to the average Princeton man. . . .

With all my love for Princeton I sometimes think, unjustly, of course, that my education really began when I left there and that not the smallest part of it has been the life here in this district. It is a sort of school which sets hard lessons and asks some difficult questions. What is our democracy worth? How shall we make it apply to our social, industrial and political problems? Are we preparing well for national safety in peace or war when so many of our workers cannot even under favorable conditions make the proper living wage? I wish more Princeton men were students in this school—but that is preaching, which is against the rules in a class letter.[39]

As America's involvement in the war became more imminent, the young minister became more convinced that on no ground could the good Christian support war. Moreover, he was inclined to believe that the war could only "be accounted for in terms of the socialist analysis." [40] He came to look upon it as an immoral struggle between rival imperialisms. By January of 1917 he had joined the Fellowship of Reconciliation, an organization of religious pacifists with a strong social-reform bent.

This was to be the beginning of Norman Thomas' long involvement with organizations dedicated to unpopular causes. "I was a long while in coming to it," he wrote to a friend in explanation of his decision to join the F.O.R., "but finally became convinced that so far as I could see, war and Christianity are incompatible; that you cannot conquer war by war; cast out Satan by Satan; or do the enormous evil of war that good may come." He went on to argue that "Christ's method of dealing with life's problems almost stands or falls with this test and that if we would honestly try His way God would guide us to unimagined solutions of our problems." He was perfectly aware that he held a view "which the great majority of Christians" reject, and conceded that men often supported war out of noble motivation.[41]

World War I had a profound impact not merely on Norman but upon the whole family into which he was born. The sermon which Welling Thomas, Norman's father, wrote on November 14, 1915, the day of his death, but which he was never able to deliver, was full of foreboding for the future of mankind. "Can it be," he asked, "that this war in Europe is going to undo in great measure what centuries of Christian effort have accomplished?" [42] Emma Thomas experienced the pain of seeing her two sons Ralph and Arthur go off to war, and also suffered what was probably even greater distress because of the fact that Norman and Evan were staunchly and openly opposed to the war. And she had cause for concern, especially in the case of Evan. Norman, as a minister, was legally exempt from military service, but Evan had no such exemption and chose to go to prison rather than accept the draft. Exceeding Norman in rebelliousness, he led a hunger strike while in prison.

Evan's correspondence with his mother and other members of the family reveals that he was probably more disillusioned with what he called "this wretched social order" than was his older brother. Norman had become an ardent critic of American society but managed to live within it with some measure of comfort. Evan's antipathy to capitalism had become so great that he seemed to find living under it unbearable. Indeed, even though in later years he was to become a professor of medicine at New York University and a world-renowned authority on venereal diseases, this uncompromising idealist never became accommodated to many of the basic values of American society. He was in it but not of it. He became chairman of the War Resisters League, and through the years his pacifism remained unabated. An eccentric blend, he is part socialist, part anarchist, part pacifist, part agnostic. He was sympathetic toward but never joined the Socialist party.

The path that Norman and Evan were taking was apparently understood, if not accepted, by their soldier brother Ralph, who was to embrace conservatism rather than radicalism. The latter wrote to Norman in February of 1918, "I am sorry we don't agree in this, the biggest affair of our lives, but you know I respect your courage of conviction and idealism." [43] Through the years, political differences were never to mar the affection and loyalty that the Thomases felt for one another.

During the war Emma Thomas, who was deeply concerned over Evan's imprisonment, wrote a moving and eloquent letter to President Wilson in which she pleaded for more humane treatment for conscientious objectors. She reminded him that "four tall Thomas boys" had been his students at Princeton. "Judging by their admiration for you," she wrote, "and their quotations from your teachings and writings, your influence over them was as strong as that of any teacher in their lives. Yet in this time of decision for thinking men, two of them have taken the line of war service for their country and two of them have felt that so inherently an evil as war is not the Christian method of bringing righteousness. . . ." [44] Her words, if they came to the President's attention, fell on deaf ears. Wilson had no tolerance or understanding for those who would not support the war effort.

As the months of 1917 went by, Norman Thomas experienced a growing radicalism, especially in his relation to the church. This was doubtless in part an outcome of his association with the Fellowship of Reconciliation. He was becoming bitterly critical of the behavior of his fellow clergymen. In January, 1917 he made his position unmistakably clear in a letter to a Presbyterian organization. He was willing to grant ". . . that churchmen and Christians should in an emergency think of war as a deplorable necessity is understandable." But that they, "without any sense of contrition for the failure of the church . . . should rush into advocacy of conscription and virtually of war in the name of Jesus of Nazareth" was more than he could accept. "It is this which tempts me to despair for the future of the church. Even in war the church ought to stand for a form of society transcending nationalism and national boundaries. Such rules as your Board of Directors have sent out make the church a handmaid of nationalism and in that very act she abdicates her highest claims upon humanity." [45]

Not only did Thomas become increasingly disturbed concerning what he viewed as the acquiescence of the church to the institution of war, but he became equally convinced that she was much too accepting of other social evils. In "The Church and Industry" (1917), one of his earliest essays on social and economic matters, he made a strong plea for Social Christianity. He vigorously criticized the church for merely going along with the status quo and argued, in effect, that it should become a basic agency of social reform. He wrote:

> . . . In that social order the church has been in general a complacent partner, yet she wonders that men reject her, and, alas, the Master whose name she bears. She ignores, tolerates, or at best, only here and there openly fights conditions which warp and twist the lives of men and women and little children.
>
> . . . The church must live and teach as the constant witness to Christ, the Savior of the individual and the regenerator of society. The two tasks cannot be separated but must be forever united as in Jesus' conception of the Kingdom. The church, then, as His witness, must confess with shame to the blindness which has made her so slow in denouncing slavery, so tolerant of war, so indifferent to child labor long after the labor unions were fighting it. On great moral issues like these she must speak out at least as clearly as she now speaks out against the drink traffic, if she is to triumph.[46]

During the same month that Mr. Thomas wrote these words the United States Congress declared war on the German Empire. This did not move Thomas to become more accepting of war. He continued to adhere to his Christian pacifism, which made him one of a small minority of American Protestant ministers who refused to sanction the war even after the United States had become officially involved.

How did Thomas justify his position to himself and others? Upon what grounds did he refrain from participation in an enterprise to which virtually the whole nation appeared to be committed? Apart from any specific criticisms of the war itself, of which he had many, he saw the problem as a matter of choosing between the dictates of conscience and the dictates of the state. His choice was clear: Man was morally required to behave in terms of conscience. "The state is not really served," he reasoned, "when she takes the place of mankind in general and God. The doctrine that there is a national conscience which must always be superior to individual conscience is the death of any vital religion and of any real sense of human brotherhood. . . . I owe much to my country. I owe more to the great company of mankind who minister to me in body, mind and spirit. As a Christian I believe I owe most to God and there can be no authority but my conscience to determine the just payment of those debts. It is, to be sure, my duty to seek all possible light from every source, but having done that I must follow conscience." [47]

An Individualist Joins a Party

Among the various American groups that continued to oppose World War I, even after the United States had entered it, the Socialist party was by far the most important and the most vocal. It was hardly surprising, therefore, that Norman

Thomas should be drawn in its direction. By this time he was not only a militant pacifist but a believer in fundamental social and economic change as well.

Probably the most important and interesting American political contest of 1917 was the mayoralty race in New York City. The incumbent candidate was John P. Mitchell, who was supported by independent Democrats, independent Republicans, and municipal reformers. The official Republican group offered William F. Bennett, and the official Democratic candidate was John F. Hylan. What might have been an ordinary campaign turned into one of the most exciting in the history of New York City by virtue of the fact that the Socialist party nominated Morris Hillquit, one of its most able and best-known spokesmen. From the Socialist-party point of view the major purpose of the campaign was to get a wider hearing for its antiwar views. Indeed, the war issue was to become the most important issue in the campaign. The Socialists themselves were surprised at the enthusiasm that the campaign engendered. In their campaign of 1913 they had put up Charles Edward Russell as candidate. Even though he was well known as a writer and speaker, the campaign did not prove to be an unusual one. Russell received only 32,000 votes. During the 1917 campaign Russell and many other former Socialists who were prowar supported Mitchell. Nevertheless, Hillquit's campaign, in which he received 145,332 votes, proved to be one of the most successful campaigns that the Socialist party has ever waged in New York City, to be exceeded only by Thomas' mayoralty campaign of 1929. The enthusiasm, especially on the East Side, somehow became contagious. Wherever Hillquit spoke, he found large audiences. It would appear that some conservative groups were truly alarmed, as they believed that he might win.

Hillquit's campaign speeches were forthrightly antiwar. The opening speech of his campaign contained these rousing words: "We are for peace. We are unalterably opposed to the killing of our manhood and the draining of our resources in the bewildering pursuit of an incomprehensible 'democracy,' a pursuit of democracy which has the support of the men and the classes who habitually rob and despoil the people of America; a pursuit of democracy which begins by suppressing the freedom of speech, press, and public assemblage and by stifling legitimate political criticism. Not warfare and terrorism, but Socialism and social justice will make the world safe for democracy. . . ." [48]

Such thoughts drew the man who was one day to become the foremost leader of American socialism closer to the Socialist party. About one month before the close of the campaign, Reverend Norman Thomas wrote a letter to Morris Hillquit indicating that he wished to back him in his campaign for mayor. But Thomas was not as yet ready, "for various reasons," to become a member of the Socialist party, essentially because he feared it would involve embracing a new orthodoxy. As one who had revolted against orthodox Protestantism, he was in no mood to accept any new creed. Yet he did make it clear in his letter to Hillquit that he believed in "the abolition of the capitalistic system," which he held responsible for the war which was then raging. "Entirely apart from the so-called peace issue," he wrote, "I think your election or even a very large vote for you must be of very great significance in the struggle for a new day." [49]

It cannot be doubted that Reverend Thomas looked upon his decision to support Hillquit's candidacy as being a very important step in his life. Indicative of this is the fact that he felt the need to write a long letter to his mother explaining the

whys and wherefores of his action. He began by intimating
that he did not expect her to be surprised at his decision. He
then went on to state his position in detail. It was as if he were
trying to clarify the issues in his own mind by committing
them to paper:

> I am not a member of the Socialist Party but, as I have
> told you, I agree very nearly with very many of their funda-
> mental doctrines and I have for some time admired Mr. Hill-
> quit personally.
>
> As for the church, I believe I am doing her the highest
> service by proving or trying to prove that she is catholic
> enough to make room for social radicals. The strife between
> radicalism and conservatism is the battle of the future. Will
> it be fought by violence or more peaceful means? If the
> church can speak now she may do much to save the future.
> For myself, I believe that the Christian ethics are impossible
> in the present order of society and that every Christian must
> desire a new social order based on cooperation rather than
> competition in which alone the highest ideals can be in-
> volved. This is the hope of the Socialist Party. I will grant
> that it is far from perfect . . . it has more idealism, though,
> than any party I know of. Its members may be less respectable
> than those in the old parties, but they are struggling toward
> the light even as were the poor to welcome Jesus. Socialism
> without Christianity is not to my mind the hope of the
> world, but you cannot Christianize radicalism by standing
> aloof from it. I believe that no opportunity has come to me
> as a minister greater than that which I have because my
> conscience has compelled me to come out now on the radical
> side. It means something when a Christian minister can
> assure an enormous audience in Madison Square Garden,

as I did the other night, that he takes the stand he does because he believes in the ethics of Jesus.[50]

Thomas was fully prepared to risk all for the sake of his socialist and pacifist ideals. He continued:

> Whether the church will tolerate me or not is for it to say. I hope it will. If it does not it will injure herself far more than it will me and I say this without conceit, because her attitude toward me will be symbolic of her outlook for the future. I am perfectly aware that the stand I am taking is costing me many friendships, every possible chance of getting another church if I should leave here, and perhaps, though I think not, my present position. I can only say that if it costs me more than I fear, it is to my mind the only way, for I could not maintain my self-respect and do differently nor could I serve the Kingdom of God as effectively.[51]

These are the words of an extremely thoughtful and deeply religious man who had come to the conclusion that the social arrangements that prevailed at that time were not compatible with the Christian principles he held so dear. With a mature awareness of the possible consequences, Reverend Thomas decided to dedicate himself to the cause of social reform. In the years that followed his participation in the Hillquit campaign, Reverend Thomas became increasingly more intent upon propagating a socialist message rather than a Christian one.

By the time of the United States' entrance into World War I he had moved far from the "respectable" groups in American Presbyterianism. He had become a member of the Executive Committee of the American Union against Militarism and even appeared before Congress as its spokesman. More significantly, he assumed a leadership role in the Fellowship of Reconciliation. He founded and edited its official magazine, the *World Tomorrow,* "a journal looking toward a social order based on the religion of Jesus." He also founded, in co-operation with Roger Baldwin, a new division of the American Union against Militarism, the Civil Liberties Bureau. And, when Baldwin went to jail for refusal to register for the draft, much of the bureau's work fell upon Thomas' shoulders. Ultimately, the Civil Liberties Bureau was to become the American Civil Liberties Union.

In the spring of 1918, about six months before his formal affiliation with the Socialist party, Thomas resigned from the East Harlem Presbyterian Church and the American Parish. He was never officially requested to do so, though it had been hinted at. Apparently, he maintained good rapport with his parishioners despite his growing radicalism. Basically, he decided to leave because he became convinced that his pacifism and emerging socialism were jeopardizing these institutions' possibilities for receiving much-needed outside financial support. The chairman of the Presbyterian Home Missions Committee accepted Thomas' resignation with delighted relief.

Thomas entered the Socialist party with some serious reservations. The character of much of its propaganda, with its proletarian verbiage, tended to repel rather than to attract him. Less than a month before joining, he indicated that he was in general agreement with its basic policies, but he also suggested that he had not yet joined because he feared "its tendency to trust to coercion of the individual mind and conscience rather than persuasion. The ultimate values in the world are those of personality," he wrote, "and no theory of the state, whether socialistic or capitalistic, is valid, which makes it master, not servant, of man." [52] Nevertheless, at this same time he began to wonder "if it would not be best to fight for the ideas of civil liberty and freedom of conscience within the party than without." [53]

By October of 1918 he arrived at his decision and wrote a letter requesting membership in the Socialist party:

> I am sending you an application for membership in the Socialist Party. I am doing this because I think these are days when radicals ought to stand up and be counted. I believe in the necessity of establishing a cooperative commonwealth and the abolition of our present unjust economic institutions and class distinctions based thereon.[54]

At that time Thomas could honestly say that he subscribed to the general principles of socialism, but he had obviously not resolved all of his doubts about becoming an organization Socialist. He continued in his letter of application:

> Perhaps to certain members of the party my Socialism would not be of the most orthodox variety. As you know, I have a profound fear of the undue exaltation of the State, and a profound faith that the new world must depend upon freedom and fellowship rather than upon any sort of coercion whatsoever. I am interested in political parties only to the extent in which they may be serviceable in advancing certain ideals and in winning liberty for men and women.
>
> My accepting of the socialist platform is on the basis of general principles rather than of details. If I were a farmer and lived in certain states of the middle west, it is quite likely that I should be a member of the Nonpartisan League and I regret the provision of the party constitution which would automatically expel me. Though I am a staunch pacifist, I should have voted for the preamble of the St. Louis platform. However, you don't want a detailed statement of my views.

I shall be glad to answer any questions that you may have to raise. If this statement is satisfactory, I shall look forward to the fellowship of the party as a real privilege.[55]

At the time of the writing of this letter Norman Thomas was no youngster; he was almost thirty-four years old. He did not embrace socialism out of some youthful enthusiasm or out of some neurotic compulsion to be unconventional. He counts himself as "an exception to the good rule of the Frenchman, 'He's no good who isn't a Socialist before he's twenty-one, or if he is, after he's thirty.'"[56] He "fought being a Socialist for quite a long time"[57] and resisted the idea of joining the Socialist party and accepting its "moderate discipline."[58] "My actual transition to Socialism," he has recalled, "was slow and gradual. There was no vision or any 'Road to Damascus.' There was no great moment of any kind."[59] Basically, he insists, his embracing of socialism has to be explained in terms of "events, not people and not books."[60] The major forces, in his own estimation, which pushed him toward socialism were the "grotesque inequalities, conspicuous waste, gross exploitation, and unnecessary poverty all about me." He saw no "adequate" progressive solution.[61] The only way out, he felt forced to conclude, was socialism, preferably of a Christian rather than a Marxist variety.

CHAPTER II

Setting the Stage

A POLITICAL leader cannot be understood apart from the movement that he attempts to lead. Leadership can never be divorced
from followership. There is always a reciprocal relationship
between the two. Leaders, even the most powerful of them, are
not free agents. Inevitably, they are confronted with situations,
not of their own making, that rise out of the history and the
culture of any given movement.

An American Socialist leader must behave in terms of situations that are rather different from those which a major-party
leader must face, for the American socialist movement has a
history and a culture—patterns of behavior and shared attitudes
—which are distinctly its own. It cannot be analyzed realistically simply in terms of the larger patterns of American society.
It must be viewed in terms of its own traditions and values.
Some of the basic facts of the history of the American socialist
movement have to be understood in order to set the stage—
so to speak—for a consideration of the political career of
Norman Thomas.

Marxism in America

The socialist movement in the United States, excluding
certain utopian colonization ventures, was not an indigenous

product of the American environment. The socialist idea in the modern or Marxian sense was apparently brought to America by German immigrants who, in large numbers, fled their homeland following the European revolutionary upheavals of 1830 and 1848. Some of these men who arrived here during the 1850's had been closely associated with Karl Marx and Friedrich Engels.

As early as 1853 a group of Germans had founded in New York the American Workingmen's Alliance. It organized branches in several other states and could even boast of a newspaper. This organization, however, had a brief life. The antislavery cause and later the Civil War itself diverted its membership from socialist activities.

In 1864 a more important and more interesting radical organization was to be born in London, England. It was called the Workingmen's International Association, later to be known as the First International. The essential purpose of this fantastic combination of men with virtually every kind of radical orientation was to promote a sense of solidarity among workers throughout the world. Among its important leaders, who were perpetually feuding with each other, were Karl Marx, Giuseppe Mazzini, and Michael Bakunin.

By 1869 the First International was to have an American affiliate in the General German Workingmen's Union, which had been organized during the eighteen fifties. The leader of the American branch was F. A. Sorge, who had been close to Marx before coming to America. The history of the First International is the history of furious debates between Marx and Bakunin and their disciples. Fearing that the anarchists would gain control of the organization, by a series of rather unethical manipulations the Marxists managed to have the organization's headquarters moved to New York in 1872. Thus

America became the home for an international debating society that debated issues of only the remotest concern to Americans. After four years of polemical discussions concerning tactics, a favorite pastime among revolutionaries, the First International was officially dissolved in 1876.

In the same year that the First International breathed its last breath, a unity convention of seven delegates from various radical faiths was held in Philadelphia, Pennsylvania. These delegates represented four different groups: the Social Democratic Workingmen's party of North America, the Labor party of Illinois, the Socio-Political Labor-Union of Cincinnati, and the North American Federation of the International Workingmen's Association. These four organizations consolidated to become the Workingmen's party of the United States. In 1877 the Workingmen's party held another convention, at which the issue of economic versus political action was debated. The opponents of political measures were actually rooted in the anarchist rather than in the socialist tradition. In any case, the majority decided upon political action, and the organization changed its name to the Socialist Labor party, which enjoys the distinction of being the oldest socialist political group in the United States. From 1877 to 1897 it completely dominated the American socialist scene.

The new organization was born into an era of growth and turbulence. During the first two years of its existence its membership more than tripled. This increase in numbers, however, was not accompanied by an increase in internal harmony. The Socialist Labor party, like virtually every other socialist group in American history, was literally plagued by factionalism. The issue of direct action versus political action was far from resolved. Some members in the party favored arming workers; others approved only parliamentary methods for gaining power.

Some favored co-operation with the established trade unions; others scorned them as instruments of the capitalist class. Some were sympathetic to the anarchist point of view; others could not tolerate it. Similar controversies were to recur throughout the history of American socialism.

To make matters more difficult, during this period of intense factionalism, the Socialist Labor party was struggling to Americanize itself. The task was not easy, for only about 10 per cent of its members had been born in the United States. In fact, the organization was never to know real success in its quest for Americanization.

A new phase in the history of the Socialist Labor party began when, in 1889, it was joined by Daniel DeLeon, a former lecturer in international law at Columbia University. From then until his death in 1914 he was to dominate the organization with an iron hand. No American radical or labor leader before or since has ever wielded such complete power. Virtually all students of American social reform agree that DeLeon was a man endowed with considerable intellectual powers but that he was amazingly egotistical and rigid in his thinking. He preached an orthodox Marxism and equated it with the absolute truth. All those who did not see eye to eye with him were viewed as traitors, not excepting his own son. "He was, perhaps, the 'purest' revolutionary Marxist the world has ever known." [1] "DeLeon's tragedy lay in the fact that he was more Marxian than his Master," conclude Lillian Symes and Travers Clement in their *Rebel America*.[2]

In most respects, the program of the Socialist Labor party under the guidance of DeLeon was not markedly different from that of other socialist groups of the time. "With the founders of this republic," declared the 1896 Socialist Labor party platform, "we hold that the true theory of politics is that the machinery of government must be owned and controlled by the whole people; but in the light of our industrial development we hold, furthermore, that the true theory of economics is that the machinery of production must likewise belong to the people in common." [3] Moreover, after ascribing virtually all of the unpleasant features of American society to the system of capitalism, it goes on, not straying one bit from the Marxist dogma, to suggest that the system is doomed. "The time is fast coming," the platform predicted, "when, in the natural course of social evolution, this system, through the destructive action of its failures and crises on the one hand, and the constructive tendencies of its trusts and other capitalistic combinations on the other hand, shall have worked out its own downfall." [4]

The unusual aspect of the Socialist Labor party's program during the years of DeLeon's leadership was the view that the party came to support concerning labor unions. In the early 1890's DeLeon attempted to do missionary work within the already declining Knights of Labor. He was apparently hoping to remake it in terms of his ever-ready socialist mold. The Knights, however, had no desire to be remade, and DeLeon was expelled from the organization. This led to his complete disillusionment with the organized labor movement as it was then constituted. He became convinced that his socialist cause could not be forwarded by working within labor, and, with characteristic bitterness, he denounced the leaders of the Knights of Labor and the young American Federation of Labor. To him they were "labor fakers." "Some are ignorant," he exclaimed, "others are corrupt; all are unfit for leadership in the labor movement." [5]

In November of 1895, soon after he was driven out of the Knights of Labor, DeLeon established the Socialist Trade and

Labor Alliance. This new labor body was industrial in form and was dedicated to the promotion of class consciousness among workers and to the destruction of capitalism. DeLeon urged all workers, even those who were already within the ranks of the Knights of Labor and the AFL, to join the alliance. This was dual unionism, pure and simple, and conservative labor leaders were quite naturally bitterly opposed to the new organization. Moreover, even many socialist trade-union officials who, for the most part, had not participated in the launching of the alliance were to become hostile toward it. They were not convinced, as was DeLeon, that the already established labor unions were part and parcel of capitalism.

The Socialist Trade and Labor Alliance had some minor victories, but it never succeeded in drawing large numbers of workers into its fold. Those who founded it did not really understand the American worker and greatly overestimated his radicalism. The formation of the alliance had two adverse results: it widened the gap between American trade unions and the socialist movement; and it precipitated the decline of the Socialist Labor party.

Even prior to DeLeon's venture as a labor leader, many members of the Socialist Labor party had become resentful of his authoritarian type of leadership; they also doubted the wisdom of his labor policies. Under DeLeon the party's history was characterized by one split after another, and a major schism in 1899 reduced the membership of the Socialist Labor party by more than half. After that year the organization was to be increasingly more of a sect rather than a party. Fearing the taint of reformism, the delegates to its convention of 1900 went so far as to eliminate from their program the advocacy of any reforms short of socialism itself.[6] By this kind of orientation they were ultimately to alienate themselves completely

from the rest of American life. Though it still has a few faith-
ful followers, who avidly read the gospel according to DeLeon
and manage to put up a presidential candidate every four
years, the Socialist Labor party has had virtually no influence
upon American thought and politics during the last sixty years.
The failure of the Socialist Labor party was grounded in its
failure to become Americanized. It neglected to heed the wisdom of Friedrich Engels, Marx's collaborator, who once wrote,
"Our Theory is a theory of development, not of dogma, to be
learned by heart and repeated mechanically. The less it is hammered into the Americans from the outside and the more they
test it through their own experience . . . the more it will become a part of their flesh and blood." [7]

The Birth of the Socialist Party

The decline of the Socialist Labor party at the turn of the
new century was due to internal factors; its failure cannot be
explained in terms of an inhospitable environment. Indeed,
American society was beginning to bubble over with the spirit
of reform. It was a period of great awakening. During the
late nineteenth century most Americans were rather com-
placent about their way of life. The criticism of the social
order which came from the pens of men like Henry George,
Edward Bellamy, and Henry D. Lloyd, and which was inherent in the activities of the Knights of Labor, the Grangers,
and the People's party, fell largely on either deaf or indignant
ears. But after 1900 reformers became respectable and were
even listened to by respectable people. The muckrakers were
to have one long heyday. Lincoln Steffens, Ida M. Tarbell,
Ray Stannard Baker, and many others began pouring out
articles which pointed up the seamy sides of American life.

The muckrakers instilled in large numbers of middle-class

Americans a deep suspicion of the large business organizations
that had held so exalted a place in American life during the
last three decades of the nineteenth century. They became especially suspicious of those persons who directed banking,
stockbrokerage, and insurance institutions—reflecting the widespread condemnation of persons who manipulated money
which was not their own. In *The New Freedom,* Woodrow
Wilson explained and described well the spirit which had over-
taken American society since the turn of the century:

> Why are we in the presence, why are we at the threshold
> of a revolution? Because we are profoundly disturbed by the
> influences which we see reigning in the determination of
> our public life and our public policy. There was a time
> when America was blithe with self-confidence. She boasted
> that she, and she alone, knew the processes of popular gov-
> ernment; but now she sees her sky overcast; she sees that
> there are at work forces which she did not dream of in her
> hopeful youth. . . . We are in a temper to reconstruct eco-
> nomic society, as we were once in a temper to reconstruct
> political society, and political society may itself undergo a
> radical modification in the process. I doubt if any age was
> ever more conscious of its task or more unanimously desirous
> of radical and extended changes in its economic and political
> practice.[8]

Perhaps Wilson overestimated the radicalism of the American
mood, but during this era of progressivism great numbers of
Americans recognized the necessity for certain alterations in
the status quo. It was an auspicious time for a radical political
party to be born.

The birth of the American Socialist party corresponded
rather closely with the beginning of the Progressive era. While

the Socialist Labor party, which was primarily an eastern group, was dissipating its energies and membership via its constant internal feuding, the socialist idea was being sponsored by several middle-western organizations during the 1890's. The most important of these was known as the Social Democracy, which counted among its leadership Eugene Victor Debs and the person most responsible for his conversion to socialism, Victor L. Berger. This group had been brought into being in Chicago, Illinois, in June of 1897. Its founders, among whom Debs was the most prominent, had just dissolved the American Railway Union, which had been virtually destroyed by the United States government injunction in the Pullman strike of 1894. In his address to the newly constituted political party of which he automatically became chairman, Debs declared, "There is no hope for the toiling masses of my countrymen except by the pathways mapped out by the Socialists, the advocates of the co-operative commonwealth." [9] Debs was convinced, by this time, that American workers needed more than a union to usher in the kind of world of which he dreamed. Had not the government, by one judicial act, been able to wreck the American Railway Union, into which he had put so much blood, sweat, and tears?

The idea that dominated this first convention of the Social Democracy was that of colonization. That is, it was proposed that the organization should found socialistic or co-operative colonies. But the convention did not fail to state some immediate demands, which included: socialization of all monopolies and utilities, a reduction in work hours, and government work for the unemployed. The colonization scheme was to stimulate a great deal of controversy within the new party and in socialist circles in general. In 1898 members opposed to colonization, with Berger and Debs at their helm, left the Social Democracy and founded the Social Democratic party, which emphasized in its program political and union activity rather than colonization.

During the same period that the Social Democratic forces were achieving organization in the Middle West, the dissident Socialist Labor party factions in the east were becoming better organized. After 1899 these factions coalesced and became an independent organization. This anti-DeLeon group, which was to be led by Morris Hillquit, held a convention in Rochester, New York, in 1900. The assemblage abandoned DeLeon's labor position and declared its intention of supporting the organized labor movement. In the same year its parent body, which was now more than ever dominated by DeLeon and was moving farther away from the world of reality, struck all immediate demands out of its platform.

The anti-DeLeon group went so far as to nominate Job Harriman and Max Hayes as presidential and vice-presidential candidates. At the same time, however, a committee was designated to confer with the Social Democratic party on the possibility of waging a joint campaign. At the Convention of the Social Democratic party in 1900 an agreement was reached whereby a new ticket was put into the field with Debs running for president and Job Harriman of the anti-DeLeon faction as vice-presidential candidate.

The election returns were rather gratifying to the two young socialist groups. Their united presidential ticket received 96,918 votes, while the Socialist Labor party candidates received only 33,450 votes. The heat of joint political action was to weld the Social Democratic party and the anti-DeLeon faction, which were themselves born of schism, into one political organization: the Socialist party. The party's birth was not to be easy, however; it was to be accompanied by severe labor pains. Pat-

terns of factionalism and controversy, which were part of its
heritage, were to be set in motion at the Founding Convention
of the Socialist party in 1901. Heated debates occurred concerning a variety of issues. The question of whether farmers
were properly considered proletarians or capitalists was debated
with vigor, and the old problem concerning the advisability
of issuing immediate demands was rehashed.

Historians of American socialism have dubbed the gathering
just described the "Unity Convention." But the Socialist party
was never to know more than formal or superficial unity.
Daniel Bell, a perceptive student of American socialism, has
aptly described the party's historical situation:

> Certainly from 1901 to 1919 the public and private doctrines
> of American socialism often seemed to bear little relation
> to each other. Publicly, the socialist message was simple and
> compelling: economic crises were endemic in the system be-
> cause the worker was not paid the full return of his labor
> and the capitalist could not find markets for his goods or
> investment; the centralization of industry, occasioned by the
> need to control markets, was insistently eliminating the small
> entrepreneur and the middle class; the growth of trusts
> presaged the necessary next step in social evolution, socialism.
> Internally, however, the new recruit would find himself in
> a morass of competing factions, each talking a special jargon,
> each claiming to point to the correct road to socialism. He
> would be assaulted by the "impossibilists" who told him that
> a fight on taxes as a political issue was meaningless because
> the workers did not pay taxes. He would find himself in-
> volved in detailed arguments concerning industrial versus
> craft unionism. And, as is typical in sectarian milieus, he

would be regaled with detailed bits of gossip and innuendo about the various party leaders.[10]

If the birth of the Socialist party did not inaugurate an era of genuine socialist unity and harmony, it did mark the beginning of a more Americanized socialist movement. From 1877 to 1901, the period of the Socialist Labor party's dominance of the American socialist movement, it was predominantly an organization composed of European immigrants and a small number of American intellectuals. The Socialist party was also, especially during its early years, to be subject to very strong European influence; but, by 1908, 71 per cent of its members were native-born. The atmosphere at its conventions from 1901 to 1912 was basically an American rather than a European one.

After 1912, however, the influence of foreign groups in the socialist movement was to be greatly increased. Finding difficulty in reaching foreign-born workers with its socialist message because of language and other cultural barriers, in 1910 the Socialist party changed its structure so that it would be able to absorb immigrants in nationality blocks of five hundred or more. Each group was provided a secretary and translator who was salaried by the party. In accordance with this plan, some fourteen foreign-language federations, as they came to be called, had been admitted to the Socialist party by 1915. Included among them were the Finnish, the Italian, the Bohemian, the German, the Polish, the Russian, and the Jewish federations.

By 1919 over one half of the members of the Socialist party belonged to foreign-language federations. These groups developed quite autonomous patterns of behavior. They had their own meetings, conventions, newspapers, and often even political programs. They were parties within a party and, as such, promoted dissension within the ranks of the Socialist party. Among these federations, the Finnish and the Jewish probably made the most significant contributions to the party, donating large sums of money and publishing extensive literature. One of the financial angels of the party was the *Jewish Daily Forward,* which was founded by Jewish Socialists in 1897. It was to become the most widely read and influential Jewish daily newspaper in the United States.

From 1901 to 1912 the Socialist party knew a steady increase in power and influence. Its membership, which had initially been less than 10,000, grew to 118,045. In 1912 its presidential ticket received 897,011 votes, or about nine times as many ballots as it had received in 1900. In this same year it could boast that 1,039 of its members were public officeholders, including 56 mayors, more than 300 aldermen, some state legislators, and a member of Congress. Press statistics for 1912 also indicate startling growth: socialist newspapers—8 foreign-language and 5 English-language dailies, 232 English and 36 foreign-language weeklies, 10 English and 2 foreign-language monthlies. There was also a voluminous outpouring of pamphlets by the young intellectuals who had been drawn to socialism. During this same period, the Socialist party, its youth organization, the Inter-Collegiate Socialist Society, and its educational arm, the Rand School of Social Science, were to count among their members and sympathizers individuals like Jack London and Upton Sinclair, who were to become important figures in the intellectual life of America.

Not only was the Socialist party making headway among intellectuals, but Socialists were also gaining ground in the organized labor movement. Relations between the socialist and the labor movements in America have always been different from those which have prevailed in Europe. In effect, the European socialist movement gave birth to the European labor movement. In American history the paths of labor and socialist development have been largely separate. As a result of the activities of DeLeon and his followers, and for other reasons, there developed a deep enmity between the leadership of the two movements. During this period of the ascendency of the Socialist party, there was much antagonism between the two groups. Repeatedly and with vehemence, Samuel Gompers denounced the Socialists. Labor men viewed Socialists as misled and sometimes dangerous dreamers; Socialists viewed labor men as opportunistic, unprincipled, and uneducated men. Yet Socialists and their ideas were definitely becoming more important within the American Federation of Labor during the period just prior to the outbreak of the First World War. Indicative of this trend was the fact that when Max Hayes, a well-known Socialist, ran against Gompers in 1912 for the AFL presidency he received one third of the votes.

Who were the men who were leading the Socialist party during the period (1902–12) which has been appropriately called its "golden age"? [11] The three names which stood out above all others were: Eugene V. Debs, Victor Berger, and Morris Hillquit. That Debs was the greatest spiritual leader that the American socialist movement—if not the world socialist movement—has ever produced cannot be doubted. John Roderigo Dos Passos, the novelist, in his *U.S.A.,* accurately dubbed him "Lover of Mankind." [12] Historian Arthur M. Schlesinger, Jr., writes of him in a not too different vein:

Under Debs' fighting leadership American Socialism . . . entered its period of national popularity. Debs himself remained curiously apart from the top direction of the Socialist movement. He could rival neither Hillquit as an organizer nor DeLeon as a theoretician; he neither dominated party conventions nor contributed important new doctrines. But he had achieved a passionate sense of urgency of the class struggle and a passionate vision of a future society liberated from capitalism. "It is simply a question of capitalism or socialism, of despotism or democracy," he would say, "and those who are not wholly with us are against us." No other Socialist could communicate the vision and the urgency with the intensity of Debs. He became one of the great American orators.

He brought to the party a devotion, an evangelical energy, and, above all, a profoundly intuitive understanding of the American people. Men and women loved Debs even when they hated his doctrines. His sweetness of temper, his generosity and kindliness, his sensitivity to pain and suffering, his perfect sincerity, his warm, sad smile and his candid gray eyes, were irresistible.[13]

The most generally accepted view of Debs coincides with that suggested by Schlesinger, namely, that he came to symbolize American socialism but that he had very little to do with the formulation of its ideas and tactics. Debs was apparently temperamentally unfitted for the fratricidal factionalism that characterized his party. The party theoreticians privately scorned him for his sentimentality and his unscholarly approach to socialism. Debs only very rarely attended national conventions of the Socialist party. During his numerous campaigns he ran on platforms that were essentially the handiwork of other men.

Ray Ginger, in his *The Bending Cross,* the best study of

Debs, however, cautions that his influence upon the socialist movement, in terms of its tactics and program, has been underestimated. "Eugene Debs deserves to be known as the political leader of American socialism," Ginger insists.[14] Though his socialist philosophy was emotionally rather than intellectually grounded, Ginger argues that Debs, nevertheless, made a large impress upon the socialist idea in the United States. Moreover, he maintains that through the years Debs's views were characterized by a consistency that was conspicuously absent from the thought of some of his better-educated comrades. Nevertheless, it would be far from accurate to categorize Debs as a socialist theorist or philosopher, for scholarship was not his forte. "In his entire life, he never made an important decision on the basis of theoretical study," concludes Ginger.[15] The task of formal theorizing Debs gladly left to others.

The party's most important theoretician was the Russian-born lawyer Morris Hillquit. He came to be an especially important leader in Jewish labor and socialist circles in the city of New York. The mold of his thought was orthodox Marxist, but it was tempered by a real devotion to political democracy. The next most important figure in the theoretical command was probably Victor Berger. He was of German birth, and his following was in Wisconsin. It was his honor to be one of the two Socialists ever to be elected to Congress. His orientation was much more practical than Hillquit's, and thus he strayed much more from the Marxist path. He tended to represent middle-western Socialists, while Hillquit spoke, more or less, for the East. Berger's brand of socialism, which Hillquit scorned as "sewer socialism," was to find its expression in the very moderate Socialist administrations which had been established in cities such as Milwaukee, Wisconsin, Bridgeport, Connecticut, and Reading, Pennsylvania.

The roles played by these three men, who led the Socialist party during the pangs of its birth and through the years that followed, which were at first characterized by apparent success and ultimately by decline, have been summarized well by Daniel Bell in one sentence: "While Debs had been the voice and Berger the windmill of action, Hillquit had been the intellectual Nestor of American socialism." [16]

What program was the Socialist party proposing to the American people during the years of its greatest strength? It was ostensibly a Marxist policy, predicated on the assumption of the disintegration of capitalist society. That capitalism would be replaced by the "classless society" was believed by the vast majority of Socialists. They staunchly believed in the inevitability of progress, which they equated with the establishment of socialism. The position and philosophy of the Socialist party was characterized by its foremost thinker, Morris Hillquit, in his *Socialism in Theory and Practice:*

> The Socialist Party represents in politics primarily the general immediate and ultimate interests of the working class as a whole. Its program consists of a number of planks calculated to strengthen the proletariat in its struggles with the dominant classes and to lessen the degree of its exploitation by the latter, and it culminates in the demand for the complete economic enfranchisement of the working class. Since the power of the dominant classes over the workingmen is based on the ownership by the former of the social tools and instruments of wealth production, the cardinal point of the socialist political platform is the demand for the abolition of private ownership in these means of production.
>
> The socialist ideal is a state of society based on organized and cooperative work of all individuals capable of perform-

ing work, and on an equitable distribution of the products of such joint labor among all the members of the community. The Socialist Party, the only party which frankly recognizes the class character of the contemporary state and politics, is at the same time the only party which advocates the abolition of all class distinctions.[17]

Even though socialism was assumed to be an inevitable and almost automatic step in the evolutionary process, there was, strangely enough, constant controversy within the Socialist party about what means should be used to bring it about. Those members who advocated violent tactics and so-called "direct action" were always in a minority. The emergence of the Industrial Workers of the World as a power in the labor movement brought the issue to a head. Many of the leading members of the IWW, who had a strong syndicalist orientation, were also members of the Socialist party. Parliamentarianism versus violence was heatedly debated at the National Convention of the Socialist party in 1912. The result was the adoption of an amendment (Article II, Section 6) to the party's constitution which read:

> Any member of the party who opposes political action or advocates crime, sabotage, or other methods of violence as a weapon of the working class to aid in its emancipation shall be expelled from membership in the party. Political action shall be construed to mean participation in elections for public office and practical legislative administrative work along the lines of the Socialist Party platform.[18]

Socialism and World War I

Not only was the Socialist party to go on record as opposing violence as a means for ushering in a socialist world, but it was also to oppose the use of force in international relations. The Socialist party did not officially accept the pacifist position on war, though it always had pacifist elements within it. Its view was that wars between capitalist nations were invariably the result of imperialistic rivalry. Prior to 1914 European socialism had also strongly indicated its determined opposition to any conceivable war. Indeed, the American socialist movement looked to the European movement for inspiration. The ideas of the American Socialist party concerning war and international relations, at least in part, must have grown out of the deliberations of the Second International, a grouping of national Socialist parties which had been founded in 1889.

American Socialists were confident, in view of the positions taken by the Second International, that, in the event of war, various European Socialist parties would quickly put a halt to hostilities by calling general strikes in their respective countries. When World War I actually broke out in 1914, the American socialist movement was profoundly shocked at the reality that, despite their pledges, European Socialists were marching against each other. "Very soon," recalls Norman Thomas, "socialists were killing socialists as cheerfully, or docilely, as Christians were killing Christians. Democratic Socialism in 1914 missed a tremendous opportunity of a sort which never could return again." [19]

The realization that nationalism proved a greater force than international socialist solidarity came as quite a shock to American Socialists. The explanation probably was that the orientation of the European socialist movement had become more "practical" and less doctrinaire because of its involvement in the organized labor movement. In addition, the very physical proximity of the European Socialists to the fighting made the maintenance of an antiwar position more difficult for them than for their American comrades. The First World War effectively destroyed the Second International.

During the period 1914–17, while the war raged in Europe, the antiwar sentiment among the rank-and-file members of the American Socialist party tended to become more solidified. Of course, Socialists were not standing alone during these years. The slogan "He kept us out of war" may not have actually elected Woodrow Wilson in 1916, but it clearly helped him retain the Presidency. Writing in the *American Socialist* of January 15, 1915, Morris Hillquit expressed a point of view which was not merely confined to socialist circles:

> American socialists should not take sides with the allies as against the Germans. The assertion that the forces of the allied armies are waging a war of democracy against militarism is a hollow catch-phrase devoid of true sense and substance. . . . From the socialist viewpoint the most satisfactory solution of the great sanguinary conflict of the nations lies in a draw, a cessation of hostilities from sheer exhaustion without determining anything.[20]

By the end of 1915, however, the Socialist party's antipreparedness stand was much less in tune with the thinking of the rest of America. The average American assumed that defense preparations made peace more likely; the average Socialist assumed, somewhat more realistically, that they made war more likely.

In 1916 the Socialist party nominated Allan L. Benson and George R. Kirkpatrick as its standard-bearers; they ran on a platform which strongly condemned not only war but defense preparations as well. The Socialist vote declined by about one third as compared to the ballots cast for Debs in 1912. The Socialist party, in general, had declined in strength since its

1912 high point. Woodrow Wilson and his New Freedom had made real inroads into potential and actual Socialist strength. People associated with labor and progressive movements were much taken by the President and his programs.

Immediately after the declaration of war by the United States in 1917, the Socialist party met in convention to consider its war position. The Committee on War and Militarism produced two significant documents: a prowar statement which came to be known as the Spargo Report, and an antiwar statement which came to be associated with the name of Morris Hillquit.

The Spargo Report was a short and rather calm resolution. It did not attempt to make any evaluation of the war that was then raging. It merely suggested that the Socialist party had failed in its efforts to keep the United States out of war, that America's involvement in it was a *fait accompli*. The role of the Socialist party should be, therefore, to "seize the opportunity presented by war conditions to advance our program of democratic collectivism. Every one of the other belligerent nations has discovered through the war," the Spargo resolution continued, "that capitalism is inherently inefficient. Whether for military or civil needs, it has been found necessary to abandon the essential principle of capitalist industry. The warring nations have had to give up the organization and operation of industry and primary economic functions for profit, and to adopt the socialist principle of production for use. Thus the war has demonstrated the superior efficiency of collective organization and operation of industry."[21] More specifically, the Spargo Report proposed that international socialist communications be kept intact in order to promote an early and "democratic" peace; that civil liberties be maintained; that wealth be conscripted in the war cause; that men not be conscripted unless such action is sanctioned by popular vote; and, most importantly, that the great industries, including agriculture, be socialized.[22]

The Hillquit Report was a very vigorous document, written with great passion and feeling and couched in the best revolutionary jargon; it constituted an unequivocal denunciation of the war in every aspect. The resolution began by announcing the "allegiance" of the Socialist party "to the principle of internationalism and working class solidarity the world over. . . ." [23] It went on to analyze the war in orthodox Marxist terms. The conflict was caused, the report maintained, by the rival imperialisms of the various European nations. In short, European workers were not paid enough by their capitalist exploiters to buy back the fruits of their labor; therefore, European nations were seeking to dispose of their goods in world markets—an act which resulted in imperialistic competition between them, which culminated in the world disaster. "Capitalism, imperialism and militarism had thus laid the foundation for an inevitable general conflict in Europe. The ghastly war in Europe was not caused by an accidental event, nor by the policy or institutions of any single nation. It was a logical outcome of the competitive capitalist system." [24] Those millions who had already died in the war were "wanton offerings upon the altar of private profit." [25]

Why did the United States enter the war? The report declared that it was drawn in by "predatory capitalists" who were seeking profits from the manufacture of war goods and who wanted their loans to the allies secured. The document presented the argument that World War I was anything but a war for democracy: [26] "Democracy can never be imposed upon any country by a foreign power by force of arms." [27] Indeed, the resolution suggested that the war, with its accompanying militarism, would imperil democracy at home. Three short, especially vigorous sentences stand out from the rest of the report:

> We brand the declaration of war by our government as a crime against the people of the United States and against the nations of the world.
>
> In all modern history there has been no war more unjustifiable than the war in which we are about to engage.
>
> No greater dishonor has ever been forced upon a people than that which the capitalist class is forcing upon this nation against its will.[28]

The Hillquit declaration also outlined a specific program of action. The major idea was that the Socialist party should carry on "public opposition to the war, through demonstrations, mass petitions, and all other means within our power."[29] Moreover, it clearly stated that this antiwar program should embrace opposition to all forms of conscription and military training, "vigorous resistance" to all attempts to restrict civil liberties, and "education as to the true relation between capitalism and war."[30] The final note was a demand for "a new society in which peace, fraternity, and human brotherhood will be the dominant ideals."[31] As was a foregone conclusion, the Hillquit Report, which was to be known later as the St. Louis Resolution, was overwhelmingly ratified by the rank-and-file members of the party.

The adoption of an antiwar position as an official policy of the Socialist party had many serious ramifications, of course. With the exception of Debs, Hillquit, and Berger, virtually all of the "big names" left the party. Those who resigned included A. M. Simons, a prominent socialist historian; George D. Herron, Christian socialist leader; Jack London and Upton

Sinclair; Robert Hunter, a famous social worker; and J. C. Phelps Stokes, the party's millionaire. The war position also alienated many prominent persons in American life who had been close to the party. It also doubtless increased the anti-socialist feeling among millions of average Americans who could not conceive of any situation that would justify an individual or a group refusing to support their country in war.

The war position also meant constant harassment of the Socialist party by the United States government and its agents. Wilson's New Freedom, insofar as civil liberties were concerned, did not survive long after the entrance of the United States into the war in 1917. Numerous members of the Socialist party, including Eugene V. Debs, ultimately found themselves behind bars for speaking out against the war. Perhaps even more significant was the fact that all of the important Socialist publications were banned from the mails by Post-Office rulings. The fear that the government would intervene hung over all Socialist meetings.

Strangely enough, during the World War I era the Socialist party did not decline much in terms of actual membership figures. From 1914 to 1918 there was a loss of about 10,000 members; but from 1918 to 1919 there was a striking increase of more than 25,000 members, which brought the figures to 108,000—close to the 1912 peak of approximately 118,000. The composition of the membership, however, was very different in 1919 from what it had been in 1912. In the earlier year only 16,000 members were in the foreign-language federations; in 1919 there were more than 57,000. Apparently, the excitement of the Russian Revolution had stimulated many immigrants to join America's best-known radical party.

Socialism and Communism

The Russian Revolution of 1917 was to influence dynamically all of the subsequent history of the American Socialist party and, for that matter, the world socialist movement. In March of 1919 the Third International was born in Moscow; the coming of World War I had destroyed the Second. The Communists who attended this initial meeting of the Third International made it clear in their first deliberations that they had no use for any but the leftwing factions of the various Socialist parties around the globe. They roundly denounced the various centrist and rightwing groups. They charged that the leadership of the American Socialist party had not lived up to the spirit of the St. Louis Declaration. The leftwing groups within the Socialist party, which wanted affiliation with the Third International, were against co-operating with attempts to establish a new Socialist international; but, in 1919, over their protests the National Executive Committee sent delegates to a conference at Berne, Switzerland, which was meeting for that purpose.

In 1920, when the Third International issued a twenty-one–point statement outlining the terms under which groups might affiliate, bitter factionalism was already raging in the world of American radicalism. The Twenty-one Points, which have become famous in the annals of radical history, symbolized the fact that the breach between socialism and communism would never be healed. The ideology expressed in this document sheds much light on the behavior of world communism during the subsequent forty years. It revealed the essentially authoritarian structure of the international communist movement.

The basic theme of the Twenty-one Points was that the communist movement must be "organized along extremely centralized lines" and that it must be "controlled by iron discipline." [32] This statement of Communist principles insisted that the "dictatorship of the proletariat" must become a reality rather than a mere slogan.[33] The program outline asserted, in virtually every one of its twenty-one sections, the principle that party members and party groups must be completely subservient to the decisions of the Third International. The notion of local autonomy was completely absent from the statement; its total emphasis was upon what the individual Communist parties were obligated to do: "Every party wishing to belong to the Communist International is obligated to offer unqualified support to every soviet republic in its struggle against the counter-revolutionary forces." [34] Thus what was expected of the member parties in the sphere of international relations was made abundantly clear.

In surprisingly bold language the antipathy of this newly established Communist high command to the older Socialist groups is revealed in Point 17: "The Communist International has declared war upon the whole bourgeois world and all yellow social democratic parties. It is necessary to make clear to every plain workingman the difference between the communist parties and the old official social democratic and socialist parties that have betrayed the banner of the working class." [35]

In a similar vein another section of the Twenty-one Points demands that parties wishing entrance into the Third International "proclaim a clean break with reformism and the policy of the 'center' and . . . propagate this break throughout the ranks of the entire party membership." [36] Leading members of the world socialist movement, including Karl Kautsky of Germany, Ramsay MacDonald of Great Britain, and Morris Hillquit of the United States, were denounced by name as "notorious opportunists." [37] Furthermore, the document makes it perfectly clear that as a requirement for joining the Communist International the various Socialist groups would have to expel such leaders. "The communist parties of those countries where the communists carry on their work legally must from time to time institute cleansings . . . of the personnel of their party organization in order systematically to rid the party of the petit bourgeois elements creeping into it," instructs Point 13.[38]

The issuance of the Twenty-one Points marked a division in the world of American radicalism that has persisted more than three decades, though there were periods of superficial and halfhearted *rapprochement*. Indeed, the rift has grown wider and more bitter as the years have gone by. It was inevitable that men with the personalities and backgrounds of Debs, Hillquit, and Berger, and their followers, many of whom had revolted against centralism as imposed by Daniel DeLeon, would not be able to tolerate a new and even more rigid authoritarianism, even if it were called "democratic centralism." Eugene V. Debs characterized the Twenty-one Points as "a policy of armed insurrection" that was "ridiculous, arbitrary, and autocratic." [39]

The announcement of the Twenty-one Points made it more dramatically clear that two socialist worlds had emerged. In the future it would be democratic socialism versus totalitarian communism. As the years went by, the division between socialism and communism became more sharp and complete, even if the general public did not always realize it.

During 1919 and 1920 American socialism was in a state of turmoil. The Socialist party and its Communist, leftwing offshoots were attempting to dominate the scene. Most of the members of the latter groupings had been in the foreign-language federations but had abandoned the Socialist party in disillusionment because it did not join the Third International. In line with the traditions of radicalism, these revolutionaries soon began quarreling among themselves, and the result was the formation of two Communist parties. One group was to be known as the Communist Labor party, which was desirous of building a party with an American orientation; the other was the Communist party, which was largely dominated by the Slavic language federations, members of which were determined that bona fide bolshevism should predominate. Almost from their inception, both of these groups were to face constant governmental persecution and prosecution under Attorney General A. Mitchell Palmer's direction and were soon forced underground. Eventually, a United Communist party developed, which subsequently became the Workers' party and ran William Z. Foster as its presidential candidate in 1924 and 1928. Since 1929 it has been known as the Communist party.

Socialism in the Era of Normalcy

During the presidential campaign of 1920 the American radical world largely rallied around the candidacy of Eugene V. Debs. The result was that, numerically, the Socialist party had its greatest electoral success in terms of total votes cast. The 919,799 votes were largely cast for Debs the man, the hero who went to prison for what he believed; it was also a protest vote, but in no way indicative of a virile Socialist party. In every way the organization was in an extremely enervated state. The foreign elements which had swelled the membership figures in 1919 left the party as quickly as they had entered it. By 1920 the membership had dropped from the 1912 peak of approximately 108,000 to the surprising low of 26,766.

The history of the Socialist party during the 1920's is hardly

an exciting drama. In these years there was little Socialist ac-
complishment. The small party, decimated by the divisions of
the war period, was just managing to survive. The membership figures for the period indicate a steady decline. In his
autobiography, *Loose Leaves from a Busy Life,* Morris Hillquit, perhaps the most influential Socialist leader in the years
immediately following World War I, commented on the state
of his party's health during the era of normalcy: "It was completely wiped out in a number of states, and all that was left
of the erstwhile vigorous and promising movement was a
small bank of stubborn die-hards, largely concentrating in a
few Eastern and Midwestern states, not exceeding 10,000 in
all." [40] The direness of the situation forced Socialists to re-
consider their traditional beliefs, strategy, and organizational
practices. They were painfully aware that their European
sister movements were infinitely more powerful. They realized
that their party had no large proletarian base.

In the structural sense the various American Socialist parties
had followed the German pattern which had been transplanted
here by the German founders of American socialism. The pattern involved having a party, composed of dues-paying members, which was primarily political rather than economic in
orientation. Extensive co-operation with the trade-union and
co-operative movements was practiced, but there was no organic unity with such organizations. Such was the case in most
continental countries where the socialist movement had ante-
dated and to a large extent founded the labor movement. In
Britain, where the labor movement preceded the socialist movement, the situation was different. The British Labor party was
and is, in effect, an amalgam of labor unions, co-operatives, and
socialist organizations, which have joined forces for the purpose of political action.

Whether to continue in the German tradition or to attempt to follow the example of the British Labor party was an issue that had frequently been debated by American Socialists. But the issue was to have more meaning in the years just prior to the presidential campaign of 1924. The trends of that time seemed to be pointing to the possibility of a major realignment in American political life.

The close of World War I found American labor in a mood of unrest, feeling the effects of the "Red scare." The year 1919 was marked by several bitter and unsuccessful strikes. Some 60,000 trade unionists in the city of Seattle, Washington, were involved in a general strike. In Boston, Massachusetts, there was the famous police strike that brought Governor Calvin Coolidge into national prominence. Strikes of major proportions occurred in the allied industries of steel and coal. The railway workers were restless; they were unhappily contemplating the prospect of a return to private ownership, since government operation had meant union recognition and generally better working conditions. During the recession years of 1921 and 1922 the Amalgamated Meat Cutters, the Seamen's Union, and the Railway Workers were involved in unsuccessful strikes aimed at retaining the gains that they had made during the war years. These reverses can be explained in part by the fact that employers were embarking on an organized antiunion campaign which was exemplified by the "American Plan," with its most important feature being the open shop. Likewise, organized labor was facing a government that was more often than not unfriendly. "Supreme Court decisions between 1917 and 1923," reports historian Nelson M. Blake in *A Short History of American Life,* "upheld 'yellow-dog contracts,' ruled that secondary boycotts were not protected by the Clayton Act, upheld the power of the courts to restrict picketing, invalidated state laws limiting the power of state courts to grant labor injunctions, and denied the power of Congress to pass a minimum-wage law for women and children in the District of Columbia." [41]

As it faced a hostile government, the organized labor movement became increasingly interested in altering the political status quo. In 1919 the United Mine Workers Union of America went on record as favoring independent political action by labor unions. A year later the Brotherhood of Painters followed suit. Similar stands were also taken by the Pennsylvania and Indiana State Federations of Labor and by many other local units of the AFL. Another development symptomatic of the mood of these times was the founding of the Nonpartisan League in 1915 by the former Socialist-party member Arthur C. Townley and its rapid subsequent growth. This movement developed its greatest power among farmers in North Dakota, South Dakota, Minnesota, Idaho, Montana, Nebraska, and Washington. Its program included various state-ownership schemes calculated to improve the lot of the farmer. It was not, strictly speaking, a third-party effort but more accurately an attempt to gain control of the old parties at primary elections. By its methods it succeeded in electing to office a number of governors, Senators, and members of the House of Representatives. Its activities ultimately led to the founding of the Farmer-Labor Party of Minnesota and to the organizing of a Farmer-Labor presidential ticket in 1920.

Conference for Progressive Political Action

These indications of labor and agrarian dissatisfaction with the two major parties led to the development of one of the most interesting third-party ventures in American history. "Towards the end of 1921," wrote Morris Hillquit in his autobiography, "I received a communication from William H. Johnston, General President of the Machinists' Union, inviting me to attend a closed and confidential conference to consider the chances of organizing an effective political party on the model of the British Labor Party." [42] Later, Hillquit was to receive a more formal invitation inviting him to attend "a conference of Progressives" in Chicago, Illinois, in February of 1922.[43] Hillquit was surprised to find that the second letter included not only the signature of Johnston, who was a former member of the Socialist party, but also those of five other rail-road-union leaders whom he definitely considered to be conservatives. Collectively, these leaders of the railroad workers represented some 1,500,000 men. Other Socialist leaders were also invited to the conference, including Victor Berger, the former Congressman; Daniel W. Hoan, who was then Mayor of Milwaukee; and Socialist editor James O'Neal.

In addition to the Socialists and the railway men, the conference included the representatives of some fifty international unions. Present, too, were representatives of the Farmer-Labor party, the National Methodist Federations of Social Service, the National Catholic Welfare Council, the Nonpartisan League, the Farmers' National Council, the Women's Trade Union League, and several other organizations. Never before had American socialism, American labor, and American progressivism met together on so grand a scale to discuss political action. This first meeting was not without mutual fear and suspicions. The labor men feared that the Socialists were too eager to found a third party; and the Socialists thought that the labor men were too cautious and conservative.

The conference, however, closed on a harmonious note. Before the delegates adjourned, they formally organized themselves into a group to be known as the Conference for Pro-

gressive Political Action. Furthermore, they agreed to expend
their energies toward the election of progressive-minded candidates in 1922. They also set the date for another conference,
to be held the following December.

During the next two years the newly formed organization
met on two more occasions. It had achieved a great increase
in national strength and established thirty-two state affiliates.
Moreover, it credited itself with liberalizing the membership
of the new Congress. Large numbers of the candidates that
it endorsed were elected, and many well-known conservatives
whom it opposed were defeated. Another significant development was that many of the nation's most important liberal
political leaders seemed to be drawing closer to the Conference
for Progressive Political Action. Among them were Senators
Robert M. La Follette, George W. Norris, Smith W. Brookhart, Burton K. Wheeler, Hendrik Shipstead, and Lynn Frazier.
Even Samuel Gompers, the AFL chieftain, seemed to be moving into the CPPA's orbit.

The most important question that faced the second conference of CPPA was whether or not a third party should be
established at that time. The support for such a move was
spearheaded by the Socialists and the intelligentsia who were
present at the meeting. The representatives of labor were not
as yet willing to sever their ties with the two old parties. The
farm elements were more inclined to use the nonpartisan
technique of capturing the old parties at the primaries. After
heated debate and a close vote, the decision was made to post-
pone action on the third-party question. The representatives
voted to make their decision on the basis of future events.

In 1923 conflicts over aims and purposes between the labor
and the Socialist factions became more apparent, but the successful co-operation of the labor men and the Socialists in the

British Labor party probably stimulated the diverse elements in the CPPA to try to keep their political effort alive. The revealed corruption of the Harding era further tended to disillusion progressives concerning the major parties. Moreover, William G. McAdoo, a Democratic presidential aspirant, to whom labor had looked with great hope, was to lose his place of favor with the progressives when it became known that his hands were also somewhat soiled by oil.

By the time of the third major meeting of CPPA in February of 1924, disillusionment with the Republicans and Democrats ran high. Plans were laid at this meeting for a convention, to be held on July 4, "for the purpose of taking action on nomination of candidates for the offices of President and Vice President of the United States, and on other questions that may come before the Convention." [44] This ambiguous statement was hardly a fighting call for a third party. Indeed, the CPPA scheduled their convention to be held after those of the Republicans and Democrats. The labor leadership was determined to wait and see if an acceptable candidate might not yet be nominated by one of the two major parties. Morris Hillquit summed up the situation well:

Had Mr. McAdoo been nominated by the Democrats instead of the conservative John W. Davis, there would have been no LaFollette campaign in 1924 or, at any rate, it would not have had the support of the organized railway workers or for that matter of the American Federation of Labor. The American labor leaders still attached greater importance to the person than to the cause; the rank and file generally followed them, and it seemed ludicrous to think that after years of patient maneuvering and hard educational work we would only arrive at a labor party without labor. [45]

Political Coalition

Just prior to the opening of the July convention, William H. Johnston, in behalf of the CPPA's National Committee, telegraphed Robert M. La Follette, asking him to be their candidate. There is no mention in this communication of the desirability of founding a new party. Indeed, in part, this preconvention nomination was probably calculated to eliminate floor nominating speeches that would have inevitably included declarations in support of the third-party idea.

To the great disappointment, but not to the surprise, of the Socialist and other third-party advocates, La Follette indicated that he was willing to run only as an "independent," not as the candidate of a new party. His strange reasoning was that "permanent political parties have been born in this country after, and not before, national campaigns." At the insistence of the third-party enthusiasts, it was agreed, recalled Hillquit, that another convention would be held the following January, in order "to consider and pass upon the question of forming a permanent independent political party." [46]

It was the hope of the Socialists that the common campaign experience would weld this political coalition supporting the candidacy of Robert M. La Follette into one cohesive political party along the lines of the British Labor party. This consideration motivated the Socialist party to support La Follette and to abandon its historic policy of supporting only candidates of socialist conviction.

La Follette ran on a platform that was refreshingly forthright when compared with those put forward by the old parties in 1924. It demanded, among other things, public ownership of the railways, the right of Congress to override decisions of the Supreme Court, the banning of injunctions in labor cases, a vote by the people before war could be declared, the direct election of the president of the United States, and the establishment of the initiative and referendum with reference to the enactment of federal legislation.

Those who supported La Follette constituted a very heterogeneous group. This strange mixture of evangelical crusaders included labor leaders, liberal journalists, single taxers, Socialists, Farmer-Laborites, and radicals of almost every hue, excepting Communists. The latter had attempted to infiltrate the movement, but their entrance was successfully blocked by La Follette and the other CPPA leaders. The American Federation of Labor broke with its tradition of nonpartisanship and supported the La Follette candidacy, but only in halfhearted fashion. The AFL officialdom let it be clearly known, moreover, that they were opposed to the establishment of a labor party and that they were not endorsing socialism.

The Socialist party probably made its greatest contribution to the La Follette campaign on an organizational level, in that it had some going state affiliates, even if they were not especially vital ones. The Progressive organization was thus largely spared burdensome tasks, such as getting the proper number of signatures in order to fulfill the election law requirements in the various states. The Socialist party was already on the ballot in forty-four states, and thus Progressive candidates often ran on the Socialist ticket or under joint Socialist-Progressive auspices. This was not an altogether satisfactory situation and undoubtedly frightened away some prospective voters who wanted to register their support of La Follette but who could not in good conscience vote the Socialist ticket.

It was during the La Follette campaign that Norman Thomas, who was then forty years old, began his long career of running for office. After Morris Hillquit declined, the "Socialist Clergyman," as Thomas was then called by the press, was nominated as the New York State gubernatorial candidate on both the Socialist and Progressive tickets. The non-Socialist Progressives, especially those in the world of labor, were much less than enthusiastic about Thomas' candidacy. They feared that a big vote for him might lead to the election of the Republican nominee, Theodore Roosevelt, and the defeat of Alfred E. Smith. In general, relationships between the Socialist and the labor CPPA leadership in New York State were strained. Here, the Socialists had an effective organization with very capable leaders, and they were inclined to assert their positions with vigor. Many years later, Thomas recalled that the New York Progressive ticket of 1924 never received extremely vigorous support from labor circles, with the exception of some of the needle-trade unions that for a long time had worked closely with the Socialist party.

This "marriage of convenience" between the Socialists and the labor unions was destined to be a short one. When the ballots were counted, the La Follette vote reached 4,826,471, as compared to 15,275,003 votes cast for Coolidge and 8,385,586 cast for Davis. Of the La Follette votes 3,797,974 were placed in the Progressive columns and 854,264 in the Socialist columns. The voting statistics came as a keen disappointment to the labor men and convinced them, with some few exceptions, that they should abandon this young movement of political protest. They concluded that the traditional AFL nonpartisan policy of rewarding friends and punishing enemies was, after all, the best. They had lost all zest for continued experimentation with the third-party idea. The Socialists, however, had become hardened to political defeat and saw campaigns in educational as well as nose-counting terms. They were not quite so ready to abandon their third-party dreams.

In accordance with the agreement reached at the Cleveland nominating convention, a postelection convention was held on February 21–22, 1925, to consider the advisability of founding a bona fide third party. The result of this meeting was a foregone conclusion. In the words of Hillquit, "This time the delegates had come to bury Caesar, not to praise him." [47] Most of the representatives of labor formally withdrew. Both Debs and Hillquit eloquently pleaded that they stay, but it was of no avail. The Socialists and the assorted La Follette followers who remained could not see eye to eye on many major issues. The Socialists, for example, were convinced that an effective third party had to have a labor base. Consequently, they also bade farewell to the CPPA. A small group of the Progressives, who refused to give up the ghost, went through the motions of founding a new national political party, but it was never to function in any real sense.

The wisdom of the Socialist party's decision to attempt to join forces with labor and progressive groups in the Conference for Progressive Political Action was to be debated in socialist circles for many years to come. But no matter how one evaluates the original decision, it is clear beyond the point of argument that the Socialist party was stronger when it joined CPPA than when it left the movement. "In the years immediately following," wrote Morris Hillquit, "it was a difficult, often disheartening, task to maintain a semblance of life in the dismembered, discouraged, and seemingly hopeless organization." [48]

The demise of the Socialist party was looked upon as an accomplished fact in many quarters even before the La Follette campaign was officially launched. In June of 1924 David Karsner wrote of "The Passing of the Socialist Party" in the pages of *Current History*. He painted a dreary picture that most political observers of the period would have accepted as accurate:

> After twenty-three years of indifferent gains and losses the
> Socialist Party goes into eclipse with the Presidential cam-
> paign of 1924. There is scarcely enough of it left to salvage
> and weld with another group. It has neither good-will nor
> bad to bequeath to another organization. It is a political
> ghost stalking in the graveyard of current events seeking
> respectable burial. The majority of its former voting mem-
> bership is back in the Democratic and Republican Parties
> from which it came. . . .
>
> It becomes increasingly clear as the Socialist Party steps
> into the shadows, that it was a one-man organization; that
> it revolved around the personality of a single individual
> whose sincerity and devoutness were sufficient to inspire
> three or four million people to take up the crusade, now
> and then, during the approximate quarter of a century of
> the party's existence.[49]

Karsner had written the obituary notice, and two years later,
in an article entitled "Collapse of Socialism in the United
States," *Current History* (May, 1926), W. J. Ghent inscribed
the tombstone. Such was the condition of the Socialist party
during the years when Norman Thomas was emerging as its
foremost spokesman.

Chapter III

A Leader Emerges

It was during the 1920's, when American socialism was at a low ebb, that Norman Thomas, then a Presbyterian minister, became a prominent leader of the Socialist party. He had joined the party just before the close of World War I. As has often been written in Socialist campaign literature, he came to the party when other people were leaving it.

Professional Radical

Beginning with his formal Socialist affiliation, Norman Thomas became, in a real sense, a professional social reformer or radical. From that point he devoted virtually all of his waking hours to organizing, speaking, and writing in behalf of a great number of organizations in the American radical and liberal worlds. So committed to radicalism had he become that he even felt conscience-bound to sever his connections with Princeton's Colonial Club. Despite his strong sentimental ties to it, he had concluded that the club system was not to the best interest of the university as a whole or appropriate to a democratic era. In later years, however, he was invited back and could not resist the temptation to rejoin.

Thomas had joined the Socialist party just at the beginning of the so-called Red scare of 1919 and 1920. "President Wilson had predicted, 'once lead this people into war and they'll forget there ever was such a thing as tolerance'; and his Attorney General, A. Mitchell Palmer, hastened to embrace the opportunity of justifying that prediction." [1] These were very difficult days for radicals or nonconformists of any hue. Thomas was being baptized into the socialist movement by the rites of fire.

Ironically, it was Mrs. Thomas' inherited income that enabled her husband to devote himself on a full-time basis to social crusading. In the years to come he became involved in cause after cause without feeling that the members of his family would have to do without necessities because he was trying to save the world. He candidly admits that "the critic of capitalism was its beneficiary." [2] However, it should be pointed out that in no year did Mrs. Thomas' income exceed $10,000, and during the 1930's there were lean years when Mrs. Thomas raised cocker spaniels and ran a tearoom in order to increase the family income.

Thomas' desire, as expressed in his letter of application to the Socialist party, to "be counted" among the radicals was coming true in the most literal sense.[3] Early in 1919 Thomas' name appeared among those submitted by military intelligence to a Senate committee investigating individuals who had not supported the war effort. The list also included the names of Charles A. Beard, Eugene V. Debs, Elizabeth G. Flynn, John Haynes Holmes, Rufus H. Jones, Louis P. Lochner, Scott Nearing, Harry Overstreet, and Oswald Garrison Villard. On the whole, Thomas was in good company, and in the years to come many of these persons were to be closely associated with Thomas in a variety of ways. Not only was his name appearing on government "dangerous persons" lists, but he was also being trailed by secret-service agents. Judging him by his various activities and writings, particularly by his association with *World Tomorrow,* Postmaster General Albert S. Burleson concluded, "Thomas is more insidious than Debs." [4] The fact is that the government officials had little insight into this radical young minister's philosophy. On no ground did he ever justify violence, not even for the sake of a social revolution.

During the summer of 1918 the United States Post Office refused to deliver three issues of Thomas' *World Tomorrow.* Postmaster General Burleson threatened Thomas with jail, largely because of an article he wrote criticizing the invasion of the emerging Soviet Union by United States troops in Siberia and at Archangel. The matter was brought to Woodrow Wilson's attention by John Nevin Sayre, a close friend of Thomas' and a brother of the President's son-in-law. Wilson defended his policies toward Russia but agreed that neither Thomas' *World Tomorrow* nor the *Nation,* which was then also under fire for the high crime of criticizing Samuel Gompers, was seditious. Wilson apparently instructed Burleson to that effect. He asked Sayre, however, to tell Thomas, his former student, that "a noted Englishman had once declared that there could be an indecent display of private opinions in public." [5] To the best of Thomas' knowledge, this was the only occasion when President Wilson personally intervened to curtail the abuse of civil liberty on the part of his administration.

Probably Thomas' most cherished cause during the war and the period immediately following was defending the rights of conscientious objectors and protesting the way in which they were being treated. These were the problems to which he addressed himself in his first book, *The Conscientious Objector in America* (1923). Never before had he become quite so disillusioned with organized Christianity. He found that it was more difficult to talk to high church officials than to military officials concerning the plight of the conscientious objectors. The intensity of his feeling was undoubtedly heightened by his indignation at the terrible suffering that his brother Evan had to endure for the sake of his pacifism. In October, 1919, when reflecting on "The Social Preparation for the Kingdom of God," he wrote with a degree of bitterness toward the church which was uncharacteristic of his earlier or subsequent works:

> True, the individual conscience may not be infallible; yet it cannot be corrected by the political state nor can Christians tolerate the doctrine that mistakes of conscience can be cured by chains and imprisonment. The church which has steadily supported the state in its policy of coercing war's heretics is a church which has denied its own right to speak with the voice of God to the hearts of men. The conscientious objectors have not asked for sympathy. One who knows the best of them would not desire to offer to their triumphant courage the insult of sympathy; rather it is the church that needs our concern—the church which is committing suicide by the neglect of things which pertain to her salvation.[6]

In the postwar years, Reverend Thomas, a minister without a church, was also involved in other crusading activities. He was arguing for United States recognition of the Soviet Union. He was actively promoting the cause of Irish freedom and served as a member of the American Committee on Conditions in Ireland along with Jane Addams, George W. Norris, and David I. Walsh. He was becoming even more deeply involved in specific labor and socialist causes. In the radical and liberal world his reputation as a courageous and effective writer and speaker was soaring rapidly.

In 1921 Thomas assumed a position of leadership in American liberalism by becoming an associate editor of the *Nation*. By the next year he had resigned in order to become a codirector, with Harry W. Laidler, of the League for Industrial Democracy—a position which he held until 1937. He did not completely sever his connections with the *Nation* but remained for some years a contributing editor and maintained a close relationship with its publisher, Oswald Garrison Villard, until the latter's death in 1949.

Thomas' activities in connection with the L.I.D. are crucial to understanding his rise to leadership in the Socialist party. Founded in 1905 as the Intercollegiate Socialist Society by notables such as Clarence Darrow, Jack London, and Upton Sinclair, the L.I.D. was at no time officially connected with the Socialist party; but it was always very closely affiliated with the party, and many of its most prominent members were also leading members of the party. The nature of the L.I.D. of the period under consideration has been summarized well in the organization's statement of purposes: "The League for Industrial Democracy is a membership society engaged in education for a new social order based on production for use and not profit. To this end, the League issues pamphlets, conducts research, lecture and information services, organizes city and college chapters and sponsors conferences, forums, luncheon discussions and radio talks." [7] Its membership has always contained many persons who were more prominent in American liberal circles than in the Socialist movement per se. Among the persons with whom Thomas had close contact, at least partially because of his directorship of the L.I.D., were Harry Elmer Barnes, Paul Blanshard, Bruce Bliven, Stuart Chase, John Dewey, Paul H. Douglas, Freda Kirchwey, Robert Morse Lovett, Francis J. McConnell, Alexander Meiklejohn, and Reinhold Niebuhr. During the nineteen twenties and thirties Thomas spoke at countless L.I.D. meetings all over the country. It was during this period that he first became a familiar figure to professors and students of a liberal or radical bent at universities and colleges throughout the nation.

Socialist Leader

As Thomas became well known as an editor of the *World Tomorrow* and the *Nation* and as a leader in organizations like the League for Industrial Democracy, the American Civil Liberties Union, and other radical-liberal organizations, he also became increasingly important within the Socialist party. His co-workers in these many activities and endeavors, especially those in the L.I.D., were frequently members of the Socialist party. Many of them became personally attached and devoted to Thomas and tended to constitute a block of his followers within the party itself.

Thomas, however, did not achieve his position of leadership in the Socialist party via a struggle for power with other contenders. During the 1920's the party was hardly overflowing with outstanding actual or potential leaders. Debs was ill after his release from prison until his death in 1926. Most of the big names had left the party because of the war issue or the question of affiliation with the Third International. Hillquit and Berger were both getting on in years, and, since neither of them was American-born, they were completely ruled out as presidential candidates. To a large degree, Thomas became the outstanding leader of the Socialist party by default. In his own view, he was "Hobson's choice." [8] Symbolic of Thomas' rise in the party was the fact that he, who never had an intimate relationship with Debs, should have been chosen to deliver the oration at the latter's funeral in October of 1926.

It was virtually a foregone conclusion that Thomas would be his party's presidential nominee in 1928. There was some speculation to the effect that James H. Maurer of Pennsylvania would be nominated, but Thomas' was the only name that was actually put before the Socialist convention. Maurer was subsequently nominated as his running mate.

Thomas delivered an eloquent speech of acceptance. He told the assembled delegates many things that in future years he was to say over and over again in different ways to audiences all over the country. He declared that Socialist "achievement" could not be evaluated merely in terms of votes, because the important task was "the steady education of men and women in the possibilities . . . of peace, of freedom, of justice, of brotherhood, for all men everywhere." [9] He maintained "that no good man as a political Messiah can save America"; [10] yet he indicated that he hoped the major parties would nominate men of high caliber. Furthermore, he gravely questioned the view, subscribed to at the time by large numbers of Communists and some Socialists, that it was wise to hope for some national disaster in that it would lead to the establishment of a socialistic society. "The sad part of it is," he stated, "that there is no promise that out of convulsion you will get salvation." [11]

Though Thomas was not one of those who desired it, the "convulsion," in the form of near economic collapse, did occur in the United States; and his doubts about whether such a turn of events would automatically lead to socialism proved well justified. The catastrophic decline of the American economy, which began in 1929, did, however, have a dynamic influence upon the history of American socialism. The Great Depression was to revitalize the American Socialist party. During the era of normalcy most Americans were inclined to believe that this was the best of all possible worlds. They were completely confident of the fundamental soundness of the economic system under which they lived; it was the golden age of optimism. Practically the only predictions that were made, and certainly the only predictions that were widely listened to, told of an ever increasing prosperity in the United States. The depression came as a rude awakening, shattering smugness and destroying confidence. Instead of pointing to the fundamental soundness of the American economic order, people began taking note of its weaknesses. Thus the situation was conducive to the development of the growth and power of the various radical political movements. In the face of this unrest Americans were prepared to consider almost any way out.

The Socialist party hardly experienced a spectacular growth, but it did gain strength on several levels. In 1928 it had an official membership of 7,793; by 1933 its numbers had increased to 18,548. In 1928, when Thomas made his first venture as a presidential candidate, he received 267,420 votes; in 1932 he polled 884,781. The changes that were taking place in the Socialist party cannot be understood, however, merely in terms of membership statistics or votes cast. The organization was attaining a new lease on life—so to speak. Its still-small membership, which had for a long time been a paper membership, began to participate more actively in the affairs of the organization. Not only were old locals restored to life, but new ones were also being founded in many parts of the country.

This reawakening of the Socialist party cannot be totally explained in terms of the external events that were related to the depression. The personal contributions of Norman Thomas to this new upsurgence can scarcely be exaggerated. From the time of his formal assumption of leadership of the party, that is, after his nomination for the Presidency in 1928, Thomas did yeoman service for the party on a strictly organizational level. To a large degree he personally established and maintained effective communications between the various locals and national headquarters.

During the early 1930's, in campaign seasons and out, he was meeting an extraordinarily heavy speaking schedule, addressing Socialist, labor, church, and university groups. Much of his speaking was sponsored by local Socialist organizations and League for Industrial Democracy chapters, but he also spoke before many groups with distinctly non-Socialist orientations. From 1932 to 1936 he addressed meetings in all states of the Union except Mississippi, Nevada, South Carolina, and Wyoming. During this period he delivered literally thousands of speeches.

Whether he was initially sponsored by a Socialist or a non-Socialist group, the end results of his speaking trips were the same: the local Socialist organizations invariably profited by his appearances. When he spoke before private groups, he was usually able to make arrangements to speak also to his fellow partisans in the area. This situation was often advantageous to Socialist groups, which were invariably pressed for money, because it saved them his transportation and incidental expenses. If his time schedule would not permit speeches under the auspices of a local Socialist group, he practically always managed to confer with local Socialist leaders. Since the 1930's Thomas has earned his livelihood primarily from public speaking, but he virtually never took fees from Socialist groups. Actually, his Socialist electioneering was personally costly to him, because during campaigns he had time to accept only a very few paid speaking engagements.

Many Socialist locals and League for Industrial Democracy

chapters were founded in connection with Thomas' speaking engagements. Moreover, during these years he came to know virtually every local Socialist leader by name, and many thousands of the rank-and-file members had developed a personal acquaintanceship with him, even if in some cases it only amounted to a warm handshake or a few minutes of conversation. In this way many of his followers came to feel that he was interested in them as individuals, and their devotion to him was untold.

In terms of maintaining party communications, his ministerial and social-work background served him well, for he was frequently personal as well as political counsel to his followers. The thousands of letters that he wrote to his political comrades throughout the country served to tie the small party more closely together. Furthermore, his personal appeals to the more affluent party members and sympathizers constituted an important means of Socialist fund-raising. There can be no doubt that, during most of the years of his leadership, Norman Thomas was better informed concerning local party conditions and personnel than any other person within the Socialist party.

The degree to which the American Socialist party was a unified whole related in large measure to Norman Thomas' personal activities. His role in the realm of communications looms especially high when it is remembered that during most of its life the Socialist party has been in a perpetual state of financial crisis. The national office could never afford to hire the paid organizers or secretaries in the numbers needed. Moreover, in all probability they could never have done so effective a job as Thomas, for he already had the status of foremost leader of American socialism and was his party's nominee for the highest office in the land.

Profile of a Leader

What manner of man was to assume the mantle of Debs? What attributes did he possess and develop for political leadership that would have to be exercised in a world with problems and challenges infinitely more complex than those in the time of Debs? Over the last thirty years, Thomas has become even more of an institution than Debs had been. As America's Mr. Socialist, Thomas has remained, realistically speaking, without a competitor as the leader, interpreter, and public advocate of socialism.

Paradoxically, despite his long record of losing elections, Thomas was probably as well equipped for the holding of high office as any other American of his time. In 1932, long before he became Senator from Illinois, Paul H. Douglas regarded Norman Thomas "as the most appealing political personality of our times. . . . Thomas' whole career is evidence of what one brave, sensitive and able man can do. The last decade was in many ways disgraceful for both its corruption and the vulgarity of its materialism. That in such a decade one man could grow in stature as Thomas has is indeed proof of the spark which lies within men and of what may happen when idealists master realities." [12] Thomas rose rapidly in a minor party largely devoid of leaders, but undoubtedly his personal attributes would have pushed him toward important leadership responsibilities in almost any political organization.

The first impression that people have when they meet him is that of his towering size, which has been a distinct political asset. He is over six feet two inches tall and has the bearing of a leader. His height plus his "strongly etched patrician features" [13] give him a unique appearance. He exudes an aura of confidence and is always thoroughly in command of himself and the situation at hand. His self-confidence, however, does not convey arrogance.

He can communicate warmth and friendliness to widely varying types of people. The handshaking art of politics, so indispensable to effective political leadership, comes easily to him because he likes people and is interested in the problems of individuals as well as those of mankind en masse. Although he is probably more keenly sensitive to the problems of society than to problems confronting individuals, it is not difficult to address him as Norman; most of his political associates have done so. An innate sense of dignity, however, has prevented him from becoming a backslapper in any sense. He is interested in the masses, but he is never quite of them. He has an abundance of charm and an unfailing sense of humor which endear him even to persons who meet him once or know him only slightly.

Physical energy—almost an absolute requirement for a successful political career—is something that he has always possessed in phenomenal abundance. As a political campaigner he has exhibited seemingly endless vitality and stamina. The consensus among the various persons who have toured with him at campaign time, many of whom were twenty or thirty years his junior, is that they found it impossible to keep up with his pace. Even in his seventy-sixth year he has been known to talk politics until three o'clock in the morning with eager young socialists. Roger Baldwin, a nature enthusiast and long-time director of the American Civil Liberties Union, has complained that Norman even insists upon discussing politics when in the woods.

Thomas has virtually no hobbies or avocations and very few nonpolitical friends. All of his tremendous energies have been devoted almost exclusively to public affairs. That these energies have been effectively and productively expended is evidenced by his prodigious output of work. His life has been perfectly in tune with a phrase from a hymn that he remembers hearing so often as a boy: "Work, for the night is coming." [14] Only fantastic and incredibly efficient industry can explain the sixteen books, the scores of pamphlets, and the multitude of articles and leaflets, the many thousand speaking engagements, the unending succession of committee meetings and conventions, and a correspondence of staggering proportions, including letters to and from most of the major intellectual and political figures of our time. All of these activities were usually carried out with the aid of one secretary plus much help from his devoted wife.

Not infrequently, such enormous productivity is associated with the ruthless, impersonal, almost inhuman type of efficiency, but this has emphatically not been the case with Norman Thomas. The main focus of his unending crusade has been the reformation of American society—indeed world society—but he has never lost sight of the fact that societies are groups of individuals. As busy as he was, as pressured as he must have felt to meet his astronomical number of lecturing and writing commitments, he never ceased to be sensitive to and concerned with the needs and problems of friends, political comrades, and total strangers. Almost never did a letter received by him go unanswered. His keenly developed sense of duty would not permit such laxness. Even small children who wrote to ask, "What is socialism?" invariably received a reply. At no time does one feel that he begrudges the time he is giving or that he is particularly rushed or pressured. Through the years there has been a stream of visitors at his office and his home, including the humble and the prominent. When at Socialist gatherings, he almost invariably singles out the humblest and least secure individuals for special attention. Obscure and relatively unimportant members of the Socialist party were surprised and delighted to find that, when they came to New York and called Thomas just to say hello, it frequently meant an invitation to join him for lunch or perhaps to come to his home for dinner. During the years of his wife Violet's life, Thomas' home was open for every sort of Socialist meeting.

Thomas' letters are replete with instances of his efforts to aid people: jobs found for friends and comrades; arrangements for medical treatment; messages of encouragement, sympathy, and condolence; protests and concrete work in behalf of persons, regardless of their political faith, who were being deprived of liberty. Even his most bitter antagonists on the left, the Communists and the Trotskyites, found that he was willing to come to their aid when their civil rights were in jeopardy during the 1940's and 1950's. Earl Browder, who was for so many years commander-in-chief of American communism, can testify to this.

Thomas is an inveterate public letter-box writer. Year in and year out he has submitted a flood of letters to newspapers over the country, answering attacks on socialism or merely stating his views on the great issues of our time. An indomitable sense of responsibility—probably rising from his Protestant heritage—seems literally to drive him toward involvement in the correction of every and any individual or social wrong that comes to his attention.

He is enormously sensitive to the condition of mankind. His appearance of physical well-being actually seems to fluctuate with the world scene. During the period of the Eisenhower-Khrushchev honeymoon, when the spirit of Camp David prevailed, he looked better, less tired, less old. When the conference at the summit in the spring of 1960 collapsed over the U-2 incident and the cold war once again grew hotter, the turn of events could be seen in his face, in his walk, in his whole bearing; he looked ill. Sensitivity to the major political, social, and economic currents in the world about one is an absolute must for effective political leadership, but perhaps Thomas possesses this attribute in too large a measure. It may be that, ideally, a political leader should also have a kind of emotional toughness that insulates him from reacting so personally to the woes of the world.

"If I Were a Politician"

To a large degree, Mr. Thomas' public life has represented a fusion of the roles of party leader and educator. Indeed, by the conventional standards of politics his role has not been, strictly speaking, a political one. This is a strange but true statement to make about the man who has run more often for the highest office in the land than any other person in United States history. To the great amusement of many of his listeners, he has often been known to introduce some thought by saying, "If I were a politician." [15] The intent of this remark was doubtless humor, but nevertheless its implication is perfectly true. The transition that Norman Thomas made was not so much from the ministry to politics but rather a shorter one from the ministry to education. In campaign season and out, observes a fellow social reformer, Thomas' role has been essentially that of a "fighting evangelist for a faith." Thomas was to say innumerable times, "I would rather be right than be president but I am perfectly willing to be both." [16] And had he been less insistent about asserting his notions concerning social injustice and its remediation, his attainment of high political office might well have been possible.

Thomas' relation to American life closely approximates the

notion that James Bryce held concerning the proper role to be played by a political leader in a democratic society. Thus, in his classic work, *The American Commonwealth,* that keen student of American civilization wrote: "The duty . . . of a patriotic statesman in a country where public opinion rules, would seem to be rather to resist and correct than to encourage the dominant sentiment. He will not be content with trying to mold and form and lead it but he will confront it, lecture it, remind it that it is fallible, rouse it out of its self-complacency." [17]

In his role of inveterate critic of American society and leading champion of unpopular causes, Thomas has rarely missed an opportunity to remind his fellow citizens of their fallibility. His political specialty has been to undertake the kinds of tasks that Bryce laid at the door of the "patriotic statesman." Probably no man of our time has been more frequently or deservedly referred to as "the Conscience of America." By both deeds and words he has given notable and continuing service to the fight against every type of injustice in the United States.

Throughout his career he has consistently fought against racial, religious, and nationality prejudice in every shape and form. This included, for example, his vigorous protesting against the forced evacuation of Japanese Americans from the west coast during World War II, whereas most other Americans passively accepted this affront to their country's tradition of liberty.

As a founder of the American Civil Liberties Union, he has been active in virtually every struggle that has involved enlarging or preserving the American heritage of freedom during the last forty years. On behalf of the American Civil Liberties Union and the Socialist party, he hastened to areas where freedom of speech had been denied to some group or individual and delivered addresses in order to establish test cases and thereby challenge civil-liberty denials. He used this technique with conspicuous success in Passaic, New Jersey in 1926, at Terre Haute, Indiana in 1935, and in Jersey City, New Jersey in 1938 against the dictatorial rule of Mayor Frank Hague.

Norman Thomas worked untiringly and openly for the cause of organized labor long before that cause became a reasonably respectable one. He has marched in picket lines and addressed workers' rallies in almost every part of the United States. Few persons in the United States did more than Mr. Thomas to publicize the facts of the enormous hardships that the share-croppers were facing during the 1930's. He played a leading role in the organization of the short-lived Southern Tenant Farmers' Union, which ultimately became the Agricultural Workers' Union.

It is of significance to note that Mr. Thomas has not merely confined his crusading to causes that have been approved by liberal and humanitarian groups in the United States. He re-sisted the "dominant sentiment"—to use Bryce's phrase—by his almost constant criticism of the New Deal and Franklin Delano Roosevelt; by his determined opposition to the entrance of the United States into World War II; by his sharp criti-cisms of the conduct of American foreign policy during the war; by his bitter denunciation of Soviet totalitarianism, when so many Americans looked upon Russia as a great and demo-cratic ally; and by his condemnation of the dropping of the atomic bombs upon Hiroshima and Nagasaki at the close of the war. These stands cost him dearly in the political sense. By taking them he alienated many of his actual and potential followers in the liberal-radical world.

The role that Bryce advised and Thomas has played re-quired much personal courage and great moral conviction. Yet it should be pointed out that in many ways Thomas' position has been an enviable one. Once he made the decision to throw in his lot with minor-party politics, the way was paved for him to become the outspoken, courageous, and incorruptible public figure. His special situation enabled him to speak out on issues that major-party leaders found too hot to handle. The situation of the political leader who has not the remotest chance of securing office is radically different from that of the person who hopes or expects to be elected. Thomas has never been confronted by the responsibilities of political office, or even by those that go hand in hand with having a reasonable prospect of assuming office. The fear of losing an election for speaking out too boldly on issues was not a problem that Mr. Thomas had to face during the long years of his political campaigning. It was only rarely that it seemed at all in the realm of possibility that votes cast for Thomas would even sway an election to one or another of his opponents. Moreover, Thomas was probably not confronted by temptations that were of the same order as those that characterize major-party politics. The rewards that could have come to him for compromise of principle or for outright dishonesty were never comparable to those that were available to major-party leaders.

Thus it is that, even though he has gone through the forms of being a political leader, he has always been somehow remote from the real rough-and-tumble of American politics. More than being the politician, he has played the role of the educator on social, political, and economic subjects. Convinced of the educational nature of his role, a Columbia University dean once referred to Norman Thomas as a traveling colleague.

Thomas' critics in the radical movement have frequently disparaged him for his educational orientation. One sensitive writer, the late F. O. Matthiessen, who first heard Thomas speak during his college days, was skeptical concerning the importance of Thomas' role. "His views were very different from those of our Yale professors," wrote Matthiessen, in his *1907–1950,* "but he was still a kind of professor all the same. . . . I continued to respect Thomas but he never served to do much more than educate some middle-class intellectuals. He was never able, like Debs, to command a real mass movement." [18] In much more bitter language an old-guard partisan hurled substantially the same charge at Thomas: "Most of your time is devoted to the L.I.D., instead of the workers in the factories, mines, and mills. I suppose Karl Marx must have said: 'Students, Lawyers, Doctors, Ministers of the World Unite' instead of 'Workers of the World Unite!' " [19]

If, in the eyes of some of his fellow radicals, Thomas has been too conventional, not enough of a Marxist, to most other Americans he has seemed highly impractical and hopelessly doctrinaire. They have found it almost incomprehensible that a man with no prospect of gaining office should have so frequently consented to be a candidate. Norman Thomas has repeatedly told his audiences, "Vote your hopes and not your fears," or similarly, "Don't vote for what you don't want and get it." [20] Large numbers of his listeners have nodded in assent when he has told them that "there is more difference within the two major parties than there is between them" and that the choice is as significant as choosing between "Tweedledee and Tweedledum." [21] Yet even many of those persons who have been basically sympathetic with his ideas have refrained from voting for him. Such persons have generally argued that it was wiser to vote for the lesser of two evils—from their point of view usually the Democratic candidate—rather than "waste" a vote on Thomas. The result has been that as a candidate he has received much in the way of applause but little in the way of votes. At the close of an election, upon being complimented for waging a campaign of high caliber, he replied, "I appreciate the flowers only I wish the funeral hadn't been so complete." [22]

Considering his vast experience with political funerals, this perennial Socialist candidate behaved through the years, to an amazing degree, as an undaunted and enthusiastic campaigner. Because of their frequency, some Americans refused to take his candidacies seriously, but Thomas always looked upon them as serious affairs. His campaigns were invariably extremely strenuous: He spoke widely and without the benefit of private trains, large hotel suites, or ghost writers; he went up and down the country to meet a speaking schedule that even a William Jennings Bryan would have found burdensome.

"Mr. Chairman, Ladies, and Gentlemen"

Far and away, Thomas' most outstanding attribute as a political leader has been his rare ability as a public speaker. Certainly, he ranks as one of the great orators of the twentieth century, in a class with Eugene Debs, Franklin Roosevelt, and Woodrow Wilson but not surpassed by them. It is hard to compare him with major-party figures, in that they have so often delivered words written by others, whereas he never had ghost writers. Indeed, because of his spontaneous eloquence he did not seem to need them. His abilities as a public speaker are well matched by his talents as a writer. His career in journalism was already well established prior to his attaining importance within the Socialist party. He writes well, consistently, and beautifully at times. His fantastic output of articles and books indicates that he reads and writes very rapidly. Such facility with a pen has been absolutely necessary for a party leader who could not afford ghost writers and who, on moral grounds, was unwilling to use them.

Thomas regards himself as being much more effective as a speaker than as a writer. To hear him from a lecture platform is invariably a stirring experience, both intellectually and emotionally. His utterances exhibit a profound grasp of man's past and a keen sensitivity to the trends of the future. His wide education serves to enrich his public speaking; his lectures abound with historical, literary, and, almost invariably, biblical allusions. Non-socialist experts in the field of speech have long regarded him as one of America's most able public speakers. He has a unique and distinctive speaking style. His speeches are punctuated by humor, by mimicry through changes in his voice, by frequent variations in the speed of his delivery, and by searching, almost haunting, rhetorical questions. His use of language is frequently vivid and striking. He likened the 1948 Democratic convention to "a carnival in a morgue lined with unburied hopes." [23]

Communications expert Harry MacArthur regards Norman Thomas as a superb actor. "Like a veteran Shakespearean player," wrote MacArthur in Washington's *Sunday Star,* "he needs but to be thrown a cue to reply with the answering soliloquy and the rest of the play. He has a perfect sense of timing and an accurate feel for dramatic values. He can let an audience and an opponent relax, then suddenly, with a verbal shaft, skewer the opponent and jerk the audience to attention. He can explode and harangue when the necessity presents itself. His personality is imposing and his wit is quick." [24]

Thomas is very stimulated by and reaches his greatest heights as a speaker in debate situations or addresses to large audiences. He excels as an orator to great crowds. So ingrained is the orator's role that one British Labor Member of Parliament has, with some justice, complained that Thomas seems to be making a speech even when in private conversation.

Thomas is at his best and prefers to speak in extemporaneous fashion from a carefully prepared outline. Thus he is enabled to make quick adjustments to the mood of his audience. He is weakest as a radio speaker, when he has little opportunity to give play to his dramatic talents and his admitted tendency to speak too fast is emphasized. In part, this acceleration occurred because the Socialist party was never able to buy enough radio time to enable Thomas to say all of the things that he thought needed to be said. Therefore, when broadcasting, he always tried to say as much as he could in the shortest possible time.

Even the great American cynic H. L. Mencken, writing in the *Baltimore Sun* on October 18, 1948, counted it "a rare and exhilarating pleasure" to hear Norman Thomas in Baltimore during the 1948 campaign.[25] Mencken might have been expected to dismiss Thomas as a "do gooder," but, instead, he regarded him as a "really intelligent and civilized man." [26] Considering that Mencken was a great authority on the American language—and never a pundit who specialized in bolstering the egos of others—his reactions to Thomas' speech are worth quoting at length:

It was extempore throughout, and swell stuff indeed. No Republican rhetorician in this campaign, to my knowledge, has ever delivered more effective cracks at the demagogy of the Hon. Mr. Truman, and no Democrat has done greater execution upon the limber triming [*sic*] of the Hon. Mr. Dewey. Most of all, no one of either party has made a greater hash of the dismal baloney of the Hon. Mr. Wallace and his Communists.

It ran on for more than an hour, but it seemed far shorter than an ordinary political speech of twenty minutes.

It was full of adept and memorable phrases, some of them apparently almost new. It shined with wit and humor. The speaker poked gentle but devastating fun at all the clowns in the political circus, by no means forgetting himself. There was not a trace of rancor in his speech, and not a trace of Messianic bombast. . . .

His voice is loud, clear and a trifle metallic. He never starts a sentence that doesn't stop, and he never accents the wrong syllable in a word or the wrong word in a sentence.[27]

There is almost always a tone of urgency in what Thomas says. Eloquently, but with apparent ease, he communicates fiery indignation at some of the less lovely features of American life: the poverty, the materialism, the racism, and the gap between our democratic ideals and practices. But his manner and his words always convey to his audiences that they are listening to one who loves his country, who treasures its best traditions, but who is determined to make it an even better place in which to live. He practically never fails to exhort his audiences to the conquest of poverty and the abolition of war, and to provide them with his plans for achieving these ends. Perhaps his greatest asset as a speaker is his ability to moralize in a fashion so persuasive and so impassioned that not for one second do his listeners doubt his sincerity. Earnestness, integrity, conviction—these qualities flow freely from his words, and sometimes, unfortunately, there are ministerial holier-than-thou notes in what he says. But his marvelous and spontaneous sense of humor has been an effective antidote to this occasional indulgence in self-righteousness.

He is a master of political humor. "His barbs are fired with a smile," observes a close student of politics, "but they hit their mark with telling effect." [28] Not infrequently, Thomas has lamented the fact that his wisecracks have been more widely quoted than the substance and meat of his speeches. He likes to say, with regard to his quest for political office, "I was catholic in my tastes." [29] His ever-willingness to run for low as well as high offices, if it was thought that the party would thus be benefited, helped to endear him to his political followers.

Decades of political campaigning for an assortment of offices, ranging from alderman to the Presidency, provided excellent play for his irrepressible sense of humor. In 1932 he asked his audiences not to hold Herbert Hoover responsible for the country's economic plight because "such a little man could not have made so big a depression." [30] Thomas' reaction to Wendell Willkie's speech accepting the Republican presidential nomination in 1940 was: "a synthesis of Guffey's First Reader, the Genealogy of Indiana, the collected speeches of Tom Girdler and the New Republic. He agreed with Mr. Roosevelt's entire program of social reform and said it was leading to disaster." [31] Always handicapped and frustrated by the inability of the Socialist party to buy enough radio time, Thomas reminded his listeners during a broadcast in the campaign of 1944, "I have minutes to discuss what Governor Dewey and President Roosevelt will have hours to evade." [32]

Just before the close of the 1948 campaign he was presented with a "diamond"-covered soapbox upon being initiated into the Circus, Saints, and Sinners Club. "I think I know why you gave me this," he said. "I'm the only man in America who can stand on a platform. In fact, I'm the only one with one to stand on." [33] He described Truman as asking his speech writers, "What's it going to be tonight?" Candidate Dewey, Thomas continued, is "clad each day in a pair of platitudes." "Harry Truman," he declared during the course of the same campaign, "proves the old adage that any man can become President of the United States." [34]

In 1929 Ramsay MacDonald, then Socialist Prime Minister of Great Britain, visited the United States. When introducing him to a New York audience, Mayor James Walker flubbed and said, "Now I present to you the Prime Minister of the United States." Quick as lightning and loud enough to be heard over the public-address system, Norman Thomas, who was in the audience, shouted out, "I heartily second this proposition." [35] Thomas' verbal quickness was also well demonstrated during one of his numerous radio debates on foreign policy. The moderator introduced him and added that Mr. Thomas had just received word of the birth of his thirteenth grandchild. Thomas instantly capitalized upon the announcement and began his speech by saying, "In other words, thirteen specific reasons for avoiding another war." [36]

The most fascinating part of a typical Norman Thomas meeting is usually the question period. Invariably, he provokes a large number of questions, to which he ordinarily gives detailed and lengthy answers; occasionally, these replies are too long. A storehouse of information, he is habitually ready, perhaps too much so, to venture an opinion on any aspect of man or the universe. It seems to be psychologically impossible for him to indicate that he has no position with regard to a question. Very occasionally he will say that a question is out of his area of competence, but then he will very often go on to say that he has a friend who is an expert on the matter at hand and will proceed to elaborate his friend's position as if it were his own. Usually, Thomas can suffer fools, if not gladly, at least politely; but, on occasion, he will give a rather angry response to a stupid question and mar somewhat the effectiveness of his main speech.

Thomas is not unaware of his remarkable abilities as a speaker. After a debate on socialism with a former New York Congressman, he remarked to a young Socialist that he could have presented the other side much more effectively than did his opponent. Despite his great confidence in his own oratory, Thomas makes a very realistic assessment in his *Mr. Chairman, Ladies, and Gentlemen*——a book of reflections about public speaking——of his impact as a speaker upon the world of politics: "It is obvious that all this speaking which I have done failed to achieve my principal object: the building of a strong democratic socialist movement. . . . I do not under-estimate the importance of effective public speech when I say that, given the circumstances, I could have made better speeches and still have failed, while under different circumstances I might have made worse speeches and succeeded." [37]

Pied Piper to Young Idealists

Nevertheless, to hear Norman Thomas, even if one does not share his political values, is to be captivated by his idealism, energy, and wit—a fact which is all the more true if the listener happens to be of college age, intelligent, and possessed of social consciousness to some degree. James Wechsler, now editor of the *New York Post,* reports that "he fell politically in love" as a consequence of interviewing Thomas for the Columbia University *Spectator*. Wechsler wrote to a friend, "He's the most impressive gentleman I've ever encountered." [38] Free-lance writer Milton Mayer also recalls his enormous youthful admiration for Norman Thomas: "I like Norman Thomas greatly, admire and respect and honor him; but once, when I was young and idolized nobody else, I idolized him." [39]

The basis of Thomas' appeal to alert young people is well explained by journalist Murray Kempton, who, as a college student, was a member of the Young People's Socialist League during the 1930's. Mr. Kempton writes, in his *Part of Our Time,* that Thomas "conveyed . . . [the] feeling that there is something glorious about being forever engaged. He seemed always just back from the side of the sharecroppers or being egged by the friends of Frank Hague. In that guise, he represented the only available piece of that buried tradition of the American radical about which Dos Passos wrote. The old libertarian dream of spending one's life in lonely combat against every form of enslavement, to the extent that it was not a Communist confusion, appeared to us to have no vessel but Norman Thomas." [40]

Young people have found Norman Thomas enormously appealing, not only because he seems to symbolize idealism and unselfish devotion to human betterment, but also because he has the capacity for talking to intelligent young men and women as if they were his peers. It may be that Thomas has put too much store in the opinions and sentiments of the young. Kempton reports that a person who once belonged to the Young People's Socialist League, and who later became a leader of the International Ladies' Garment Workers Union, has said "that, when he was eighteen . . . he was flattered to have Thomas take his advice so seriously, but that, when he was twenty-one, he was simply appalled." [41]

To conclude, however, that Thomas makes a practice of flattering youth and thereby wins their adulation would be inaccurate. He does not hesitate to admonish his youthful audiences for what he believes to be their shortcomings. He demands that they face up to their responsibilities in a troubled world. When he addressed an overflowing meeting at a large midwestern university in April, 1959, a student complained during the question period that Thomas had criticized "this generation for its fatalism, its silence . . . for its failure to organize in opposition to the foibles of our government." The young man argued that it was not "the fault of his generation" but rather, he implied, the fault of the kind of world youth had inherited.[42]

At such sentiments Thomas becomes greatly aroused. He replied:

> None of us is wholly responsible for anything. We've all got parents, and now it's a fashion to hold that parents are responsible for most that we do wrong. I've rewritten the parable of the prodigal son: When the young man comes home to his father and says, "I've sinned against heaven and in thy sight; I'm no more worthwhile to be called thy son," he adds, "But, after all, it was all mother's fault; I'm the victim of momism." [*laughter*] I'll agree that his mother may have done wrong. . . . She didn't have the right text-books and all the rest of it. And I'll agree that my generation, and my sons', and all the generations have made lots of mistakes. But I get awfully tired of hearing this kind of apology so that in the last analysis it's the people I'm talking to . . . who have never made mistakes. It has been, in the past, youth who have done things, even when their elders have made mistakes.

Thomas was in no mood to let his youthful audience off the hook. He went on to tell the story, one of his favorites, about the religious mother who had a boy who liked to fight:

She used to tell him, "Jimmy, when you think of fighting, remember that it's the Devil that's telling you to fight." He said, "Yes, mother." So she went downtown—and when she came back she pulled Jimmy off the neighbor, Johnny. And she said, "Jimmy, Jimmy, didn't I tell you that when you felt like fighting it was the Devil, and you should say, 'Get thee behind me, Satan'"? And he said, "Yes, mother, it's true the Devil told me to hit him, but I thought of kicking him all by myself." [43]

Again, there was laughter, but Thomas' listeners got the point: All of us, young and old, must be held accountable for the tragic condition of mankind.

His ability to fire the enthusiasm of youth, even as he chided them, has been so great that innumerable young people joined the Socialist party or came to identify themselves as socialists largely as a consequence of having heard or met Norman Thomas. Ironically, he was much more successful at carrying the socialist message to other people's children than to his own. It is true that of the young people who came to the Socialist party during the 1930's, its most recent period of vigor, only a tiny minority have remained; yet the influence of Norman Thomas and their Socialist experience has in countless cases had a lasting effect.

The measure of a leader is not merely his direct impact upon the events of his time; he has to be judged as well by the influence that he may have had on others who also come to play roles of leadership. In surprisingly large numbers, those persons who came under the spell of Norman Thomas in their youth have played important leadership roles in contemporary American society. They are to be found chiefly in the labor movement and in the liberal wing of the Democratic party.

The most dramatic example of the power that Norman Thomas' political offspring wield is provided by the United Automobile Workers. Virtually every member of the high command of this outstandingly vigorous, progressive, and powerful labor organization, including the three Reuther brothers, once belonged to the Socialist party. As relatively young men, they met and came under the influence of Norman Thomas, and established close relationships with him. With varying degrees of enthusiasm, the UAW leaders have attached themselves to the Democratic party. They are now ardent liberals rather than Socialists. Generally, it follows that disenchantment with a cause means disillusionment with its leader, but not so in the case of the UAW chieftains and their attitudes toward Thomas. Almost to a man, they regard him with affectionate admiration and tremendous respect. Walter Reuther, Victor Reuther, and Emil Mazey have loaned their names in recent years to celebrations in Thomas' honor.

For years, even though he repeatedly came to Detroit, Thomas avoided visiting Solidarity House—the UAW's palatial headquarters. He was anxious not to cause any embarrassment to his former followers, whom he knew to be less than eager to have attention called to their Socialist pasts. Perhaps he was hurt that years went by and he was never officially invited. Yet publicly and privately, he always said that he regarded Walter Reuther as the leader of labor to whom the United States could look with the most hope. During approximately the first decade of his presidency of the UAW, 1947–57, Walter Reuther seemed to avoid any public association with Norman Thomas, not because of any personal antipathy but apparently because he thought such association would be tactically unwise. Doubtless Thomas had the UAW leadership in mind when reminiscing about his experiences as a public speaker: "There was a time that I was in much demand by labor groups. . . . However, as the labor movement grew stronger and more deeply indebted to the New Deal it seemed to most of its leaders, including some ex-Socialists once inclined to deplore my relative conservatism, rather inexpedient to invite so prominent a Socialist as Norman Thomas." [44]

By the time Thomas was in his seventy-sixth year, public communication between him and the UAW was re-established. Perhaps the leadership had a change of heart; perhaps they felt more secure in their positions of power; or perhaps they never deliberately intended to remain aloof from their former leader. Whatever the explanation, in February of 1960 Thomas was invited to appear on the UAW's television program, "Telescope." Also, what was to be a small luncheon with a few UAW staff members was arranged, but when the word got around that Thomas was to be at Solidarity House, requests to attend began pouring in. Many people were turned away, but some eighty guests from in and around the Detroit labor movement did have lunch with the veteran Socialist. It was a sentimental, nostalgic occasion; the atmosphere was permeated by warmth and good feeling. These very practical labor leaders were intent upon paying homage to the grand old man who had never ceased to fight for the causes of their youth—causes from which they had somehow never managed to disassociate themselves totally. They delighted in being in the presence of this witty, urbane man who had had such an enormous impact on their formative years. Perhaps they were in a mood of self-congratulation because the idol of their youth had proved worthy of their youthful allegiance and admiration.

Thomas thoroughly enjoyed the reunion and was apparently in fine public-speaking form. As one labor educator recalls, "He poked fun at some of labor's shibboleths, gleefully pointed

out the antics of some of 'labor's friends,' made jocular references to the Union's professions for peace on the one hand
and to its plea for more defense work on the other—and so on
and so on. The audience loved it. He received a standing
ovation." [45] He was probably the only man in the country who
could have talked to these unionists in so critical a vein without rousing their rancor. It seems that they felt he had almost
a parental right to scold them.

In the Circle of His Family

While Thomas was trying to remake the world, he was also
a husband and a father. As their offspring and friends have
testified, his marriage to Frances Violet Stewart proved to be
a remarkably happy and satisfying one. A daughter-in-law has
described it as "the most wonderful marriage I ever saw in
my life." [46]

There is no doubt in Norman Thomas' mind that his be-
loved Violet shared his basic beliefs and generally saw eye to
eye with him on the day-to-day issues that arose in a rapidly
changing world. Yet one of their children insists that "she was
by no means a socialist." [47] Socialist or not, she loved her husband deeply, was enormously loyal to him, and cheerfully ad-
justed her life to his incredibly demanding schedule, which
so often took him away from her and their children. Thomas
was always keenly aware that many other public men were
not so blessed. During the years of their marriage and since
the death of Violet in 1947, he repeatedly acknowledged his
"debt" to her "for extraordinary happiness in difficult years
and for strength to carry on. Whatever happens in these times
of trouble, I am convinced that there is no substitute for the
kind of family life that she made possible for me and for our
children." [48] Perhaps it was his love for his wife, which ex-

tended to her aristocratic relatives, that accounts in part for the fact that Thomas has never advocated class warfare. Thomas has spoken of his marriage as "perhaps the only real success of my life." [49]

Norman and Violet reared a large family. After Norman, Jr. (b. 1911), who died in childhood, came William (b. 1912), Polly (b. 1914), Frances (b. 1915), Becky (b. 1918), and Evan (b. 1920). There are fifteen grandchildren. The Thomas off-spring are conventional people who lead conventionally successful lives. William holds an executive position with the American Red Cross. Evan, a successful editor, was recently made a vice president of Harper and Brothers. Both sons attended Princeton. Polly is married to a physician, Frances to a banker, and Becky to a personnel officer for a large firm.

Early in his career as social reformer Thomas pledged himself to exert no pressure upon his children to embrace his socialism or any of his other causes. In retrospect, he wonders "if he leaned too far backwards." [50] Of his five children perhaps only one can be accurately called a socialist. Yet they are all interested participants in the affairs of their own communities, a fact which pleases their father greatly.

All of Norman Thomas' children have warm and satisfying relationships with him. If they no longer entirely share his politics, they continue to love and respect him and regard him as a great man. Considering the amount of time he was away from home, his relationship with his children is uncommonly good. His children feel that his repeated and long absences were somewhat compensated for by the fact that he had the capacity for being all father when he was with them. Another compensation was that their uncle Evan Thomas, whom all of the Thomas children came to adore, lived with them during most of the years of their childhood, and perhaps in some ways this warm, unforgettable human being was a father figure.

The children of busy public figures frequently do not fare well in the psychological sense, but Norman and Violet developed for their children a healthy and harmonious family life. As Mr. Thomas is the first to admit, the credit for this achievement must go to his late wife. All who knew her, including her in-laws, maintain that she was a remarkable wife and mother, a person capable of great loyalty and devotion.

In family and in other nonpolitical matters, Thomas is no radical. According to the tradition of his forefathers, he believes in and lives by a rather strict code of individual morality. Perhaps he understands human failing better than his own parents did, but he is still rather intolerant of it. If any of his children did not receive top grades in all academic endeavors, he was inclined to consider it a matter of moral dereliction. During an interview with a *New York Herald Tribune* reporter on the occasion of his seventy-fifth birthday, he announced proudly, "There's not one divorce among my five children and that ought to set some sort of record." [51]

Thomas is as conventional in his reactions to art as he is about family relationships. "I must confess that I am a great conservative in art and music," he has remarked, "and in the presence of modern art I am speechless. . . . I get all my modern art from the drawings of my grandchildren." [52]

One of the major leaders of the UAW, who deeply admires Thomas, perceptively evaluates him as a "moralist-idealist," [53] and he has been this both at home and in the arena of public affairs. Thomas is an outstanding example of the moral man in the immoral society: the incorruptible Puritan of American politics. His selfless devotion to the public weal for a half-century has few parallels in United States history. Either in the ministry or in major-party politics his combination of phenomenal energy and ability would have assuredly brought to him more of the conventional symbols of success. He did not deliberately set out to make his life almost a constant crusade against injustice. He never expected to become a Socialist. In all probability he would not have become a political radical had he not gone, after his graduation from Princeton, to New York and been exposed to religious modernism at the Union Theological Seminary and to desperate urban poverty. Even though he demitted the ministry in 1931, over the protests of the New York presbyters, the Christian minister fighting against evil symbolizes best his decades of championing unpopular causes. He felt compelled to propagate his socialism much as his ancestors had been moved to bring the Word of God to their parishioners.

CHAPTER IV

The Roots of Factionalism

AMONG THE many situations that confronted Norman Thomas in his role as a leader of the Socialist party, recurring factionalism, which resulted in schism after schism, was the most basic. Factionalism is inherent in all politics, but within major American political groups it has generally not been so intense, constant, or destructive a phenomenon. Had Norman Thomas been able to cope successfully with the situation of factionalism, the whole history of American socialism during the last three decades might have been significantly different. Possibly, by some miracle, the period would have been characterized by growth rather than by unprecedented Socialist decline.

Factionalism was at its height within the party between 1930 and 1940. At the beginning of that decade there was still some remote hope that the Socialist party would develop into a powerful force in American political life; by the end of it all such hope had been abandoned by realistic men. It was during that period that Norman Thomas faced his most significant tests as a party leader.

Socialist factionalism of the 1930's cannot be understood apart from other larger, more or less external situations that were dynamically affecting the leadership role of Norman Thomas and the history of the Socialist party. It was condi-

104

tioned by a complex of forces rising fundamentally from fascism, communism, the New Deal, the upsurgence of labor, and the outbreak of World War II.

Factions Emerge

Rumblings of factionalism in the Socialist party were to be heard even before the opening of the 1930's. In December of 1928, just after the close of the presidential campaign, a series of meetings was held under the informal sponsorship of the League for Industrial Democracy to discuss the possibility of founding a third party. Norman Thomas played a leading role in these discussions. Other party members who became involved were Edward Levinson, Paul Blanshard, McAlister Coleman, Reinhold Niebuhr, and Paul Porter. Also represented were prominent American liberals John Dewey, Oswald Garrison Villard, Morris L. Ernst, Paul H. Douglas and W. E. B. DuBois. Thomas had apparently not been completely disillusioned by the 1924 Progressive honeymoon and still thought in terms of a Socialist-liberal political alliance.

Out of these deliberations came the founding of the League for Independent Political Action. John Dewey was named chairman of the new organization. Its first important political venture was to give active support to Norman Thomas in the New York mayoralty race of 1929. He received 175,000 votes, which was a good showing by Socialist standards. Nevertheless, many of the more influential members of the party in New York, whose thinking was strongly influenced by Morris Hillquit, were deeply suspicious of the League for Independent Political Action. To them it symbolized a watering down of socialism, and they resented Thomas' affiliation with it. This group of New York Socialists, soon to be known as the old guard, was made up for the most part of Jews who were

European-born and self-educated. They were closely tied to needle-trade unions and the *Jewish Daily Forward*. For long years this newspaper has been the most important Yiddish-language daily in the country. It was a key instrument of Socialist education in the early part of this century. Through generous financial aid, the *Forward* and various old-guard organizations enabled the party to survive during the 1920's. To a great extent during these years the New York party was the Socialist party.

The old guard, which was Marxian in its avowed philosophy but not radically inclined when it came to action, feared that the activities of the League for Independent Political Action would mean the corruption and dilution of "their" Socialist party. They were panicked by the fear that some of Thomas' associates wanted to abandon the name of the Socialist party. When John Dewey asked Senator George W. Norris to co-operate with the League for Independent Political Action, the New York Socialist party was quick to pass a resolution reaffirming the notion that it was "the party of the working class" and that it wanted no connection with individuals who disagreed with the capitalist parties only in little ways.[1]

The group that gathered around Thomas in the party—sometimes called the progressives—was much less inclined than the old guard to worship at the shrine of Marx. The progressives were inclined to be pragmatic in their political thinking. They thought that the Socialist traditionalism of the old guard was hamstringing the development of a vigorous Socialist party. For the most part, the progressives were American-born, middle-class, and university-educated. A number of them were pacifist ministers. They had had intimate association with Thomas via the League for Industrial Democracy and the *World Tomor-*

row. As appears to be characteristic of liberals, however, the progressives were not a cohesive group.

Another group, to be known as the militants, emerged. It was probably smaller than the progressives but significantly more vocal. It was essentially composed of young people who were embittered and disillusioned by the depression. Their ilk was coming in large numbers to all of the radical parties during this period. As one might expect, they were demanding action. The militants were contemptuous of both the old guard and the progressives. They viewed themselves as radical Marxists who opposed gradualism and reformism. Thus they automatically found themselves apart from the essentially non-Marxist progressives. In the years to come, however, they worked jointly with the progressives in opposition to the old guard. They viewed the Marxism of the old guard as a façade. To the militants, who were enamored of the Russian experiment, it was inconceivable for the old guard to pledge allegiance to Marxism and at the same time to be highly critical of Soviet Russia. Among the more important leaders of the militants were Maynard Kreuger, Franz Daniel, Theodore Shapiro, and Andrew J. Biemiller.

The lines that separated these Socialist factions were, of course, not always clearly drawn. Large numbers of party members remained essentially aloof from what was eventually to develop into fratricidal warfare. Nevertheless, intense factionalism was prevalent within the Socialist party during the 1930's.

A number of factors appear to have caused this disunity. In the first place, it was an aspect of the revitalization that the Socialist party was experiencing in the years of the Great Depression. Socialists had seen the first part of their economic prophecy come true. They had rather consistently rejected the idea that the American economy was fundamentally sound, which was a widely held notion during the 1920's. They predicted that the boom would be followed by bust; and it was. Now they awaited the fulfillment of their prophecy's second part: the collapse of capitalism and the establishment of a socialist society. If capitalism was breathing its last breath, then it followed that it was of crucial importance to arrive at the correct tactics for ushering in a socialist order. With the millennium presumably so near at hand, it was of critical importance to arrive at the correct socialist theory and action. One could not risk letting the dream slip away, and each group within the party was convinced that only it knew the sure road to the utopia.

Secondly, the ensuing years of party history were to precipitate conflict between generations. To a certain extent it was to be the younger people in the party against the older people. The old guard represented the conservatism of age; the militants and progressives, the radicalism of youth. Similarly, it was to be a struggle between those who had long held control of party machinery and policy, and newcomers who were anxious to break what they viewed as a power monopoly. Moreover, since the Socialist party had lost rather than gained members during the 1920's, there was no sizeable in-between age group to temper the behavior of the disputants.

Thirdly, the factionalism of the 1930's was to a degree a manifestation of sectionalism. Almost from the founding of the Socialist party, members in the country at large were suspicious of their New York comrades. The New York branch of the organization was always very powerful in terms of numbers and influence, and westerners and middle westerners were fearful that the New Yorkers were attempting to dominate the party. Also, it was charged over and over again that the New Yorkers were intellectually arrogant, that they had a know-it-all attitude, that they were condescending in their relationships with members from other parts of the country. Conflict on this level was partly an aspect of tension between native and foreign-born members of the party. It was also symptomatic of the distrust with which people from smaller communities frequently view the residents of the giant metropolis. With consciousness of these geographical divisions, Socialist-party headquarters have been variously located in Springfield, Massachusetts, St. Louis, Missouri, New York, New York, and Chicago, Illinois.

Finally, it should be kept in mind that this was the period during which Norman Thomas was trying to secure his leadership position. He was trying to become the leader of the Socialist party in fact as well as in name. There is some reason to believe that Thomas feared that Hillquit wanted to relegate him to the position of a figurehead, which some maintained had been the role of Debs. Another factor contributing to Thomas' changed attitude toward Hillquit was that in 1931 Hillquit, acting in the courts as attorney in behalf of the former owner of certain Russian oil interests, appeared to question the sacred socialist principle of public ownership of natural resources—or so it seemed to Thomas and numbers of other Socialists at the time. Thomas, however, never denied Hillquit's great abilities or his enormous contributions to the development of American socialism.

1932: Convention and Campaign

Factionalism tangibly got under way at the Milwaukee, Wisconsin, National Convention of the Socialist party in 1932, during which Norman Thomas was nominated for the second

time as the presidential candidate. At this convention a progres-
sive-militant alliance was achieved in an attempt to depose
Morris Hillquit as national chairman of the party. The aim
was to replace Hillquit with Mayor Daniel W. Hoan of Milwaukee. It was a strange union in that the militants did not
dislike the progressives less but disliked the old guard more.

The maneuver was unsuccessful; Hillquit was re-elected by
a convention vote of 105 to 85 and a membership vote of 7,526
to 6,984. Hillquit, who was an adroit public speaker, had made
a speech loaded with sarcastic allusions to the youthfulness and
inexperience of his opponents, and by his closing remarks he
clinched his election: "I apologize for being born abroad, for
being a Jew, and for living in New York."[2] These indirect
accusations of prejudice, however, were less than just. The
attempt to unseat Hillquit was apparently part of Thomas'
strategy to Americanize the Socialist party, but it was in no way
an antiforeign campaign. Undoubtedly, Thomas believed that
the American-born Hoan, the mayor of a large American city,
would be a more appealing figure and a more suitable chairman than Hillquit. This was probably true, but in terms of
the internal politics of the Socialist party it proved to be a very
unwise position to take. To oppose Hillquit, who, since Berger's death, was indisputably the grand old man of the party,
the most distinguished living founding father, was a large
and perilous undertaking.

Charges, mostly by innuendo, that Thomas and his followers
were anti-Semitic had no basis in fact, but in later years even
Thomas was to admit that one speech delivered by an unimportant backer of Hoan could have been so interpreted. More
significantly, many of Thomas' most ardent supporters were
Jews—including Charney Vladeck, an important official of the
Jewish Daily Forward—and they emphatically denied the

The American Socialist party met in Chicago, Ill., during September, 1932, to map out its national campaign for the coming presidential election. Party leaders shown conferring above are, left to right, National Party Chairman Morris Hillquit, Mrs. Victor Berger, Socialist presidential candidate Norman Thomas, and Daniel W. Hoan. (UPI)

Socialist party standard-bearers in the 1932 presidential campaign were vice-presidential candidate James Maurer and presidential candidate Norman Thomas. (UPI)

Presidential candidate Norman Thomas speaks to a crowd gathered in Rayburn Plaza, Philadelphia, Pa., in October, 1932. (UPI)

charges of anti-Semitism. Nevertheless, in human affairs what is believed to be true is often as important as what is true. The number of people who actually believed these unsubstantiated charges is difficult to estimate, but without a doubt the whole attempt to unseat Hillquit inflicted deep wounds that were to fester for years to come. Indeed, they were never to be completely healed.

During the campaign of 1932 the Socialist leadership behaved publicly as if there were peace and harmony within the party. In actuality, relationships between the various factions in the party were becoming more strained. Despite this fact, 1932 proved to be the most successful campaign of Thomas' long career as candidate for the Presidency.

In addition to the usual Socialist call for the "public ownership and democratic control" of the "basic industries," the platform on which Thomas ran in 1932 included the following series of twelve immediate demands that remarkably anticipated many of the essential features of the New Deal:

1. A Federal appropriation of $5,000,000,000 for immediate relief for those in need to supplement State and local appropriations.

2. A Federal appropriation of $5,000,000,000 for public works and roads, reforestation, slum clearance, and decent homes for the workers, by Federal Government, States and cities.

3. Legislation providing for the acquisition of land, buildings, and equipment necessary to put the unemployed to work producing food, fuel, and clothing and for the erection of houses for their own use.

4. The 6-hour day and the 5-day week without reduction of wages.

5. A comprehensive and efficient system of free public employment agencies.

6. A compulsory system of unemployment compensation with adequate benefits, based on contributions by the Government and by employers.

7. Old-age pensions for men and women 60 years of age and over.

8. Health and maternity insurance.

9. Improved system of workmen's compensation and accident insurance.

10. The abolition of child labor.

11. Government aid to farmers and small home-owners to protect them against mortgage foreclosures and moratorium on sales for non-payment of taxes by destitute farmers and unemployed workers.

12. Adequate minimum wage laws.[3]

Certainly the 1932 Democratic and Republican platforms gave no comparable evidence of understanding the needs of the nation in this time of great crisis.

Prior to the election, optimistic Socialists and their friends were thinking in terms of a vote of 2,000,000 to 3,000,000. Thomas indicated that he would be encouraged by a vote as high as 1,500,000. The official count was 884,781, which came as a deep disappointment to Thomas and his supporters.

Fascism, the New Deal, and Communism

Between the closing of the 1932 presidential campaign and the next national convention of the Socialist party, which was scheduled for the spring of 1934, Socialists of the various factions spent more time maneuvering for position and planning strategy for the next national party meeting than they did at their avowed major functions of socialist education and organization. It would seem that during this period the so-called Thomas progressives and the militants tended to coalesce. Men who were closely associated with Thomas, like Reinhold Niebuhr, Paul Blanshard, and Coleman Cheyney, were becoming increasingly identified with the militants. Thomas consistently refused to identify himself formally as a militant, largely because his non-Marxist stand made such action impossible. Indeed, he always maintained that he belonged to no faction. Nevertheless, the militants increasingly regarded Thomas as their leader, and his own growing opposition to the old guard made it appear as if he were.

In most ways, the militants seemed to be gaining strength in the months leading to the 1934 convention. The old guard, however, retained a tight hold on the party's powerful subsidiaries: the *Jewish Daily Forward,* the *New Leader,* the Rand School of Social Science, and Camp Tamiment. Old-guard prospects were seriously dimmed by the death of Morris Hillquit on October 8, 1933, for they had no other leader of comparable stature.

The world situation between 1932 and 1934 was driving the already hostile Socialist camps farther apart. The assumption relied upon by Socialists for years, that the downfall of capitalism would automatically be followed by the establishment of socialism, had already been proved wrong in Italy by Mussolini and his Fascist cohorts. Hitler's seizure of power in Germany dumfounded the whole Socialist world. German socialism had long been looked upon by the more conservative Socialist groups as a shining example. After all, it was the movement that had produced Bebel and Kautsky; its membership ran into the millions; it had organized powerful and wealthy labor and co-operative movements. Why did it surrender to Nazism with hardly a murmur? The militants answered that it was because of its inherent conservatism and because it had been unwilling to undertake the necessary co-operation with the German Communists in order to avert the disaster. They also concluded that fascism was imminent in the United States and that only some kind of "united action" between the Socialists and the Communists could save America from the fate of Germany.

Even more disheartening to American Socialists, if possible, than what happened in Germany was the pattern of events in Austria. Just as the German socialist movement had been looked upon as a model by the less radical Socialists, the so-called revolutionary Socialists had looked to the Austrian movement for their inspiration. It had been led by the renowned theoretician Otto Bauer; it had had an extremely well-organized membership, which included groups with military training. And yet Chancellor Dollfuss, responding to external and internal Fascist pressures, effectively destroyed Austrian socialism.

The militants were convinced that the threat of rising fascism not only required more co-operation with the Communists but also necessitated other changes in Socialist practices and thinking. Just prior to the opening of the 1934 convention they issued *Towards a Militant Program for the Socialist Party of America,* in which they demanded more centralized party control over the various state organizations. They favored establishing "socialist fractions" in the trade-union movement. They indicated a willingness to abandon parliamentary procedures under certain emergency conditions; for example, they conceded that the establishment of a "workers dictatorship" might be justified in order to forward their socialist cause.[4] Thomas was never to embrace the militant doctrines, but he was attracted by the youthful enthusiasm of the militant group.

The critical nature of the early 1930's led to the formation of still another group within the Socialist party, namely, the Revolutionary Policy Committee. It took a position that was even to the left of the militants. In its resolution, the "Road to Power," it declared: "We make no fetish of legality . . . no institution or instrument set up by the capitalist class can be depended upon to establish the Workers Republic." [5] Almost every reform group is cursed with a lunatic fringe, and such was the R.P.C. It functioned very much as an autonomous group within the party and was composed of flaming revolutionists of the romantic variety, including various types of former Communists, some of whom were actually acting as spies within the party.

Thomas was to reject totally the R.P.C. point of view. Indeed, the militant outlook was to the left of his own; yet his thinking had clearly become more radical between the 1932 and 1934 Socialist conventions. He was greatly irked by the conservatism and general inaction of the old guard in New York. During these years both he and the militants were vigorously favoring industrial unionism; he felt that the New York party was too subservient to the AFL. So great was his dissatisfaction with the New York organization that he, uncharacteristically, refused to be a candidate in the New York mayoralty race in 1933.

More significant than his specific differences at the time with the New York party was the fact that he, too, was profoundly disturbed by both the world situation and the American domestic situation. In *The Choice Before Us* (1934), Thomas argued that "Germany was the supreme tragedy," but was quick to add that the situations in Austria, Italy, Hungary, and Poland were virtually as discouraging. Rather ironically, in view of later history, he pointed to Spain as the "outstanding exception" to this dismal picture, for she "had achieved a peaceful revolution politically and had embarked upon a series of profoundly significant social changes." [6]

Thomas' analysis of the domestic scene in America was also on the grim side. He candidly admitted that the various minority parties, with a combined vote of 1,232,824, made a very poor showing in 1932. Moreover, he was apparently not convinced that America was on the verge of a Socialist or Communist revolution. He granted that in its first nine months of power the New Deal had represented a great improvement over the Hoover approach to the problem of depression; nevertheless, he manifested a distrust and skepticism about the whole "Roosevelt Revolution" that he was never to abandon. He marshaled many impressive arguments against the new administration: In the first place, he took great pains to point out that the New Deal was not socialism, by any stretch of the imagination. He argued that it did not even put into effect in a complete or satisfactory way the traditional socialist immediate demands—which did not in themselves constitute socialism. To him the New Deal was a haphazard attempt to save capitalism. He indicted the Roosevelt administration for its lack of an underlying philosophy or a comprehensive plan.

Thomas lambasted the National Industrial Recovery Act, one of the major New Deal legislative efforts. He pointed out as of January, 1934 that under it "chiseling" was widely prevalent, that "minimum wages tend to become maximum," that the "great employers" were managing to circumvent it, and that the interests of the consumer were almost completely neglected. As he saw it, this was "another illustration of the fact that capitalism and desirable social planning, or indeed any effective social planning, are incompatible." [7] Thomas was in no sense an enthusiast of the New Deal program, and he was frankly contemptuous of the party that directed it. He was convinced that Roosevelt was not "giving us what we ought to have," but he conceded that the President was "miles in advance of his party. . . . You must remember that the Democratic Party nationally—and we've got to think in national terms—is a party of the Bourbon South, of Tammany Hall, and God knows what else. Most of our Democratic State administrations are as bad as their Republican predecessors." [8]

Before the New Deal was a year old, Mr. Thomas was already convinced that, "with the possible exception of the Tennessee Valley Authority," it could best be described as "state capitalism." [9] Writing to Maury Maverick, in December, 1933, he indicated that Roosevelt was proving more able and more liberal than he had expected. "I am, however, very skeptical," he declared in the same letter, "of the way in which the New Deal will eventually lead us." [10]

His great fear at this juncture in history was not that Roosevelt himself would lead America to fascism, but that his "ideal" of "capitalistic collectivism" could set the stage for it. The President, he argued, "in the best sense of the word, is an aristocrat" whose "accent" alone would disqualify him as a potential Fascist leader.[11]

Nevertheless, Thomas viewed the aspirations of the New Dealers as both incredible and dangerous. He chided them for their attachment to a program that lacked a consistent or solid philosophical base. Thus, "they rather exult," he wrote, "in a pragmatism of an opportunistic sort. They will increase social control, they will protect the underdog, they will stabilize business, and yet somehow or other preserve individual initiative, private profit, and the rights of the little man." [12]

An understanding of the New Deal is basic to an understanding of the leadership problems that confronted Norman Thomas in the depression decade. The New Deal was not simply an invention of Franklin D. Roosevelt and his "brain trust." The roots of the New Deal were deeply imbedded in the social-reform movements that preceded it. Populism, Theodore Roosevelt's New Nationalism, and Woodrow Wilson's New Freedom all helped to prepare the way for Franklin Roosevelt's New Deal.

The theme song of the historic New Deal movement was improvisation and experimentation rather than adherence to any well-formulated doctrine. The huddles were frequent, and the plays were changed repeatedly. Thomas was not far from the truth in his characterization of the New Deal as opportunistic pragmatism; yet this very quality, which alienated the theory-conscious Mr. Thomas, probably drew the American people closer to the movement.

The New Deal was essentially an attempt to save capitalism rather than an attempt to abandon it, as some persons on the right fearfully believed and some leftists hopefully anticipated. Yet, that it involved radical modifications of the American economy cannot be denied. It signified the end of laissez-faire capitalism; federal regulation of economic processes, which had begun before the turn of the century, was substantially broadened. Moreover, the New Deal did not restrict itself to the essentially negative function of regulation; under it the notion of the positive state or welfare state received great impetus. There was no marked trend toward the socialization of the means of production, but the government assumed new and important functions in its attempt to promote the general welfare. It endeavored to prime the economic pump when it had virtually ceased functioning. More significantly, by the establishment of a Social Security program it gave partial protection to large segments of the population against the hazards of old age and unemployment and, at the same time, promoted the stability of the whole economy.

By contrast with the inaction which had characterized the era of normalcy, the New Deal seemed dynamic. It did not always mean well thought out or carefully planned action, but it was action, nevertheless. The New Deal displayed a willingness to experiment with new remedies in a period when the old remedies had conspicuously failed. Its leader, Franklin Roosevelt, came to symbolize qualities of optimism and daring —qualities that drew the American people to the new administration.

Socialist Americans were, in general, no more immune to the magnetism of the Roosevelt personality and administration than were their fellow citizens. It was to be part of the New Deal's destiny to attract to its banners the bulk of America's socialists and socialist sympathizers. Some erroneously looked upon it as the fulfillment of their socialist dreams; others realized that it was not socialism but thought that part of a loaf was better than none; still others concluded that socialism was not for America and became bona fide New Deal liberals.

In his *The Politics of Upheaval,* Arthur M. Schlesinger, Jr., sympathetic historian of *The Age of Roosevelt,* has well characterized Thomas' response to the Roosevelt administration:

In part, the attack on the New Deal was essential if the Socialists were to maintain an identity of their own. But in

Thomas' case it also stemmed from a growing moral concern over aspects of New Deal Policy. He feared the militarism of the Roosevelt administration. He sharply criticized its indifference to the plight of tenant farmers and sharecroppers. He raised his voice courageously and insistently on questions of civil liberties and civil rights. His essential contribution, indeed, was to keep moral issues alive at a moment when the central emphasis was on meeting economic emergencies. At his best, Thomas gave moving expression to an ethical urgency badly needed in politics, to a sense of the relation between means and ends and of the inestimable value of the individual human being—to the hope for "the end of the long night of exploitation, poverty and war, and the dawn of a day of beauty and peace, freedom and fellowship." [13]

Thomas was to continue his vigorous criticism of the New Deal throughout the 1930's. Yet, as he seemed to be painfully aware, his criticisms made little impression, even upon traditionally socialist groups. Roosevelt and the New Deal continued to make inroads into the world of American socialism, and, if there was a formula for blocking these inroads, the leader of the Socialist party did not find it.

The New Deal was not the only force during the 1930's that was having a disintegrating influence upon the American socialist movement and the Socialist party in particular. The Communist party, in terms of both its aboveground and underground activities, was at its height of power. During that decade the disciples of Lenin and Stalin penetrated far and wide into American life. During most of the years following the Russian Revolution the Communists throughout the world were constantly making vigorous and vicious attacks not only upon conservative groups but upon liberal and socialist groups as well. All other groups with left and center orientations were looked upon as rivals that had to be destroyed. Indeed, the Communists behaved in accordance with a theory that suggested that Socialists were more of a threat to their ambitions than Fascists. They reasoned that the Fascist movement represented the last stages of capitalism, and thus its days were numbered. Hence, the Socialists, whom they referred to as "Bourgeois Socialists" or the "Social Fascists," were regarded as their real competitors—obstacles to the advance of Communism. Working on this assumption, Communists helped to precipitate the downfall of the German Republic in 1932—a fact that was not to be generally known in America until years later.

During the early months of the Nazi regime, the Communists sought *rapprochement* with the Fascists, but the former were soon to realize that they had misjudged the potential of a Fascist Germany. They were apparently jolted by the pro-Hitler results of the free Saar plebiscite and the growth of the power of fascism in Austria. Consequently, the Soviet leaders outlined a new set of tactics for world communism, and the Communist parties in every part of the world hastily and docilely embraced the new line.

The era of the popular or united front had dawned. The essential ingredient of the new line was co-operation between and, if possible, the unification of all anti-Fascist forces. Under the guise of opposition to fascism, rather than candidly placing the emphasis on their desire to defend the interests of the Soviet Union, the Communists disingenuously wooed liberals and radicals of every hue. Countless numbers of American liberals, including some of the most prominent ones, were ensnared at one time or another. Innumerable liberal organizations, which were founded in good faith, were captured by what has been well described as the "Communist Trojan Horse."

Socialists, in general, knew the Communists better and were somewhat more wary of them than were the liberals. Yet during most of the 1930's, even though they were strongly inclined to reject Communist tactics, Socialists tended to look upon Communists as fighters in a common cause. The Communists, however, were under no such illusion. For example, there is little doubt that they successfully planted spies in high places within the Socialist party and that they did everything within their power to alienate young Socialists from their party leaders. When competing for the allegiance of the young with the Communist party, the Socialist party was always at a disadvantage. The Communists were able to present to prospective converts something concrete: In the Soviet Union they had a fatherland to offer. Apart from the more devious attempts to undermine the Socialist party, during the mid–1930's the Communist party repeatedly made overtures to the Socialist party with the aim of persuading it to participate in various kinds of united-front activities. Questions relating to the degree and type of co-operation with the Communists, if any at all, provided the background for an important share of the destructive factionalism that plagued the Socialist party during the depression decade. Few questions debated by Socialists at the time were so emotion-provoking.

To Thomas, the American domestic situation seemed so grave that he came to conclusions concerning co-operation with the Communists that he was no doubt to regret in the years to come. In *The Choice Before Us,* he stated his position:

Short of organic unity or a general coalition, Communist and Socialist parties might logically be expected to work out a united front to achieve certain immediate ends upon which both sides are agreed. There is nothing illogical about an international united front against war and Fascism. While the Communist party still believes in the inevitability of new world war and the possibility of turning it into world revolution, it does not want, and it knows the workers do not want, that war right now. It wants Fascism as little as any Socialist party. Here the thing that stands in the way of unity is neither philosophy or tactics. It is mutual suspicion. I happen to belong to that group of Socialists, at present in a minority internationally, who believe that the urgency of the situation and the chances of success make it worth while to try boldly and carefully for a united front with the Communists upon certain specific issues, especially if and when that united front includes elements which as yet are neither Socialist nor Communist." [14]

Lest Thomas' position on communism at that time be misunderstood, it should be clearly pointed out that this was hardly a blanket endorsement of Communist principle or practices. In *The Choice Before Us,* in which he argued for a united front with Communists on specific issues, he also suggested that it was extremely difficult to work with a group that "openly boasts that good faith is a 'bourgeois' virtue and which has proclaimed not once but repeatedly . . . that the purpose of the united front maneuvers is to undermine the Socialist parties and destroy Socialist leadership." [15] He rejected emphatically and specifically the Communist emphasis upon violence and dictatorship. As he saw it, socialism would be "the fullfillment of what is best in the democratic tradition and the guarantor of a heaven which can be reached without compelling men to pass through the lowest circles of a hell of violence and disorder." [16]

Despite his fears and misgivings, Thomas was convinced that it was essential "that Socialists and Communists act together in certain matters," or they would have to face the prospect of being "destroyed separately." [17] Such a position, of course, pushed Thomas closer to the militant faction and farther from the old-guard group. Somehow or other, the pattern of events in Germany and Austria did not fundamentally alter the outlook of the old-guard members. Although they professed orthodox Marxism, they were in practice committed to legal and evolutionary socialism. A logical concomitant of their gradualist position was a deep hatred of the American Communists and a deep suspicion of Soviet Russia. Their skepticism concerning the Russian experiment and its adherents around the globe began with the establishment of the Third International in 1919 and grew steadily in the years that followed. Undoubtedly, what the militants alleged to be the conservatism of the old guard was partially a reaction to the excesses of communism. In retrospect, Thomas readily admits that the old guard perceived the ugly realities of Soviet totalitarianism before he and the militants did. He maintains, however, that they did so, more or less, on an intuitive basis. As he remembers——or rationalizes——they presented few facts to support their charges against the Communist regime.

In a matter of a few years Thomas' evaluation of the Communist party and its adherents was to coincide almost completely with that made by the old guard. He became reluctantly convinced that communism was little better than fascism. History has a way of settling some differences of opinion.

CHAPTER V

Fratricidal Warfare

CONTROVERSY WITHIN the Socialist party of America among the several factions had already been brewing for more than two years when its eighteenth national convention began its sessions in Detroit, Michigan, on May 31, 1934. The opening atmosphere was a strained one, to put it mildly. The two major factions, the old guard and the militants, had come to Detroit prepared to do battle. Mr. Thomas made it perfectly clear in his words of welcome to the delegates that he intended to use his vote and, more importantly, his power and influence in behalf of the militant position. "The outstanding task before all lovers of peace, liberty, and economic justice is," he declared, "the fight against Fascism. The way to fight Fascism is to build Socialism. There is no time to be lost. We have various beginnings of Fascism in America, but not as yet Fascism. The drift, however, is to Fascism." [1] He went on to denounce the Communists for boasting of "dictatorship and great scale violence" as being necessary to the establishment of socialism. Yet he also spoke of the need for a "glorious and revolutionary change" and added that "Socialists in their war against Fascism will not submit tamely to Fascist violence or put a mechanical conception of democracy ahead of Socialism." [2] The radicalism of Thomas' statement bolstered the confidence

of the militants and cast a shadow of gloom among the old
guard.

The militants had the initial advantage in the convention
warfare which was about to be waged, for they had acquired
control of all of the major committees, including the Resolu-
tions Committee, the Platform Committee, and the Committee
on Constitution. The militants quickly put before the convention a resolution concerning foreign policy. Among others, it
contained the following statement concerning the "road to
power": "The conference declares that it is not the task of the
Socialist Parties to attempt to straighten out the capitalist world
or even to collaborate in such an attempt. It declares, on the
contrary, that by whatever means they are going to achieve
power they must not secure the exercise of power within the
structure of the capitalist regime, but must utilize power in
order to destroy the bourgeois state and to install the dictatorship of the revolutionary masses during the period of Socialist
reconstruction." [3] The old guard was deeply suspicious of the
whole notion of a dictatorship of the proletariat. After heated
debate the resolution was voted down, by a narrow margin, on
a roll-call vote by the assembled delegates. Thus the old guard
knew victory with respect to the first major issue to be decided by the convention.

This initial old-guard triumph was to be marred by the
fact that, despite the opposition of some of that faction's most
important leaders, constitutional changes concerning Socialist-
party membership requirements were effected. The new ruling
adopted by the convention made the acceptance of the theory
of the class struggle a prerequisite for membership in the party.
This proposal was put before the convention by Daniel W.
Hoan, who was then mayor of Milwaukee and, therefore, exerted considerable influence in the internal affairs of the Social-

ist party. It would appear that during the first few days of the convention an alliance was cemented between the militants and those persons whom Hillquit used to dismiss as the "sewer Socialists" of Milwaukee. Ideologically, these two groups were hardly in tune, but politics does make strange bedfellows.

The Declaration of Principles

These initial controversies at the convention proved to be mere skirmishes or practice maneuvers when compared with what was to follow. On June 3, 1934, the warfare really got under way. This date marked the formal beginning of a series of bitter internecine struggles that continued for some six years. The final result was the virtual destruction of the American Socialist party.

At this convention, and in the party as a whole, sharply divergent attitudes toward the Declaration of Principles, a militant resolution, came to symbolize the rifts that had been developing in the Socialist party for years. The document was authored, in the main, by Devere Allen, a young minister and a Thomas supporter. It was a four-page statement of general principles, formulated as a guide to Socialist behavior in those troubled times. Those Socialists who framed it no doubt looked upon it as the new *Communist Manifesto,* and in the bombast of its style it did resemble that famous handiwork of Marx and Engels. The Declaration of Principles was a flamboyant outburst; its language was characterized by that peculiar phraseology which was typically Marxist and radical. It was undoubtedly assumed that this revolutionary language would appeal to the American masses, but in reality it was totally lacking in such appeal. Only the authors of the resolution and the old guard were stirred by it.

It began with a burst of revolutionary rhetoric:

The Socialist Party is the party of the workers, regardless of race, color, or creed. In mill and mine, shop and farm, office and school, the workers can assert their united power, and through the Socialist Party establish a cooperative commonwealth forever free from human exploitation and class rule.

If the workers delay and drift, they will prolong their period of enslavement to a decadent capitalism.[4]

It went on to say that "those who labor with hand and brain in their concerted might, can overthrow this monstrous system and replace it with a socialist order."[5] To understand some of the vehemence of the language of the Declaration of Principles, the time during which it was composed has to be kept in mind. It was written in the midst of the depression, when American society appeared mortally wounded, when workingmen and their families were suffering great hardships, when almost ten million persons were unemployed, and when the national income was only a little more than one half of the 1929 figure.

The declaration contained the usual socialist demands, panaceas, and platitudes. It attacked the inequities of capitalism and proposed as an alternative a society wherein the basic industries would be socially owned and democratically managed. It encouraged Socialist-party members to join and support labor unions. Its most controversial section pertained to what the Socialists should do in the event of America's involvement in war, in the event of the collapse of capitalism, or in the event of the establishment of fascism. Thus one of the most bitter conflicts in American socialist history was to begin ostensibly because of differences of opinion about methods of coping with a predicted pattern of events that often did not happen. Here was clearly an instance of what has been called the otherworldly orientation of the American socialist movement. Both sides appeared perfectly willing to wage battle over a highly uncertain and often inaccurately perceived future. The grist for the debates that were to be fought on the convention floor and for the next two years within the Socialist party was contained in the following closing paragraphs of the Declaration of Principles:

The Socialist Party is opposed to militarism, imperialism, and war. It proposes to eradicate the perpetual economic warfare of capitalism, the fruit of which is international conflict. War cannot be tolerated by Socialists, or preparedness for war. They will unitedly seek to develop trustworthy working class instruments for the peaceable settlement of international disputes and conflicts. They will seek to eliminate military training from schools, colleges, and camps. They will oppose military reviews, displays, and expenditures, whether for direct war preparedness or for militaristic propaganda, both in wartime and peacetime. They will loyally support in the tragic event of war, any of their comrades who, for anti-war activities, or refusal to perform war service, come into conflict with public opinion or the law. Moreover, recognizing the suicidal nature of modern combat, and the incalculable train of wars' consequences which rest most heavily upon the working class, they will refuse collectively to sanction or support any international war. They will, on the contrary, by agitation and opposition do their best not to be broken up by the war, but to break up the war. They will meet war and the detailed plans for war already mapped out by the war making arms of the government, by massed war resistance, organized so far as practicable in a general strike of labor unions and professional groups in a united effort to make the waging of war a practical impossibility, and to convert the capitalist war crisis as a victory for Socialism.

In its struggle for a new society, the Socialist Party seeks to attain its objectives by peaceful and orderly means. Recognizing the increasing resort by a crumbling capitalist order to Fascism to preserve its integrity and dominance, the Socialist Party intends not to be deceived by Fascist propaganda or overwhelmed by Fascist Force. It will do all in its power to fight Fascism of every kind all the time and everywhere in the world, until Fascism is dead. It will rely nevertheless on the organization of a disciplined labor movement. Its methods may include a recourse to a general strike which will not merely serve as a defense against Fascist counterrevolution but will carry the revolutionary struggle into the camp of the enemy.

The Socialist Party proclaims anew its faith in economic and political democracy, but it unhesitatingly applies itself to the task of replacing the bogus democracy of capitalist parliamentarianism by a genuine workers democracy. Capitalism is doomed. If it can be superseded by a majority vote, the Socialist Party will rejoice. If the crisis comes through the denial of majority rights after the electorate has given us a mandate we shall not hesitate to crush by our labor solidarity the reckless force of reaction and to consolidate the Socialist state. If the capitalist system should collapse in a general chaos and confusion, which cannot permit of orderly procedure, the Socialist Party, whether or not in such a case it is a majority, will not shrink from the responsibility of organizing and maintaining a government under the workers' rule. True democracy is a worthy means to progress; but true democracy must be created by the workers of the world.[6]

The issues that the Declaration of Principles raised were many. The controversy that it precipitated revealed that genuine differences in thinking about socialist principles and tactics had developed within the Socialist party. Although it would appear that the underlying question probably did not hinge so much upon differences of opinion as it did upon which grouping—the old guard or the militant-progressive caucus —was to have control of the party, it is still important to understand the ideological differences that emerged from the crucible of debate.

Those Socialists who supported the resolution argued that the times were extremely critical and justified such proposals. They viewed war and fascism as being imminent and concluded that it was incumbent upon the Socialist party to announce to the American people what policies it would pursue should either or both of these events occur. As they saw it, American socialism would have to become more radical, more revolutionary, if it was to avert the fate of German and Austrian socialism. Thus they exulted in the fiery words of the Declaration of Principles. Their orientation was essentially democratic and nonviolent; yet they were cynical about the quality of American democracy. They believed that in the event of war or fascism strict adherence to parliamentary and nonviolent methods would be questionable policy. They had the impetuousness of youth.

The old-guard group and the older people in the party, in general, had formulated the prevailing policies of the party and were content to leave them unaltered. They had lived through the trying days of World War I and the ensuing Red scare, and they were not eager to find themselves once again among the hunted. Many of them had achieved a reasonably comfortable standard of living under capitalism. They were still interested in altering "the system," as they called it, but they had little zest for the idea of revolution either of the violent or the nonviolent variety. To them the Declaration of Principles seemed Communist-inspired doctrine and an invitation to governmental prosecution.

In short, the militants and progressives felt that defeat of the resolution would represent a victory for the dead hand of conservatism within the party; the old guard believed that its passage would signify that the party had succumbed to communism. Thus it was not surprising that the Declaration of Principles precipitated one of the most vigorous and interesting debating sessions that has ever occurred at a Socialist-party national convention, which customarily involves stormy debates.

Virtually all of the party's leading figures were to take the floor. Charney Vladeck, a leading official of the *Jewish Daily Forward,* but not completely committed to any of the party's rival groups, acted as chairman of the convention during this debate over the Declaration of Principles. Among those who spoke against the resolution were the following old-guard leaders: Louis Waldman, a prominent labor attorney who had been the Socialist candidate for governor of New York in 1932; Algernon Lee, the director of the Rand School; Jacob Panken, who was a New York municipal judge; and George Kirkpatrick, vice-presidential candidate in 1916 and a prominent Socialist author. Those who spoke for the resolution and, in effect, for the militants included: Norman Thomas; Devere Allen, who had authored the resolution and who was an editor of the *World Tomorrow;* Andrew J. Biemiller, who was later to represent Wisconsin as a Democrat in the United States Congress; and Powers Hapgood, a labor leader who was later to help organize the steelworkers.

One of the less well-known members of the old-guard faction, "Comrade Sharts," was to take the floor early in the debate. His words were indicative of the fact that the old guard was becoming increasingly appreciative of the virtues of American democracy:

> Comrades: As this may be the last time I shall speak to the Socialist Party of America I beg of you to listen with some patience to what I have to say. We are meeting today in a capitalist-ridden hall in Detroit, in a capitalist-ridden city, in a capitalist-ridden state, in a capitalist-ridden land known as the United States of America. You will observe that we are meeting here with no policeman present. You will observe that there is no agent of the government on the platform to stop this meeting at the first criticism of the government. You will notice that we are here enjoying absolute freedom of discussion without the slightest danger that we will be flung into prison for what we say against the prevailing government and the prevailing capitalist system. We can, today, discuss with perfect freedom the tearing down of this system.[7]

Devere Allen was, of course, to take the floor in support of his handiwork. He declared, "that, whether it is a case of war or a case of a fascist *coup d'état,* the question of whether or not our activities are to be considered lawful will be decided not by ourselves but by the opposition. . . ."[8] Many references were made to the St. Louis Declaration of 1917, and most of the militants were arguing that the Declaration of Principles was in that tradition. Algernon Lee retorted to such arguments

by pointing out that he had "served with Morris Hillquit on
the Committee in 1917," that the latter had been opposed to
some of the recklessness of that resolution's language, and that
later those who had favored such wording asked him to try to
prove to the courts that the words really did not mean what
they said.[9]

Thomas' position at Detroit was an awkward one. He did
not regard himself as a member of the militant or old-guard
faction and did not want to be so identified. He did not subscribe to the bombast or the studied radicalism of the former
or to the conservatism of the latter. He was not inwardly enthusiastic about the Declaration of Principles. In all of his
own writing and speaking the traditional Marxist-radical language was conspicuous by its absence. The very style of the
declaration was not pleasing to him. Though he regarded
American democracy as very imperfect, he was not quite willing to dismiss it in cynical fashion as was done in the declaration and as most of the militants were inclined to do. Many
years later, he felt that the Declaration of Principles in the
form presented had been a mistake. He also regretted that
he had not written the resolution himself instead of allowing
Devere Allen to do so.

If Thomas did not see eye to eye with the militants, he
nevertheless viewed them as a hopeful group. He was attracted by their youthful enthusiasms, their potentialities, and
their ardent devotion to the cause of socialism. To him the
old guard was a "sterile" group with little or no promise. If
it were to continue under old-guard direction, he was convinced that the Socialist party could neither grow nor prosper.
So, at this Detroit convention, he chose to co-operate with and
virtually become a member of the militant group.[10]

When Thomas rose to speak on the Declaration-of-Principles

question, the militants greeted him with a round of enthusiastic cheering. Nevertheless, according to the remembrances of old-guard leader Louis Waldman, Thomas appeared "pale and nervous as he faced the noisy convention. . . . I felt, as I sat watching him on that occasion, as if he were more like a captive than a leader." [11] In any case, whether motivated by expediency or real conviction—or a mixture of both—he spoke out strongly and eloquently in behalf of the Declaration of Principles:

> The issue that has been raised this afternoon ought to lift up our hearts. . . . I am glad that we have come to this place of decision. I do not believe, for my part, the inference that might be drawn from some speeches, that any comrades will leave us as some comrades—not Morris Hillquit—left us after the St. Louis convention, I do not believe that such an inference will be just.
>
> But the issues here are as serious as they were then. . . . We say that in the event of war we will do thus and so. We say that in the event of the complete collapse of government we will do thus and so. We say that if, after achieving power by constitutional means—I would have thought that the left would have attacked this part, not the right, if, after achieving power by constitutional means, there is a struggle against us, then we will act as brave men ought to. Now what is there in that. What, but what Socialists have always said? . . .
>
> We live in a time when the Social Democracy of Germany —Socialism's Neue Beginnen Group, the Austrian Social Democracy, and even the British Labor Party have adopted in retrospect resolutions at least as bold as this. We live in a time when audiences in churches have stood up and have

openly announced that they were not going to support war and would register their objection to war in advance. Shall not the Socialist Party do as much? What is it that we are being asked to do? Simply this: first of all we are asked to present a declaration of principles, that deals with the things people want to know about. Most folks know that Socialists believe in certain things. They don't believe in capitalism; they don't believe in the profit system; they do believe in social ownership. But they are saying to us: what are you going to do about it? And now for the first time in the American language, in language that supports democracy, we have, thanks to Devere Allen, an answer that we are proud to stand on, to the kind of questions we shall be asked.[12]

Louis Waldman, who was emerging as the old guard's foremost leader and who was an orator in his own right, made a powerful reply to Thomas' arguments:

Let me answer another statement which sounds well from the platform, but in fact is untruthful. My eloquent friend, Norman Thomas, made a plea, a plea I love to hear him make, that we are opposed to the carnage, the cruelty of war. Good Heavens! Is there a man or a woman in this convention that doesn't agree with him? Is there a man or a woman who will not join him in a cry against war? What we are opposing is not a protest against war, and that is what speakers like Norman Thomas present to you—a picture not of the revolution but of a common aspiration, and its sounds plausible. We aspire to the day when we can have a great sentiment opposed to war, but what we oppose, comrades, is writing into a Declaration of Principles a resolution which will bind us, fetter us, paralyze us, and frustrate our efforts to build, in the U.S., a public opinion opposed to the cruelties, the disasters and the carnages of war. That is why we are opposed to this resolution.[13]

Finally, when the debating was over, the Declaration of Principles was referred to the assembled delegates for their approval or disapproval. They indicated their support of the Declaration of Principles by a "weighted membership" vote of 10,822 to 6,512. The talk of split was so prevalent, however, that both sides agreed to refer the Declaration of Principles to a membership referendum vote upon the petition of 25 per cent of the delegates to the convention. The convention also elected a National Executive Committee composed largely of Thomas supporters.

The close of the Detroit meeting marked an end to the wrangling on the convention floor, but it was only the beginning of the protracted and bitter struggle for control of the Socialist party. Detroit signified a breach in the ranks of American socialism that was never to be healed. As was a foregone conclusion, the final decision concerning the Declaration of Principles was referred to the party membership at large. Thus each of the two opposing groups at the convention prepared to wage a campaign to convince the rank-and-file members of the soundness of their respective positions. Each side issued a formal summarization of its stand. The "Statement for the Majority in Defense of the Declaration of Principles" was as follows:

We live in a time of obvious and acute world crisis. At no period since 1918 has the menace of new war been so serious. We dare not risk confusion in our ranks when an

American emergency arises, nor hope successfully to cope with a well prepared opposition unless we are equally well prepared to act.

The new conditions make a more resolute, aggressive, and revolutionary policy imperative for Socialism. The proposed declaration is in line with the development of socialist thought all over the world. The Socialist Party of America cannot lag behind.

From the debate published as a supplement to the American Socialist Quarterly and from a careful reading of the declaration itself, it can easily be seen that it does not call for illegal action, terroristic acts, or the abandonment of the democratic way. The declaration expresses our faith in economic and political democracy, but recognizes the fact that in countries where democracy really became dangerous for capitalism, it was capitalism itself that abolished it. For this eventuality, socialists must prepare. As to legality it is the opinion of a group of eminent lawyers that the declaration does not violate the law and is not inhibited by any statute.[14]

The "Statement for the Minority in Opposition to the Declaration of Principles" read:

> As a statement of basic principles, the document is inadequate and confused. Approval of its closing paragraphs would end our normal political activity and turn our party into an underground organization. Space permits bare mention of its worst features.
>
> Existing democracy, incomplete though it be, is immensely valuable to the workers, through whose struggles it has been won. Let communists and fascists call it "bogus." Our duty is to defend and to perfect it.
>
> The pledge to support any "comrade" coming into con-

flict with the law by any anti-war activity invites fanatics and provocators to join the party and involve it in responsibility for acts inconsistent with socialist principles. It is also an incitement to unlawful acts. Such incitement is itself a crime, for which courts could hold every party member liable.

The threat to establish minority government when capitalism "collapses" is ambiguous. . . . It is dangerous because it challenges the majority to crush the party before it gains strength, and because membership in an organization avowing illegal purposes is in several states a penal offense.

Defeat this document and thus retain the sound and clear declaration of 1924.[15]

Preparation for Split

After the Detroit convention Thomas naturally became involved in the struggle to secure the acceptance of the Declaration of Principles by the party membership. His correspondence, however, indicates that he sensed the seriousness of the situation and that he was attempting, though not very successfully, to patch up the rift that was widening within the party. One of his first moves was to write a warm and conciliatory note to Louis Waldman, reminding him of their years of working together and telling the old-guard leader that he was still mindful of the fact that it was Waldman who had twice nominated him for the Presidency. Moreover, Mr. Thomas ventured the opinion that they should be able to continue to work together in the same organization.

Thomas' plea, however, fell upon deaf ears. After agreeing as to the pleasantness of their past relationship, Waldman wrote frankly, in reply: "Upon sober reflection, I feel more convinced than ever that only bitter partisanship and factional loyalty could have made you support that Declaration of Principles. I have no other explanation for it. I certainly cannot believe that you changed your convictions on the question of violence and illegality over night; and I know from the many years that we worked together that you never held those views." [16]

Waldman's charges cannot be easily dismissed. There is nothing in Thomas' previous writings or speeches to indicate that he could have gone along ideologically with the philosophy announced in the Declaration of Principles. Perhaps his willingness to support the resolution cannot be explained so much in terms of "loyalty" to the militant faction as in terms of the disgust that he felt for the old guard.

Some of Thomas' bitterness toward the old guard is reflected in a letter that he wrote during the same period to Charney Vladeck, who was personally close to both Thomas and the old-guard leaders. His tone is more candid and less compromising than in his letter to Waldman. "I want party harmony or as much of it as we can have," he declared, "but I can't for the life of me see that we can afford to purchase party harmony, or indeed that we could get it at all by a policy of knuckling under to a small group armed with a bludgeon, financial or otherwise." [17]

Vladeck wrote an interesting, thoughtful, and almost touching reply:

> Comrade Thomas, you know how deeply and sincerely I have been attached to you. You know how much I sacrificed in order to protect your leadership. You failed at Detroit, and it is now up to you to assist in a new orientation. Before the Declaration of Principles goes to the members for a referendum, it must be clarified and modified. If possible some of us should be consulted on the manner in

which it can be done without violating the proprieties. I consider the situation very grave. With all our faults and deficiencies, of which you know I am thoroughly aware, it is the older comrades who are still the backbone of the party. It is still the "Forward" that gives the Party votes on election day. And it is still the old timers with whom Socialist work is not merely a duty or an adventure, but a vocation.[18]

Thomas answered Vladeck:

I am afraid however that the action of the right wing has made it altogether too late to try to do what you suggest. The extraordinary lengths to which the right wing or some spokesmen for it have gone in personal abuse, misrepresentation, in implied threat of split, have created a situation which to my mind makes a modification of the Declaration look like capitulation and which would certainly antagonize as many as it could possibly win. May I point out that these tactics originated on the right, not on the left. They began with Louis Waldman's remarkable release to the capitalistic press. They extended to articles in the "Forward" which, if they have been correctly translated for me, show not a chemical trace of Socialism and very little spirit of fairness. They include the organization of a committee for the preservation, mind you, not of a point of view but of the Socialist Party, to which committee I understand, there has been pledged from $5,000 to $50,000 by a group which has not yet been able to raise its modest quota for the National Drive for Socialist work. How is it possible to yield to this sort of bludgeoning and retain one's self respect or the respect of others? . . . I think the Declaration will strengthen rather than weaken Socialist morale in the country. Conceivably I may be mistaken, but I am not mistaken about the tactics that the rights have employed.[19]

Though Thomas rejected Vladeck's suggestion about re-writing the resolution, he had already proposed to Leo Krzycki, a vice president of the Amalgamated Clothing Workers and also chairman of the National Executive Committee of the Socialist party, that something be done to allay the fears of the old guard. "It might be a good plan," he suggested, "for the N.E.C. to adopt a careful statement reiterating the historical Socialist opposition to physical force, anarchy, and terrorism. This might meet the fear of some comrades who seem to be-lieve that we are committed to the support of it." [20]

Two weeks after the delegates left Detroit, Thomas attempted publicly to minimize the gravity of the situation. In this con-nection he wrote in his weekly column in the *New Leader,* which was at that time the official organ of the Socialist party:

> One of the gratifying things about the discussion of the Declaration of Principles here in New York is that already sober second thought is asserting itself and that group after group in the party is declaring itself explicitly against wild rumors of split which unfortunately were being circulated and reached the ears of capitalist reporters. I think there will be no more intemperate discussion of the declaration in the capitalist press. Whatever happens to this particular Declaration of Principles, the Socialist Party is going to stick together in order to assert leadership in a mighty movement of city workers and farmers in these critical days of struggle against fascism. We have been together too long to divide now on a question of how to say what in their hearts most Socialists agree ought to be said.[21]

Thomas' reassuring words were hardly in keeping with the realities of the situation. The chasm between the two Socialist factions was becoming increasingly wider; bitterness was growing on both sides. Daniel Bell, in his "The Background and Development of Marxian Socialism in the United States," has colorfully and accurately described the situation:

> The passage of the Detroit declaration unloosed a civil war in the Socialist Party and many members welcomed the party strife. "Capitalism," after all, was an abstract enemy, speaking on street corners was dull, arguing with unconvinced workers tedious. Here the struggle was real, the enemy tangible, and most important, victory promised organizational power. For a year and a half guerrilla warfare raged in the party to the exclusion of almost all other problems. Meetings of the branches and of the city central committees became battles planned weeks in advance. Letters, telegrams, and communiques would call members to caucuses; debates at meetings would rage fiercely for hours and spill over into the neighboring cafeterias until the small hours of the morning. Youngsters boned up eagerly on Marx, Lenin, Kautsky, and tirelessly locked phrases over long windy resolutions on "the road to power." All world history was ransacked for glittering metaphors, while in the corridors, petty gossip would zestfully circulate regarding one or another party leader, spies were planted in the opposing ranks and membership lists were packed. The barricades of Petrograd were being repeated in New York, especially one evening when the Old Guard abruptly raided the Yipsel offices in the Rand School and snapped new locks on the doors. Nor was this a mimetic debate. Capitalism was doomed; the only problem at hand was to capture the Socialist Party, issue the correct manifestoes, and victory would be assured.[22]

The "civil war" developed into a public battle of words. The old guard issued a propaganda paper entitled *Socialist Voice*.

Its masthead included the names of Jasper McLevy, mayor of
Bridgeport, Connecticut; James H. Maurer, Thomas' running
mate in 1928 and 1932; Algernon Lee, the Rand School director; and Charles Solomon, prominent New York Socialist.
It carried a lead story entitled "30 Reasons Why the Declaration Should Be Defeated." [23] Included among the more important reasons listed were: that the Declaration of Principles
broke with party traditions; that it would lead the party upon
the violent road; that it would create an unlawful movement;
that it discredited democracy; that it would promote chaos
within the party; that it was equivalent to the acceptance of
fascistic and communistic methods; and, finally, that it would
alienate the labor movement. The *Socialist Voice* also carried
a statement by Reverend John Haynes Holmes, an old friend
of Thomas' and an important leader in the American pacifist
movement, in which he bitterly denounced the Declaration of
Principles and Mr. Thomas:

> The Detroit Declaration of Principles is Communism, pure
> and simple. . . . I am utter-opposed to the Declaration and
> hope that it will be defeated in the referendum. It is foolish
> and rather pitiful for Norman Thomas to say that there
> must be no split in the party. The Declaration, of course,
> makes a split inevitable. If the Declaration is carried in the
> referendum, then all socialists who believe in democracy and
> cherish pacifist principles and ideals must get out of it. If,
> on the other hand, the Declaration is defeated, then its pro-
> ponents must go over to Communism, where they belong.
> The Detroit convention was as futile as an ecclesiastical
> council and as fatal to true Socialism as such councils have
> been fatal to true Christianity. Its work must be undone be-
> fore we can move an inch forward to our goal.[24]

The most bitter and largely scurrilous piece of literature to be published in this verbal battle was a pamphlet, *Some Pages of Party History,* by James Oneal, a leading old-guard member and at the time the editor of the *New Leader*. Writing his pamphlet in the characteristic radical polemical style, he established a major thesis that the militants constituted a pseudo left. The old guard, he argued, strangely enough, represented bona fide Marxism. What were the militants in actuality? They were indeed not radicals at all; they were basically liberals and reformists who were playing at the game of revolution. Where did these middle-class playboys come from? It was their misfortune, in Oneal's view, to have come from colleges, universities, and theological seminaries rather than from the working class itself. He scorned the League for Industrial Democracy, whose members had such origins by and large; he charged that the L.I.D., of which Thomas was codirector, functioned as a rival organization to the Socialist party and that it thus drained energies and funds from the latter. Running through the whole of his pamphlet, of course, was the idea that the militant caucus was infiltrated by the Communists. His major plea was for a genuine working-class party that was not corrupted by middle-class intellectuals. If the militants had redeeming qualities, Oneal was not willing or able to discover them, but of their defects he wrote with relish:

> One type is the younger militant who is all too common. He also comes from the middle class and professional families. Six months or a year in the party and he becomes a "theoretician" swaggering with erudition. One immediately understands that the Socialist movement began when he joined it. He discusses problems with the gusto of one who has digested everything written since the days of Marx. He is

an expert on "tactics." In fact, that is his specialty. He solves problems of the class war here and abroad with the ease that he flicks ashes from his cigarette. One cannot throw a club ten feet without hitting one of these little Trotzkys, Lenins, and Stalins.[25]

Thomas' pen was, of course, also busy during this period, but nothing that he wrote at the time was in the nature of a polemic. Indeed, he consistently refrained from publicly attacking the old-guard leaders as individuals; and, considering the kinds of attacks that were being made against him, his private correspondence was amazingly free from personal abuse directed against the opposition leaders. Oneal's pamphlet was in large measure directed against him. After all, Thomas' background and those of the persons closest to him in the party were distinctly middle-class and university; their orientation was clearly intellectual. Thus, as Thomas himself was to point out, the fact that he did not answer Oneal was some evidence of his desire to maintain party unity. Also, Thomas wrote a letter to James Maurer, not asking him to change his position on the referendum but urging him to refuse to loan his name to inflammatory organs such as the *Socialist Voice*.

In reflecting upon "What Happened at Detroit," Thomas elaborated the reasons for his support of the Declaration of Principles in the *World Tomorrow* of June 28, 1934. He wrote, in part:

> I like the Declaration of Principles because it is an aggressive and stirring statement of Socialism. It does not borrow trouble by trying to answer all possible questions about the future. It does answer some questions which my experience in all parts of America convinces me that we must answer

if we are to get the support of thoughtful and eager spirits in the task we have in hand.

The Declaration reiterates Socialist allegiance to peaceful and orderly methods of struggle, and to democracy in industry and politics. War and violence are neither blessed nor accepted as inevitable. On the contrary, it is because war is such a monstrous evil that Socialists are determined to offer "mass resistance" to it. . . . The history of the world might have been different and infinitely happier if the Socialist parties of Europe had long before 1914 set out to educate and organize the workers for a refusal of conscript service and for a successful strike against mobilization. To establish peace means to change the system which breeds war. To prevent particular wars while we change the system depends more upon the firm opposition of masses of workers with hand or brain than upon any panacea a capitalist world will consider. Hence the importance of our warning to our lords and masters.

I have repeatedly said and written that Socialism and democracy each requires the other for the perfection of either. But we cannot afford to put or seem to put loyalty to a mechanical, nose-counting type of capitalist democracy ahead of loyalty to Socialism. It is this which the Declaration says in its own words. It contrasts a bogus capitalist democracy with workers' democracy but it neither says or implies that American capitalist democracy is as yet equivalent to Fascism or that "workers' democracy" is merely another way of saying dictatorship of the proletariat. If it does not yield to a Socialist majority at the polls, or if the capitalist order breaks down in general collapse, Socialists will not say, "There is nothing more we can do about it, we hate Fascism but we must accept it." It says that we will use the solidarity of the workers to crush antidemocratic forces, and it suggests the general strike as the most likely weapon. In the event of a complete collapse, we will not try to carry out a nose-counting election in a lunatic asylum, but if we have power will establish the kind of rule which will make order and true democracy possible. In so saying, the Declaration delivers us from the criticism of futility. It is thoroughly in line with historic socialism.

Why, then, the strenuous attack upon the Declaration in Party circles? In part, that attack is a rationalization of the bitter disappointment of the Right-wing Old Guard at losing to a large degree its control over party machinery. In part it is a rationalization of the obsession some Socialists have lest any departure from liberal parliamentarianism mean a drift to communism.

What are the facts? As for legality, the only practical question is this: Under the absurd and wholly undemocratic laws of some states might this Declaration be used to involve the party and tie up its finances and energies in endless criminal cases? This matter, as it affects phraseology, is being examined by a committee of Socialist Lawyers. My own opinion is that possibly the Declaration might be used against Socialists in any wave of anti-red hysteria. But then so would any Socialist speech. The Declaration of itself does not create the danger except, perhaps, as the extravagant statements of few of its Socialist critics may help to awaken hysteria. Of course, if and when a New World War comes the socialism that is not illegal will not be true socialism.[26]

Thomas was quite confident that the Declaration of Principles would be passed in other parts of the country, but he was dubious about the outcome in his home state of New York. Moreover, the old guard was becoming increasingly bitter toward him as an individual. Thus he reported to Clarence Senior, the national secretary of the Socialist party, concerning the 1934 New York State convention:

> After one of the most disgraceful conventions you have any idea of, I was nominated for senator. The Old Guard, when Oneal finally declined to run against me, stuck grimly to the last but were beaten something like 58 to 38. For myself, of course, the campaign will be in some respects a torture. I expect to go off on my own in a car as much as possible to try to speak and organize. . . . I expect to give the fall pretty solidly to it. . . . Thank God you don't live in New York! [27]

Despite his feeling of discouragement, he was still intent upon trying to lessen the intensity of the conflict with the old guard. Accordingly, he wrote a letter to Charles Solomon, who had been nominated by the old guard for governor at the same state convention. Thomas tried to make it clear to Solomon that his reasons for not supporting the gubernatorial candidate were not personal ones. His explanation was that he had reason to believe that Solomon was about to leave the party, and he wrote that, under those circumstances, "I could not support my own brother for nomination to a high office." [28]

Thomas continued to support the Declaration of Principles with vigor; but, whenever he wrote or spoke about it, he also included some words calculated to promote the unity of his party. For instance, in September, 1934, he began a message that he sent to a Socialist meeting at Stevens Point, Wisconsin, by saying that the declaration effectively asserted Socialist opposition to war and fascism; but he closed by pointing out that it was "a kind of insanity for people who want to organize the workers now for Socialism and make the best use they can of such democratic tradition as we now have to split because we cannot agree about what may be necessary in future contingencies that the wisest of us cannot wholly foresee." [29]

The confidence of Thomas and the militants concerning the outcome of the referendum proved to be justified. On October 17, 1934, it was announced that the party members had affirmed their support of the Declaration of Principles by a vote of 5,993 to 4,872. Yet it was hardly an overwhelming victory.

Just after the result of the referendum vote was reported, Thomas sent a letter to Clarence Senior, with whom he had a very close personal relationship and to whom he always appeared to speak with the utmost frankness. "The right wing is very sore," he commented, "but somewhat impotent. I do not want a split. I think that we shall have to bear that in mind in negotiations about the united front and other activities. Our problem is to be patient without capitulating in New York to a minority. . . ." [30]

Thomas appeared to be attempting to soften the blow of defeat for the old guard. Hence, less than two weeks after the referendum vote was officially announced, he sent a conciliatory message to the members of the New York State Committee, which was largely old guard in composition. It read, in part:

> From every point of view I think we want an inclusive party rather than an exclusive sect. That means I want to see men in the party both to the right and to the left of my own position. We don't have to agree on everything in order to work together toward the cooperative commonwealth. It is for that that we should plan and to that that we should

direct our energies. Any split of the Party will be suicide for both factions, or at least it will make the job of rebuilding enormously difficult.[31]

It becomes clear from the above that Thomas was not inclined to gloat over his side's victory in the controversy over the Declaration of Principles. Nor was he interested in punishment and vengeance, as were some of his fellow Socialists in both factions. By December of 1934, it was obvious that he had become disgusted with some members of both groups. In another letter to Clarence Senior he complained that it was "pretty hard to carry on the work of the Party with the extreme right and the extreme left both crazy." [32]

What were Thomas' attitudes, as 1934 drew to a close, concerning the strife within his party, and what kind of a party was he interested in building? Above all, he was still determined not to identify himself formally with any faction in the party. He admitted that he was "most nearly sympathetic with the Militants," though he was not able to agree "altogether with their theoretical position." Moreover, he was convinced that it was his "duty," in his special situation, not to be bound by the "caucus" of any group.[33] Whether he liked it or not, however, he was already regarded as a militant by most of his fellow Socialists. Yet it cannot be doubted that he honestly did not consider himself as such.

He was hoping to build "an aggressive Socialist Party" that would "serve as an inspiration and spear head for a great farmer-labor movement." He believed that the party could and "should include men and groups who conceivably may be forced later on to part company on some important questions of tactics," [34] and he also realized that "the party" had "to guard itself against the . . . dangers of an extreme romantic revolutionary insurrection."[35] But the philosophy of this or that faction was not what disturbed him most; his constant complaint, as indicated in a letter of December, 1934, was about the organizational deficiencies of the Socialist party:

> My own great concern about the party is lack of efficiency and I think that to get greater efficiency we sometimes have to struggle for changes in the party machinery and personnel. None of us as an individual and no group is as efficient as might be desired. In general, however, I am bound to say that in most places—not everywhere—the hand of the Old Guard upon us tends to become a kind of dead hand on the Party. I am making a generalization of the sort that unfortunately has to be made, though it ought to be made with caution.[36]

Thus, Thomas felt it important that the old guard should not control party organization. Despite his reservations with regard to the militant outlook, he looked to them with hope because of their youthfulness and because he believed that they possessed efficiency, energy, and enthusiasm—qualities that the old guard, in his judgment, conspicuously lacked.

Time widened rather than healed the breach that had developed within the Socialist party as the struggle for party control became intensified during the passing days and months of 1935. Thomas was increasingly barraged by vituperative letters from old-guard partisans, to which he generally replied with an amazing degree of restraint. It would seem he was determined not to answer his detractors in kind. For example, his reply to an especially slanderous and bitter letter in which he was called "a tool of the militants" was, in part:

> I belong to no faction and do my best to serve a party which is destroying day by day its chance of usefulness by

the absorption in the internal struggle of the sort your letter indicates. I cannot tell you how much harm has been done by the tactics sometimes employed by the *Forward,* by the *New Voice,* and which find their echo in your pages. Your definition of tool, probably, is anyone who does not agree with a comparatively small group in the Party which claims proprietary interest over it.[37]

In February of 1935, Thomas took the decisive step of resigning from the *New Leader,* which was then the official newspaper of the Socialist party and was dominated by the old guard. "You put yourselves above the Party," he declared in his letter of resignation, "and are no longer a Socialist paper in the sense that you once were." [38] In the same month the militant group founded its own newspaper, the *Socialist Call,* to which Thomas contributed a regular column. It was a newspaper with a strange masthead, which read: "Official organ of the Socialist Party of Arkansas, Illinois, Missouri, Ohio and West Virginia. Endorsed by the Socialist Party of the states of Indiana, Massachusetts, and Michigan, and by the Young People's Socialist League of America." [39] It became the voice of those segments of the party that were dominated by the militants.

The major episodes of the struggle between the old guard and the militants took place within the New York environs, although the controversy had serious ramifications for the Socialist party all over the United States. But, generally speaking, outside of New York the lines that divided the two groups were never so sharply drawn, and the controversies were not characterized by such intense bitterness.

In March, 1935, the militant-dominated National Executive Committee of the Socialist party, which had been elected at the Detroit convention, officially intervened in the New York State controversy. It charged that the old guard was not adhering to the Declaration of Principles and, furthermore, that it was blocking the entrance of younger persons into the party. The old guard was apparently working on the fairly correct assumption that all young party members were potential militants. The National Executive Committee did not merely prefer charges; it requested that members of the New York State old guard appear before it in order "to show cause why the state organization's charter should not be revoked and the state reorganized."[40]

This move by the National Executive Committee initiated long months of legal maneuvering by both sides. Some attempts at compromise were also made, of which the most notable was that of Mayor Daniel W. Hoan of Milwaukee. At his suggestion the National Executive Committee issued a statement in repudiation of "dictatorship and the use of violence" and in support of the "doctrine and policies of democracy." Further, it specifically made ineligible for membership in the Socialist party "any advocates of violence and communism."[41] Obviously, this part of the statement was an attempt to reassure the old guard that the party was not taking the violent or Communist road. Another part of the Hoan statement, however, insisted that the New York State organization would have to allow the Young People's Socialist League to come back into its fold. Furthermore, it stated that party members who made "unauthorized statements to the capitalist press" were to be disciplined.[42] From the enviable vantage point of one looking back at the past, this attempt at compromise seems to have made sense; yet it apparently came too late, for neither side was in the mood for conciliation.

An event that added much in the way of fuel to the conflagration was Thomas' decision to engage in a public debate with Earl Browder, who was at that time general secretary of the American Communist party. The old guard defined the debate as a prelude to a united front with the Communists and feared that it was a step toward organic unity between the Socialist party and the Communist party. Thomas justified his decision on various grounds: From a strictly practical standpoint, he argued that the debate, which was to be held in Madison Square Garden, would bring to the Socialist party funds that were sorely needed, as it was to be sponsored by the *Socialist Call*. His most important motivation was that he considered it a good opportunity to clarify publicly the Socialist position of opposition to a united front with the Communists. Moreover, he wanted to eradicate the notion that Socialists were afraid to meet Communists in debate situations—an idea which he believed to have currency among the younger party members. Also, he contended that the proposed debate did not conflict with traditional party policy, because he had debated with Communists on many previous occasions. On November 28, 1935, Mr. Thomas announced in a press release:

> So far as I am concerned, tonight's debate will be a genuine debate. It will, I trust, be a constructive debate. We are not boxers trying for victory on points or by a knock-out. Communists and Socialists, however sharp their past and present differences, recognize that they are in common danger from Fascism in America and if it is by any means possible intelligent Socialists and Communists do not want to have to learn to get along together only in a concentration camp here in America.[43]

In its assessment of the debate, the *New York Times* reported: "Last night Mr. Thomas took a strong stand in favor of democracy against dictatorship."[44] But Louis Waldman, the official old-guard spokesman, came to no such conclusion; he implied that it was a debate founded on mutual love. Furthermore, he contended that Thomas had no right to engage in the debate, because, according to a National Executive Committee ruling, Socialists could not engage in united-front activities without first gaining the consent of the party local to which they belonged. Since the New York City party organization, which was old-guard–dominated, of course, had never granted Thomas such permission, there would seem to have been some substance in this technical charge that Waldman made; yet Thomas' participation in the debate was not, strictly speaking, united-front activity. Indeed, Thomas' main consideration in agreeing to the debate had been to try to explain to both Socialists and Communists why he thought that a united front was inadvisable at the time. It is true, however, that he did not believe that a united front with the Communists was completely out of the realm of possibility in future times. To a surprising degree, part of Waldman's public statement on the Thomas-Browder debate sounds like what Thomas himself was to say over and over again in the years to come on the issue of unity with the Communists:

> We regard unity with the Communists, either on specific or general issues, as suicidal from a tactical standpoint and as thoroughly dishonest as a matter of principle. The Socialist Party has traditionally and constantly adhered to the principles of democracy and freedom. The Communist Party believes in dictatorship and the suppression of civil rights. Between the two there is an unbridgeable gulf.[45]

In the days that immediately followed the debate between Thomas and Browder, the split within the New York Socialist party was taking on more serious proportions. The party's New York City Central Committee was literally torn apart. Resenting its old-guard domination, most of the militant Socialists bolted the group and established a rival central committee—a move of which Thomas indicated his approval by addressing the rump committee. Matters progressed to the point of discussion in old-guard circles about expelling Thomas from the New York party. The chairman of the New York Socialist party, Algernon Lee, and its secretary, Julius Gerber, issued a joint statement attacking Thomas: "It is regrettable that Norman Thomas, against his own better judgment, allowed himself to become the window dressing for a minority group which for six months has been persistently working to split the party. Instead of leading, he is being led." [46]

To suggest that Thomas was being used by others distorts the truth, but there is no doubt that he was receiving advice from many quarters. One person who clearly attempted to influence him at the time was Maynard Kreuger, a young professor of economics at the University of Chicago who was to be Thomas' running mate in the presidential campaign of 1940. Eventually, he became second in importance only to Thomas as a leader of the Socialist party. Kreuger was an avowed militant and tried consistently to encourage Thomas to take a more adamant position in his relations with the old guard. Even though the militants had a majority in the National Executive Committee, including Kreuger himself, the committee's orientation was not sufficiently anti–old guard to satisfy the young professor. Hence, early in December of 1935 he wrote to Thomas in the following vein:

If the N.E.C. does not quickly take the necessary steps to back up you and the Militants by eliminating Waldman and his like from the party, I intend to resign from the N.E.C. and fight at the next convention as a resigned member. I suggest January 31st as a reasonable time limit. I am proposing this to Coolidge, Leo, Powers, and Franz. Will you join us in the move, and let us make it, that is, let us take the initiative in threatening resignation? I am quite prepared to go all the way through with it if the threat does not get us a substantial majority for reorganization of New York State by the N.E.C. and that quickly.[47]

Later in the same month Kreuger tried once again to persuade Thomas to take a stronger stand concerning the old guard. "We can dump the Old Guard now," he wrote, "without serious defections anywhere except in New York and among the Finns. If we act now we can still stage a successful convention. But every week that passes will be a handicap to that convention unless we force the issue now."[48]

It is impossible to say what effect, if any, Kreuger's prodding had upon Thomas' attitude toward the old guard, but there is no doubt that Thomas was becoming more hostile and more uncompromising—a fact which is well evidenced by his statements during December of 1935. In a memorandum on negotiations that were taking place at the time between the old-guard and the militant groups, he wrote:

I am aware of the advantages of peace if it can be honorable. A peace which looks as if we, however, had conceded anything in our criticisms of the Old Guard misleadership or that in any way we acknowledge any justice in the usurpation practiced by the Old Guard misleadership would alienate the people who must build a real Socialist Party and confuse and not help us in the future.[49]

In reply to a letter from Charney Vladeck, one of the few officials of the *Jewish Daily Forward* who remained personally close to Thomas and reasonably sympathetic with the militant position in the controversy, Thomas suggested that he was aware of the "difficulties" and complications that would arise in the Socialist party's relation to the unions if the internal conflict continued. "But it is my sober opinion," he declared, "based on many hours of thought by day and night, that those troubles are not as great as the continuance of the dry rot in the party and the lack of enthusiasm for the party which the old situation involved." [50] He indicated his disdain for the old guard even more vigorously in a public statement of the same period:

> They have slandered the Party and sabotaged its national work.
>
> They have spent their energies on red-baiting, assailing the national party in the *New Leader, Forward,* and the Capitalist press. They have neither money nor energy to wage a proper Socialist political campaign or to help in the Socialist fight for the unemployed, for the organization of the cotton sharecroppers or for the defense of liberty in Terre Haute.
>
> Repeatedly they have compromised Socialist principles by a labor policy which is merely subservient to reactionary leadership and which too often has ignored or condoned racketeering.
>
> They have alienated youth and turned hopeful recruits away from the Party in disgust.[51]

Despite the bitterness of his words and the lateness of the day, Thomas still thought of himself as being apart from the militant group. He was dubious concerning their notions with respect to the "road to power" but felt that they had the right to state their position on such matters. "You can't have free discussion in the party," he wrote to a Socialist comrade, "without permitting men and women—even youngsters—sometimes to say things that you and I may think foolish about the future." [52]

By mid-December of 1935 the situation in New York was such that the two contending Socialist groups were reading each other out of the party. Each claimed that it had the support of a majority of party members in New York City and State. The fact that the controversy was, to a degree, a matter of the younger persons in the party against the older persons was confirmed by the alacrity with which the Young People's Socialist League announced its allegiance to Thomas and the militant group.

Early in January of 1936 the National Executive Committee of the Socialist party took official action on the New York controversy: It revoked the state charter that was held by the old-guard group and appointed a committee to administer party affairs in New York, but Thomas' secessionist group was not as yet given official recognition. The old guard suggested publicly that it had no intention of recognizing the decision of the National Executive Committee, on the ground that the action was unconstitutional. The issue was, in effect, put to a test in the New York State primaries of April 7, 1936, when the enrolled Socialists voted to send a predominantly militant or Thomas delegation to the national convention. The final tally indicated that New York State would send thirty left-wing delegates, six old-guard delegates, and seven undesignated delegates. After the primary, Thomas announced that those persons who had fought against his group at the polls were still, of course, welcome in the party. But this attempt to soothe hurt feelings had little significance in the context of the bitterness that had preceded it.

Bitter Fruits

The last chapters of the struggle between the old guard and the militants for control of the Socialist party were enacted when the party met in convention in May, 1936. Two delegations from New York, one headed by Louis Waldman, the other by Norman Thomas, asked to be seated at the convention. Daniel Hoan tried desperately to work out some kind of compromise between the warring factions. He suggested that both delegations be seated and that each delegate be accorded one half of a vote, but his plan unfortunately went unheeded. Only one man at the convention, Norman Thomas, could have conceivably effected a last-minute compromise, but he had no such inclination. His reply to Hoan's proposal amounted to a roundabout but unmistakable rejection. "The Old Guard," he declared, "has simply walked out of the party. I should like to see them come back but not at the expense of socialism. I am not the dictator of the matter. I don't know what the convention will do, but I am personally for anything within reason. I will do anything for party unity except sacrifice socialism." [53]

The convention's decision was foreseeable: The old-guard delegates were not seated. They departed from the convention and at the same time from the Socialist party. Some of the persons who left had helped to found the party in 1901, and many of them had tears in their eyes as they walked from the convention hall. Waldman announced that they would form a new party based upon "social-democratic principles . . . and devoted to genuine Socialist ideals as distinguished from

Communist doctrine and practices."[54] Thomas predicted a
dismal political future for those who were leaving the party:

> I can almost find it in my heart to be sorry for them. Some
> of them are intelligent enough politically to know that what
> they have done is a magnificent gesture and certainly not
> more.
>
> At the best interpretation it is a mere face-saver. At its
> worst it is a mere spite party doomed to futility unless here
> and there it can pick up a few jobs by bargaining with the
> Democrats.
>
> Certainly it will not draw any support on the one hand
> from practical folks or on the other hand from eager young
> enthusiasts.
>
> It may hold for a little while the old, who live on past
> memories, but I expect that the best of them, or at any rate
> the right wing Socialists for whom they profess to speak
> will be back with us. Anyway out of this group will come
> no new party.[55]

Aside from any question of political bitterness, it would
appear that Thomas experienced some sense of relief at the
old guard's departure. It was common knowledge that the
old guard was sorely tempted to follow the political lead of
the top officials of the needle-trade unions, to whom it was tied
emotionally and in some respects economically. David Dubinsky
of the International Ladies' Garment Workers Union, Sidney
Hillman of the Amalgamated Clothing Workers Union, and
Emil Rieve of the Hosiery Workers Union had already declared their support of Roosevelt and the New Deal. Thomas
reasoned wisely that it was "far better for the Socialist Party
that those who intend actually or tacitly to support Roosevelt
should be outside the party."[56]

The old guard named its new organization the Social Democratic Federation. Its official statement of principles declared, "We rely for the attainment of our aims upon the use of democratic methods. In the United States there is no justification for a resort to insurrection and violence, nor for any open or veiled propaganda in favor of preparation for such action." [57] "The continued implication," Thomas replied, "that the Socialist Party as opposed to this little group advocates violent insurrection and dictatorship is, of course, false." [58] "The Social-Democratic Federation is neither Socialist, Democratic or a Federation, but merely a half-way port to Tammany Hall," he charged.[59]

The day following the old guard's departure, Thomas was nominated as the Socialist party's 1936 candidate for Presidency of the United States. The nomination was made by Harry W. Laidler, who for many years had been closely associated with Thomas in the direction of the League for Industrial Democracy, and seconded by Daniel Hoan. There were some shouts of protest, including objections by Jasper McLevy, but in the end the nomination was effected by almost unanimous consent. In his acceptance speech Thomas anticipated the issues he was going to stress during the course of the campaign. With his customary eloquence he hammered away at Roosevelt and the New Deal:

Mr. Roosevelt has not delivered us from poverty, exploitation, and war. . . . In short, the New Deal has not worked. Even if the temporary achievements of the New Deal were infinitely greater than they are, it could not long deliver us against the relentless threat of a civilization disintegrating to war or a new cycle of wars, to a new birth of tyranny in a Fascist form. It is not the Old Deal that has failed or the

New Deal that has failed, but the capitalist rationalism of which both are the expression. . . . Add the debits and the credits of the New Deal with as optimistic an estimate of the credits as you will, and the sum total is not prosperity or abundance or security or freedom from war or exploitation. It is not even an organization of forces assuredly on the march to these great, great ends.[60]

The closing of the 1936 National Convention of the Socialist party signified a victory for Norman Thomas. Theoretically, he had consolidated his leadership. With the removal of the old guard, he was now apparently free to build the Socialist party into the kind of a political instrument that he desired it to be.

The victory was in many ways a hollow one, however, and bitter were its fruits. The Socialist party that Thomas now ostensibly presided over had lost much in terms of power and influence between its 1934 and 1936 national conventions. Many members, who had become disgusted and discouraged by the constant internal strife during these years, had drifted away. Between September, 1934, and September, 1935, official party membership declined from 22,943 to 16,270. It has been estimated that during the two years between the conventions the Socialist party lost about 40 per cent of its membership. The old-guard withdrawal resulted in significant membership losses in New York, Connecticut, Massachusetts, and Pennsylvania and in the loss of the two major foreign-language groups —the Finnish Socialist Federation and various Jewish Socialist organizations.

Probably of more significance than these membership losses was the fact that the party's most important unofficial subsidiaries disaffiliated, in effect, along with the old guard. The organizations that largely severed their intimate connections with the Socialist party included the Workmen's Circle, the *Jewish Daily Forward,* radio station WEVD in New York City, and the Rand School of Social Science. Furthermore, the split involved the general disintegration of relationships between the Socialist party and the leadership of the various needle-trade unions.

Just prior to the opening of the 1936 National Convention of the Socialist party, Norman Thomas commented to some of his followers concerning the party split that appeared to be in the offing. "Personally I do not believe," he wrote, "that a mere defection of Old Guard groups in New York, Massachusetts, or even Pennsylvania or Connecticut is so terribly serious." [61] Reinhold Niebuhr was similarly convinced and in the winter of 1936 reported that ". . . In New York there is already a remarkable burst of new energy in the party since the hand of the Old Guard has been removed from the wheel of power." [62] Such optimism was hardly justified in view of the pattern of future events. In the months and years that followed the departure of the old guard, by virtually every test and in almost every part of the country the Socialist party underwent unremitting decline.

Thomas Answers Ten Questions

Thomas did not fully recognize the disastrous implications of the split in the Socialist party. As he entered his third presidential campaign, his spirits were high and his morale unabated. Shortly after his nomination he was interviewed by Willis Thornton for an article entitled "Smoking Out the Candidates," which appeared in the *Cleveland Press* (Ohio) on June 3, 1936. The interview focused around ten questions, which Thomas readily agreed to answer; but he did so only after prefacing his answers with assorted comments, which were as revealing of his thinking and his mood as his actual replies to the questions:

I'll be glad to answer these questions. Of course they are all based on the existing order of capitalism, in which I don't believe. But if a Socialist government were to be elected on Nov. 3, that wouldn't mean Socialism on Nov. 4. There would have to be a period of transition even then, of cleaning up the problems piled up by decaying capitalism.

* * * * *

Since I am running for the presidency, it is only fair that I answer these questions as to immediate measures that would be taken on the matters covered by the questions.

* * * * *

Socialists this year will be expected to vote the Socialist ticket. . . . There will be no trucking with plans like voting for Roosevelt to help defeat a reactionary Republican, or trying to support a hastily-contrived farmer-labor party with neither farmers nor labor behind it. No "united front" with Communists or others.

* * * * *

The plan of supporting a "liberal" regime to keep the reactionaries out has been exploded by experience. I voted for Wilson in 1916 because "he kept us out of war." What did we get? War. The German Social Democrats voted for Hindenburg to defeat reaction. What did they get? Hindenburg and Hitler, and then just Hitler.

* * * * *

We have rejected a united political front with the Communists. If they should decide to support our ticket rather than have one of their own, of course we can't help that. But I want to make it clear right now that we haven't asked, won't ask and don't want their support, and that they will have no part in directing our campaign.

Thomas indicated that he would view with favor a Farmer-Labor ticket in 1940, providing that it was organized far enough in advance: "It's got to be well started by 1938." He reiterated his opposition to capitalism: ". . . I must make it clear as a Socialist that you are asking me how to run a capitalist system in which I do not believe." [63] Then, "without a hem or a haw," he proceeded to answer the ten questions "almost faster than one could write them down."

1. Do you favor balancing the budget? If so, do you advocate reducing relief expenditures or increasing taxes? If by taxes, what kind?

Ideally, yes. Practically, a budget so far out of balance can't be continued much farther without very serious inflation. It is ridiculous, however, to talk of a balanced budget by reducing relief expenditures until we have done far more than we have up to now to get rid of unemployment. Taxes will have to be increased and the increase should fall on incomes, inheritances, and corporation surpluses (this is no endorsement of the House Bill). There should also be a land value tax and for purposes of debt reduction and for hastening Socialism, a graduated capital levy rising to virtual expropriation in the higher brackets. But I would leave Mellon enough to keep him out of the poorhouse.

2. Should relief be by direct cash payments or as wages? Should relief be paid for and administered by the Federal Government or by the states, or both?

Relief should be through the payment of the prevailing wage for useful work wherever it is possible to provide useful work. It could have been provided on a much greater scale under an adequate program of public housing. Direct relief is better than "made work"—on the whole, it is less destructive of morale. It is hypocritical nonsense to talk of states bearing the burden of relief. In their present hardpressed situation only a few could do it. The first states to holler if this burden were returned to them would be the Democratic states-rights states of the South.

3. How should the problem of permanent unemployment and care of the aged and unemployed be handled?

Through adequate social security legislation. I favor in principle the Frazier-Lunden Bill. I regard the present security bill as an insecurity bill. But I doubt if our disintegrating capitalism can bear the cost of really adequate security.

4. Do you favor further devaluation of the dollar or stabilization at the present gold content? Do you believe in any form of currency change, currency inflation or credit inflation, a return to the gold standard, or a managed currency?

I am entirely opposed to currency or credit inflation. I believe in the principle of a managed currency, but not in the form of any of the plans cranks send to me. I do not believe that under the present system we are likely to get an effectively-managed currency without ownership of the banks and credit machinery. I am opposed to further complication of the situation by continuing the unsound silver purchase policy which has proved so disastrous to China.

5. Do you favor any program whose aim is to control or fix wages, working hours, or a shorter work week?

As a Socialist, my whole interest is in democratically-managed, socially-owned industry rather than in control by government of private industry, but as things are, most emphatically I do favor all these controls, as imperfect means of improving the unemployment situation.

6. Do you favor an amendment to the Constitution authorizing the Federal Government to deal with economic and social problems, national in scope, or in limiting the courts as to their rights to declare laws of Congress unconstitutional?

Emphatically, yes! Our party is the principle advocate of the "farmers' and workers' rights amendment" originally drafted by that very able lawyer, Morris Hillquit, and introduced in modified form by Senator Benson and Representative Marcantonio.

7. Do you favor modification or suspension of the antitrust laws to enable businessmen to get together (a) to agree on trade practices, (b) to agree on labor relations, (c) to attempt to fix prices?

It doesn't interest me much. Neither the anti-trust laws nor any modification of them will work, under capitalism, for any desirable social ends.

8. What is your remedy for the farmers? Do you favor the curtailment of production, industrial or agricultural?

I do not favor any curtailment while the legitimate needs and wants of Americans are unsatisfied. For the farmer, I believe in the socialization of marketing agencies, agricultural councils of the most representative farmers on the use of land, socialization of the great plantations, especially those in the cotton country, to be cropped co-operatively under expert guidance. In general, as a Socialist, I favor abolition of private landlordism and occupancy of homes and one-family farms on the basis of titles based on actual occupation and use of the property.

9. Are you in favor of the policy making reciprocal trade treaties to encourage foreign trade or reduce tariff walls?

Yes, but it has a limited usefulness.

10. Do you favor a policy of public power development, the continuance or expansion of TVA and control of public utilities through the utilities holding company act?

Yes, but if a Socialist had been in office, he would not have subjected the utilities to regulation by the holding companies act, but would have used such an act through the holding company setup to take over the utilities of the country for the people.[64]

Despite the dismemberment of his party, Thomas was resolute in his determination to conduct a vigorous campaign—all difficulties notwithstanding.

CHAPTER VI

The All-Inclusive Party

THERE CAN be little doubt that Norman Thomas assumed that the old guard's departure would inaugurate a new era of peace and harmony within the Socialist party. Such an assumption was clearly not justified by the party's history in the years that followed. Factionalism within the party was to continue almost unabated after the 1936 national convention. Communism, fascism, the New Deal, and the upsurgence of labor continued to be the situations that underlay much of this dissension. In addition, during the last years of the depression decade another source of conflict was the question of whether or not America should intervene in World War II.

The Communist issue, which had enormously complicated relationships between the various Socialist factions prior to the withdrawal of the old guard, was not to be easily resolved. As early as August of 1934 Thomas had argued in favor of an all-inclusive Socialist party. He was strongly inclined to welcome the various unattached radicals into the party in order to broaden the base of the organization. The unaffiliated radicals whom he had in mind were, in the main, the various breeds of former Communists. They included former Trotskyites as well as a group known as the Communist Party Opposition, led by Jay Lovestone and Benjamin Gitlow, who had been key mem-

bers of the American Communist party before becoming involved in an internal struggle with William Z. Foster, which
was arbitrated in Moscow to their disadvantage. Thomas admitted frankly that he did not see eye to eye with these assorted radicals on many important issues, but he was convinced
that their presence would improve the Socialist party. He was
especially impressed by the fact that many of them had had
rather extensive experience in the labor movement.

The old guard had vigorously opposed admitting such persons—even if they had formally disaffiliated from the Communist party. While the old guard and the militants were
debating the advisability of an all-inclusive Socialist party, Benjamin Gitlow and Jay Lovestone were carefully observing the
struggle and issuing condescending public statements. Gitlow
announced that he and his followers intended to join the Socialist party because it had finally abandoned the reformist path
and had become a revolutionary party. In a public statement,
Jay Lovestone suggested that the Declaration of Principles was
"feeble" and "hesitant" but indicated that his group was encouraged by recent trends in the Socialist party and would be
glad to help it move leftward.[1]

In November of 1934 the National Executive Committee of
the Socialist party adopted Thomas' position and extended an
invitation to join the party to all those persons who believed in
"the Cooperative Commonwealth."[2] "To gain his point," Louis
Waldman commented bitterly, "Norman Thomas is apparently
willing to make a saint out of Stalin and a mild radical out of
Trotsky. He has suddenly decided that there is no difference
between Ben Gitlow, Communist candidate for vice-president
in 1924 and 1928, and his followers and the Socialist Party."[3]
During the months that it remained in the party, the old-guard
group continued to oppose the all-inclusive membership policy

and did everything within its powers to frustrate its implementation.

End of a Dream

When the old guard finally severed its ties with the party in June of 1936, Thomas and his followers were free to carry out their program for building a party that they hoped would unify the various leftwing forces in the struggle against fascism. The membership of the Socialist party was roughly divided into three groups in the period that followed the 1936 convention. In the first place, there was the militant group, which was becoming increasingly less militant in its policies as the years passed. Essentially, it was led by Jack Altman, secretary of the New York party, and Paul Porter, of Wisconsin. Many of its members were inclined toward the formation of a mass labor party; they were eager to work with organizations like the American Labor party in New York and the Progressive party in Wisconsin. Thomas tended to agree with them concerning the advisability of co-operation with these third-party movements, but a rigid party policy against supporting non-Socialist candidates made such action extremely difficult.

Secondly, there was the clarity group, which was composed of some former militants and Revolutionary Policy Committee adherents plus an assortment of other leftists. Its leaders were Herbert Zam, a former Communist, and Gus Tyler, then editor of the *Socialist Call*. The clarity Socialists were skeptical concerning the peaceful achievement of the new society. Their language was traditionally Marxist, but in their views on party organization they owed more to Lenin than to Marx. They opposed a broadly based labor party and argued, instead, that the Socialist party should become a "revolutionary vanguard" group that would lead the masses.[4]

Thirdly, there was the appeal group—the Trotskyite faction.
Large numbers of them, at Trotsky's suggestion, joined the
Socialist party individually immediately after the old guard
had left it. These disciples of Trotsky were in an instructive
mood; they were eager to give direction and purpose to what
they believed to be a confused and wondering Socialist party,
and it is probably true that they were better educated in socialist theory than were most of the Socialist-party members at the
time. It was true, also, that the Trotskyites did not join the
Socialist party in good faith—a fact which was made abundantly
clear by James P. Cannon, their leader, in his *The History of
American Trotskyism*:

> . . . I never encountered anything so fabulous and fantastic
> as the negotiations with the chiefs of the "Militants" caucus
> in the Socialist Party. They were all transient figures, im-
> portant for a day. But they didn't know it. They saw them-
> selves in a distorting mirror, and for a brief period imagined
> themselves to be revolutionary leaders. Outside their own
> imagination there was hardly any basis whatever for their
> assumption that they were at all qualified to lead anything
> or anybody, least of all a revolutionary party which requires
> qualities and traits of character somewhat different from the
> leadership of other movements. They were inexperienced
> and untested. They were ignorant, untalented, petty-minded,
> weak, cowardly, treacherous and vain. . . . Our problem was
> to make an agreement with this rabble to admit us to the
> Socialist Party. In order to do that we had to negotiate. It
> was a difficult and sticky job, very disagreeable. But that
> did not deter us. A Trotskyist will do anything for the party,
> even if he has to crawl on his belly in the mud. We got
> them into negotiations and eventually gained admission by

all sorts of devices and at a heavy cost. . . . When, a little later, the leaders of the Socialist Party began to repent the whole business, wishing they had never heard the name of Trotskyism . . . it was already too late. Our people were already inside of the Socialist Party and beginning their work of integrating themselves in the local organizations.[5]

Once in the Socialist party, the Trotskyites proceeded to organize themselves as a party within a party, contrary to the assurances of co-operation that they had given at the time that they were seeking admission. They even went as far as publishing their own newspaper, the *Socialist Appeal*. The general result of the admission of the Trotskyites was bedlam.

Factionalism within the Socialist party got under way with a new fury. Pamphlets were issued; caucuses were organized; furious debates were waged; and once again it was full-fledged fratricidal war. These debates, waged primarily by the party's leadership, were largely concerned with the labor-party issue and the proper course to follow with respect to the Spanish Civil War; rank-and-file members were alienated by the constant bickering in the party and were leaving it in large numbers. The Trotskyites challenged the party's official position of extending aid to the Loyalist government under Largo Caballero and argued, instead, for the support of some of the more radical Spanish anti-Fascist groups. They evaluated almost all matters in terms of the Russian experience and were hoping for a sovietized Spain.

As late as March of 1937 Thomas was still optimistic concerning the new party structure. Though he was becoming concerned about the factional quarrels, he still argued for "an inclusive party of Socialists with unity of action but freedom of discussion." [6] He became increasingly doubtful, however, concerning the wisdom of having allowed the Trotskyites to enter the party. By June of the same year he was convinced that "the Trotskyites had joined not with the aim of building a united Socialist Party but rather for the purpose of capturing it for Trotsky." [7] By August the process of expelling the Trotskyites had begun. More than fifty in New York City were banished outright, and the remaining ones were warned that they would have to choose between "building a revolutionary party or devoting their lives to futile sectarian war." [8] Jack Altman issued a fair and largely accurate statement concerning the expulsion of the Trotskyites, which appeared in the *Socialist Call:*

> They were expelled for attempting to undermine the Socialist Party, for loyalty and allegiance to an opponent organization, the Bureau for the Fourth International, and for refusing to abide by the decisions and discipline of the National Convention, the National Executive Committee and the City Central Committee of the Party and for no other reason. . . .
>
> The Trotskyites entered the Socialist Party on the same basis as all other applicants. They were never invited into the Party as a group by Norman Thomas or anybody else. They asked to come in as individuals after they had voluntarily dissolved their own party, giving assurances that they came as Socialists. The only invitation ever extended was a general invitation by the National Executive Committee to unattached radicals to affiliate themselves with the Socialist Party and accept its discipline.[9]

Thomas was in thorough agreement with the action taken by the New York party concerning the Trotskyites. He had come to the position that the problems confronting the Socialist party could not be solved by the inclusion of members whose real loyalty was to communism rather than to socialism. "And at this point," he maintained, "it doesn't matter whether the loyalty is to Stalin's Communism or Trotsky's." [10] The Trotskyites, as he saw it, were concerned more with the Russian than with the American situation. He held them responsible for the fact that so many party meetings developed into fruitless wrangles about Spain and Russia. He felt that they were no more scrupulous about tactics than the Communists who had managed to maintain power in Russia. Not the least of his objections to the Trotskyites was that they confined "their major attention to sectarian quarrels rather than to socialist campaigning." [11]

The criticisms that Thomas and other Socialists were making of the behavior of the Trotskyites during the period that they were in the party are rather well substantiated by the cynical boasting that James P. Cannon was to indulge in during later years:

> Partly as a result of our experience in the Socialist Party and our fight in there, the Socialist Party was put on the sidelines. This was a great achievement, because it was an obstacle in the path of building a revolutionary party. The problem is not merely one of building a revolutionary party, but of clearing obstacles from its path. Every other party is a rival. Every other party is an obstacle.[12]

The Trotskyites did succeed in doing real damage to the Socialist party. When they had entered it, several hundred persons belonged to their sect; but when they were finally expelled, they took with them approximately one thousand members. Especially disastrous for the Socialist party was the Trotskyites' success in drawing many of the party's younger people into their fold.

The Trotskyite debacle marked the beginning of the end of Thomas' dream of an all-inclusive party. He finally realized—and the cost of the lesson was great—that a party composed of left splinter groups was not a compatible whole. Moreover, Thomas and most of those who had once belonged to the militant caucus became increasingly wary of all persons who had been trained in the Communist tradition. ". . . I rather think that if Trotsky had won rather than Stalin," commented Thomas to his aides, "we might have had much the same story with the positions reversed." [13]

A Reappraisal of Communism

One of the great ironies of the history of the American Socialist party is that the old guard ostensibly left the party because of fear that it was going in a Communist direction. The irony is strengthened by the fact that the old guard was to become involved almost immediately in the American Labor party, where it was to work side by side with the Communists. The old guard's prediction of party trends was wrong, of course. From the time of the old-guard departure in June of 1936, the Socialist party, under the leadership of Thomas, became increasingly skeptical concerning domestic and international communism and had reached a state of complete and final disillusionment in September of 1939. Indeed, the old-guard charges that Thomas was leading the party down the road of communism never had much substance. It is true that from 1934 to 1936 Thomas believed in limited co-operation with the Communists on specific issues and that to him the Soviet Union still represented one of mankind's great hopes; yet it is also true that during this period, and even long before, he was a bitter critic of many aspects of Communist doctrine and practice both at home and abroad.

As early as January of 1935, one and one-half years before the old guard left the party, Thomas wrote that he was "profoundly disturbed by some recent reports from Russia. It does look to me as if there were some force in Trotsky's criticism that the present bureaucracy tends to become a new class in the state. As a Socialist I see no excuse at this time for the kind of terrorism the Stalin government is applying." [14] By December, 1935 he was to support a plea which was at the time being directed to the Russian government for "mercy and justice" to Soviet political prisoners. He argued that it was basically a question of "justice rather than mercy." "Surely today the Soviet government is so strong," he declared, "that it no longer has even the excuse of urgent revolutionary necessity to deny elementary civil liberty." [15]

During 1936 and 1937 the Communists continued to press for a united front—urging which Thomas resisted with increasing determination. He continued to favor joint action with the Communists on specific issues, but he bluntly spoke out against "organic unity" in August of 1936:

> The differences between us preclude organic unity. We do not accept control from Moscow, the old Communist accent on inevitable violence and party dictatorship, or the new accent on the possible good war against Fascism, and the new Communist political opportunism. We assert genuine civil liberty in opposition to communist theory and practice in Russia.[16]

The purges that took place in Russia from 1936 to 1938, which involved the liquidation of many of the top leaders of the Bolshevik revolution, confirmed Thomas' worst fears and suspicions concerning the Soviet Union. Again in August, 1936 he wrote that, if Zinoviev and his associates were guilty of con-

spiring with Trotsky and the Nazis, as was charged, in order
to undermine the Soviet regime, they deserved "the severest
possible punishment and the scorn of the workers. But everything we know of the character and beliefs of these men makes
the story highly improbable. The Stalin Government must be
made to understand that intelligent public opinion will not
accept its charges as proof. Neither will it accept the results
of the ordinary political trial as conducted in Russia." [17]

The year 1937 brought more word of Russian purges and
more disillusionment on the part of Thomas. He was seriously
disturbed by the pattern of events in Russia and more and
more convinced that the purge trials were not being conducted
fairly. He was not willing to accept the famous confessions
at face value. His doubts hinged upon the fact that the Soviet
government did not present factual substantiation of these confessions. Yet Thomas took pains to point out that he had not
abandoned all faith in the Soviet Union. Moreover, he suggested
that it was not incumbent upon all Socialist-party members to
evaluate the Moscow trials in precisely the same way. He insisted that the American Socialist party was confronted by its
own tasks and duties which it had to perform, that Socialists
could make their greatest contribution by building a strong
party in which "civil liberty" and "constructive criticism"
would flourish.[18]

By February of 1937 he was already a leading member of
the Committee for the Defense of Trotsky. The fact that the
Trotskyites were, at the time, wreaking havoc within the Socialist party did not deter him from defending their leader,
whom he believed to be the victim of unjust accusations. An
excerpt from a public letter that he wrote to the *New York
World Telegram* in February clarifies the position that Thomas
took:

I am not a Communist neither a Trotskyist nor a Stalinist. I believe that behind the present tragic situation lies the initial failure of the Communist Party to provide within its own party structure and within the structure of the government which it controls in Russia any proper means of discussion or criticism or protection for what we commonly regard as civil liberty. This I have said long before the Trotskyist issue became acute, and the original structure and theory of the party on this matter were determined while Trotsky was still a powerful figure in it.[19]

Also by February of 1937 the Socialist leadership had largely abandoned the hope and the desires of maintaining effective co-operation with the Communists on almost any level. "In recent weeks," declared the National Executive Committee of the Socialist party, "the Communist Party has resumed its practice of making vicious and falsified attacks upon the Socialist Party and some of its members. These attacks are accompanied by hollow-sounding appeals for unity."[20]

In the spring of the same year Thomas decided to go to Europe, and, of course, one of his major purposes was to see Russia. At first, the Russian government denied him a visa, apparently because he was a member of the Committee for the Defense of Trotsky. Thomas wrote a rather irate letter concerning the situation to his good friend Sir Stafford Cripps. In it he defended Trotsky's right of asylum in countries other than Russia and suggested that the "incredible trials" were doing damage to the Socialist cause. "It is a rather fascist performance," he added, "to exclude a man [Thomas] who has been a loyal supporter of Russian recognition from the days when it was dangerous to support that cause in America down to today."[21]

Finally, after considerable negotiating, the Russian government reversed its position and granted Thomas a visa. Thomas visited Russia in the late spring of 1937, and, writing from Amsterdam in June, he reported his impressions of the Soviet Union in his weekly column in the *Socialist Call*. Obviously, he left Russia with mixed feelings. For example, he gave high praise to "Bolshevo," which appeared to him to be a model prisoners' community; but at the same time he was extremely disquieted by the sight of "a big gang of prisoners under armed guard finishing the aqueduct which is part of the Moscow Volga Canal project. None of these prisoners was eligible for 'Bolshevo.' They were presumably 'murderers, bandits or political prisoners'—kulaks, real or alleged, and members of that large group of Russians who suddenly disappear from their homes and accustomed places, usually without any trial worthy of the name." [22]

It was with obvious pleasure that he found himself able to commend Russia for its handling of minority-group problems. Specifically, he seemed convinced that the Russian government was successfully coping with the problem of anti-Semitism. It was with less satisfaction that he noted a severe shortage of housing and other consumers' goods, but he was inclined to explain and excuse these lacks on the basis of military expenditures caused by the Fascist threat.

Thomas was impressed by the successful operation of various social-service programs, but even in this area he suggested that he was infinitely more satisfied with what he saw in Denmark and Sweden. "I breathed a purer air of democracy as between man and man in Denmark than I did in Russia," he wrote.[23] It was his "strong feeling . . . that Russia was not moving towards a classless society, but on the contrary, perpetuating and even strengthening new class divisions." [24] This opinion he substantiated by citing great disparities in the remuneration received by various Soviet workers. The conditions under which Russians worked, he observed, left much to be desired. "There is much to be said in support of the necessity of various spurs to teach Russians to work, but the speed-up system as practiced in Russia seems to me to contain many perils not only to individual well-being, but to Socialist ideals." [25]

There would be hope for the improvement of some of these regrettable situations through the processes of discussion and criticism, he maintained, if Soviet Russia were a genuine "Socialist Democracy." But he argued, in effect, that the Soviet Union was not a democracy. "Criticism may apply to the carrying out of a policy," he noted, "but not to its formation. The Russian peasant and worker live under about the strictest passport system in the world; they have unions and workers' clubs; they are allowed to go to church; but they have no right of free association, political or otherwise." [26] Another feature of Russian society that disturbed him was that one man appeared to possess overwhelming power and authority. "Every issue," observed Thomas, "is settled by a quotation of Stalin. In Kiev and Moscow around May 1, I saw rather more pictures of him than of Lenin." [27]

There can be no doubt that Thomas' visit to Russia considerably lessened his faith in the Soviet experiment, but it should not be concluded that he was as yet completely disillusioned. To him Russia was still a land of socialist promise, and he apparently looked upon the task of criticizing it as necessary but personally painful. The following appear to be the words of a man who is wavering between optimism and despair:

It is just because there is so much to admire in Russia, just because I want Russian life and conditions to stand out in complete contrast to those in fascist countries, that I grieve over the matters to which I have briefly referred. Nothing is gained for Socialism by ignoring them, and to see them need not blind one to the great achievement of the Soviet government. Some observers hope that the secret ballot will bring a little democracy at the bottom, and that Stalin himself has enough of his old revolutionary idealism to want to narrow the gap which is now widening between the classes in Russia. Of his probable successors they are more doubtful.

Certainly Russia has cleared the ground for real Socialist building, but the Socialist building requires for its safety as well as for its beauty an atmosphere of liberty.[28]

During the months that followed his return from Russia, Thomas became increasingly skeptical and bitter concerning the Soviet Union. He wrote a pamphlet for the League for Industrial Democracy, entitled *Democracy versus Dictatorship,* in which he made unmistakably clear his view of the Russian government as a dictatorship. By the close of 1937 he was already on the verge of abandoning all his dreams and hopes concerning Soviet Russia. As the news of what appeared to be an unending succession of Russian purges became known to the outside world, Thomas became more cognizant of the parallels beween the behavior of Russia and the Fascist nations. Indeed, he had even come to believe, rather prophetically, that there was the possibility of an alliance between Hitler and Stalin. He was no longer content to have his socialist dream identified with the Soviet Union. "More and more it becomes necessary for socialists to insist to the whole world," he declared, "that the thing which is happening in Russia is not socialism and it is not the thing which we hope to bring about in America or in any other land." [29]

By the spring of 1938 his disenchantment with Soviet Russia

was almost complete. His feelings were no longer mixed; he was no longer the friendly but critical observer; he was now more foe than friend. His earlier criticisms of Russia had been somewhat restrained; now he became the relentless critic. In March, 1938, he wrote:

What has happened in Russia represents the degeneration of Socialism, the complete subversion of revolutionary idealism, and an all but fatal wound to working class integrity and confidence in its own destiny. There is no hope for Socialism, which indeed deserves no support, unless it can divorce itself completely from everything that the Moscow trials stand for. . . .

The only important thing that is left for us to do is correctly to learn the lesson of these Russian tragedies. To my mind it is clear. No society can be decent, certainly no society can be Socialist, under the regime of the totalitarian state ruled by the iron hand of the dictator of a monolithic party, which party from the beginning professed to believe that the end completely justifies the means and that good faith is a contemptible bourgeois virtue.[30]

The publication of Thomas' pamphlet *Democracy versus Dictatorship* caused considerable controversy among American liberals and radicals. Thus Thomas was asked by the League for Industrial Democracy to write another pamphlet more specifically oriented to Soviet Russia. Many leading Communists and Communist sympathizers, including Earl Browder, were asked to write rejoinders to the proposed Thomas essay, which the league agreed to publish under the same cover; but none were forthcoming. Thomas wrote this well-documented pamphlet entitled *Russia—Democracy or Dictatorship?* in collaboration with Joel Seidman. It was published in December of 1939, but it had actually been written a year earlier. Publication had been delayed by the unsuccessful attempt to find an author who was willing to answer Thomas' charges.

The central thesis of this pamphlet is contained in the following passage:

> Clearly the Russians are not free, if that term has any real meaning. The rights that they possess are vastly inferior to those possessed by citizens of the United States and the other western democracies. In the first "workers" state the worker is permitted fewer liberties than in capitalist democracies. Rights of free speech, assembly, organization, and press are non-existent. The Russian worker enjoys the real advantage of employment and of a certain degree of security, provided he is not critical of the regime; but living standards are terribly low, even for the more fortunate skilled workers. Officially there can be no exploitation in Russia, and productive equipment and the national income are the property of all workers. Actually the workers have little to say as to distribution of the national income, and a very high percentage is drained off for capital investment, for armaments, or for the high bureaucracy. The state can exploit, just as private capitalists can.[31]

Thomas and Seidman argued, however, that "communism, with all its denials of human rights and civil liberties, is far superior to fascism." [32] They took this stand because of the economic gains that they believed the Communist regime had brought to the Russian people. More significantly, they concluded that, regarding "the lack of civil and democratic rights and the use of terror to crush all opposition, fascism and communism are similar. The word totalitarian may equally be applied to both." [33]

The Moscow-Berlin Pact of August, 1939 destroyed the last vestiges of Thomas' faith in the Soviet Union. Even though he was not completely unprepared for the agreement, there was a strong sense of outrage in his reactions to this new international friendship:

> . . . Stalin's agreement with Hitler becomes a piece of infamy beside which Munich was an adventure in ethics, and the hypocritical nonintervention agreement in Spain a model of international good faith. . . .
>
> By every test of civil liberty Russian life is at least as much regimented as in the Fascist countries. The press, schools, and radio are if anything more absolutely controlled. . . . To strike is as dangerous in Russia as in Germany. . . .
>
> Stalin's infamous pact with his fellow dictator has at last made the issue plain: His Communism is the ally not the foe of Fascism; the enemy, not the friend of democracy and the worker's cause.[34]

The Moscow-Berlin Pact ushered in a new era in the history of the American Socialist party. Its members, under the leadership of Norman Thomas, were now totally disillusioned with communism of both the Russian and the American varieties. They had come to view communism as a dangerous totalitarian force and became its dedicated, relentless, and fearless critics. It would be no exaggeration to assert that since 1939 vigorous opposition to communism has been one of the guiding themes in the Socialist party history.

It should be noted that Thomas and his followers understood the totalitarian nature of communism long before certain important segments of American liberalism saw Russia in a true light. Indeed, Thomas was often denounced as a Red-baiter by liberals, because he so frequently and bitterly criticized Russia and the Communists. It should also be pointed out, however, that by 1939 many persons who were prominent in the radical-liberal world did see eye to eye with Thomas on communism. Although there is no conclusive proof, the likelihood is that, by taking his uncompromising anti-Communist stand, he succeeded in alienating more persons among the radical-liberal clientele than were drawn to him because of it.

The New Deal and Labor

If Thomas' views on communism alienated some potential followers, his position on the New Deal did even more damage. During the 1930's and 1940's virtually all of those persons in America who were actual or potential Socialists embraced the New Deal—some sooner and some later. The New Deal gathered to its bosom not only liberals and radicals, but, more significantly, the leaders of organized labor as well as the rank-and-file membership were also won over to it.

As early as 1933 important Socialists were leaving the party and moving in the direction of the New Deal. In September of that year Paul Blanshard, who had worked closely with Thomas in many causes and who had collaborated with him in writing the book *What's the Matter with New York,* resigned from the party in order to assume a position with the La Guardia administration. There was sadness but not bitterness in Thomas' reaction to Blanshard's defection, as he wrote to Blanshard explaining that it was not possible for him, as the leader of the Socialist party, to avoid making a public statement concerning the resignation. Moreover, he tried to reassure Blanshard that he felt no ill will toward him. "I have," he wrote, "enjoyed and counted on your friendship and comradeship in common tasks. I hope that we can continue the latter as far as possible and that the days will come when it can be renewed in close intimacy." [35] Considering the situation, Thomas' public statement concerning Blanshard's desertion was surprisingly free from rancor. "None of his old friends and associates," he declared, "questions his sincerity or ability, but only his judgment. . . . We suspect that the Republican Mayor La Guardia has gained more in this new member of his 'brain trust' than the 'practical' Socialist Mr. Blanshard from his change of allegiance." [36] In all the years since, Thomas and Blanshard have maintained a warm friendship.

Another leading Socialist who was becoming more "practical" during this same period was the well-known writer Upton Sinclair. Before making his End Poverty in California plan public, he sent a draft of the idea to Thomas in September, 1933 for "criticisms" and "suggestions." [37] Thomas was more than willing to criticize and suggest. Indeed, his basic suggestion was that Sinclair abandon the whole plan, and he tried to persuade him to do so:

> What you are now trying has on some scale been tried over and over. Impatient Socialists have said we will capture the old parties. Have they ever succeeded? Do you really think you will be nominated for governor? If you are not nominated will you return to the Socialist Party, perhaps bringing some of your new Democratic adherents with you? Will you once more don sack cloth and ashes as you did after you left us in the world war? If so, we shall again welcome you back. But remember each defection will weaken your influence. [38]

In 1934 Thomas feared that the EPIC campaign would destroy the Socialist party in California, for Sinclair had run as its gubernatorial candidate in the previous election and, because of his prominence as a writer, was very influential among California Socialists. In fact, during the course of the 1934 campaign Thomas felt it necessary to write to the Socialist

candidate for Governor in order to encourage him to stay in
the race. Despite the grave light in which Thomas regarded
the situation, he was not inclined to harbor bitterness against
Sinclair, any more than he had against Blanshard. "As you
well know," he wrote to Sinclair, "I am not in the least interested in what reactionary Democrats say against you, and for
you personally, aside from what I think is your serious error
in tactics in furthering the cause you have loved, I have nothing
but good will and friendship. . . . Above all, let me tell you
how very keenly I feel your loss [from the Socialist party]." [39]

The process of Socialist defection to the New Deal began to
take on serious proportions immediately preceding the presidential campaign of 1936. In May, 1936 it was announced that
David Dubinsky, president of the International Ladies' Garment Workers Union, and Emil Rieve, president of the Hosiery
Workers, had resigned from the Socialist party in order to
support President Roosevelt in the coming campaign. There
can be little doubt that the old guard was motivated, at
least in part, to leave the Socialist party by a desire to follow
the political lead of the needle-trade unions in throwing their
support to Roosevelt. The old guard had long been closely
tied—some said subservient—to the leadership of these labor
organizations. The important union leaders who continued to
support Thomas in 1936 included Julius Hochman of the International Ladies' Garment Workers, Joseph Schlossberg of the
Amalgamated Clothing Workers, A. Philip Randolph of the
Brotherhood of Sleeping Car Porters, and Jerome Davis of the
American Federation of Teachers.

The American Labor party in New York State was formed
in 1936 almost exclusively by former members of the American
Socialist party. Those who essentially brought it into being were
Louis Waldman of the Social Democratic Federation, David

Dubinsky of the International Ladies' Garment Workers Union, and Sidney Hillman of the Amalgamated Clothing Workers Union. One of the major considerations that led to the establishment of the American Labor party was to give the residents of New York State who had formerly voted the Socialist ticket an avenue for voting for Roosevelt without voting Democratic. To many of these liberal and socialist persons the Democratic party, which they equated with Tammany Hall, was an anathema, and they quite literally could not cast a vote in the Democratic column without severe gastrointestinal upset.

Early in the presidential campaign of 1936 Mr. Thomas vigorously criticized the political behavior of organized labor, though he was pleased to note its increased participation in American political life. He maintained that it had an "exaggerated fear of the consequences of a Republican victory" and that by its behavior "it helped the workers to forget that Roosevelt has solved no fundamental issue." [40] Thomas further contended that it was unwise for organized labor to accept Roosevelt uncritically and at the same time to overlook the composition and principles of the party that the President headed. "Basically, it is proof of labor's weakness," wrote Thomas, "not its strength, that its leaders feel themselves compelled to risk so much in devotion to one man. It is a faith in a man, not a party, for the more intelligent of the workers have no faith in the Democratic Party as such." [41] As the presidential campaign of 1936 was drawing to its close, Thomas declared, "It is the tragedy of this campaign, not that there was a kind of labor stampede to Roosevelt, but that it asked so little and permitted Roosevelt to ignore all issues." [42]

The degree of pressure to support Roosevelt that was being exerted in labor circles is illustrated by a situation that arose in the 1936 campaign—a situation which caused the Socialist party and Norman Thomas no end of embarrassment. In the midst of the campaign and without prior warning, Leo Krzycki, an important Amalgamated Clothing Workers official who was chairman of the National Executive Committee of the Socialist party at the time, announced, to the chagrin of Socialists all over the country, that he, too, had joined the Roosevelt band wagon. What was the explanation? It was not that Krzycki had as yet abandoned his Socialist faith; rather it was his inability to withstand the strong pressures that were being put upon him to quit the Socialist party by his boss, Sidney Hillman. Krzycki felt so strongly about the situation in which he found himself that he broke down and wept in Norman Thomas' office.

Relationships between the Socialist party and the organized labor movement were never of a satisfactory nature, especially from the point of view of Socialists. They were more harmonious in Europe, where socialist groups had generally launched the unionization of labor and where both movements were committed to the building of socialism. There, divided loyalties were not so prevalent. In America, where the socialist movement and the labor movement have had separate but interrelated histories, there have always been elements of discord. The individual who participated actively in both movements was continually being involved in situations in which his loyalty was being questioned by one group or another. Krzycki may well have reasoned that, had he remained loyal to the Socialist party, he would have been disloyal to the Amalgamated Clothing Workers.

Formulas for coping with this situation of divided loyalties were often laid down by Socialist leaders. "In general, I feel strongly," wrote Norman Thomas to Julius Gerber, a fellow

Socialist, in September, 1933, "that we have a right to expect Socialists in labor unions to act as Socialists and not as Republicans or Democrats. Certainly we may expect them not to use the tactics of political compromise with dubious elements that so often are used. At the same time I agree with the proposition that we ought not to interfere in the day by day internal affairs of the unions." [43]

James Oneal wrote in a similar vein, although he gave more emphasis to the importance of trade-union autonomy. In the pages of the winter 1933 edition of the *American Socialist Quarterly,* he argued that the Socialist party had no more right to dominate the behavior of its members with respect to their union activities than the various unions had to determine the behavior of Socialist unionists with respect to party activities. The attempt at party domination of the Socialist unionists, Oneal maintained, only alienated the workers from socialism. Just as Thomas, however, he felt that no Socialist unionist had the right to support capitalist candidates. The basic function of the Socialist party in its relations with the trade-union movement, Oneal concluded, was to win over the workers through education to socialism. His implication was that, if the party confined itself to an educational role, relationships between it and the unions would be more satisfactory.

Despite the various suggestions that were made for avoiding it, most Socialist unionists were sooner or later caught in a dilemma of divided loyalties. The pattern of relationships that existed between the Detroit Socialist party and many of its members who were rising to positions of power and influence in the CIO's United Automobile Workers well illustrated the character of this dilemma.

As has already been said, for a variety of reasons the early 1930's was an era of revitalization for the Socialist party. Far more important to the American people as a whole, it was also a period of renewed vigor for the American labor movement.

In June, 1933, the National Industrial Recovery Act was passed by the Congress. Section 7a of this statute, the principles of which were later incorporated into the Wagner Act of 1935, enabled organized labor to achieve unprecedented power in American life. It provided for governmental encouragement of the organization of the nation's workers. For the first time in American history, collective bargaining was given sanction by the federal government. Section 7a gave employees the right to bargain collectively through representatives of their own choosing.

Immediately after the passage of the National Industrial Recovery Act, organized labor began to capitalize on its new legalized status. During a period of little more than three months, total union membership in the United States grew from two and one-half million to almost five million. Feverish organizational drives had been set in motion. Moreover, this was the phenomenal period during which workers were holding spontaneous mass meetings and sending telegrams to the American Federation of Labor requesting entrance into the organization.

Organized labor's new lease on life was, of course, to have its ramifications in the automobile industry, which had long been a target for union organization. There was periodic labor unrest in this industry even prior to World War I. During the 1920's there were various and sporadic attempts by the American Federation of Labor to unionize the industry, but they were dismal failures. Such failure must be attributed largely to the fact that the AFL attempted to organize the automobile industry along craft lines, and this form of organization was simply not suited to mass production industry. The craft-union form functioned successfully where skill was the important factor among the men to be organized; this was clearly not the case in the highly mechanized automobile industry. The AFL organizational plans involved dividing the automobile workers into numerous different unions. The result was almost invariably jurisdictional squabbling leading to general bedlam. It should also be noted that, for various reasons, the 1920's was not an auspicious time for labor organization, even when founded upon the best plans possible.

After the enactment of the National Industrial Recovery Act, several attempts at the unionization of the automobile workers got under way. The earliest significant attempt to organize the automobile workers was led by the Mechanics Educational Society, a semi-industrial union which knew considerable success in bringing tool- and diemakers into its ranks in 1933 and 1934. This union was soon to be overshadowed by the entrance of the AFL into the automobile industry. However, even the AFL's dominance was temporary. Controversy over appropriate organizing policies for the automobile industry became a crucial issue in the struggle between the AFL and the Committee for Industrial Organization, which had grown up within the AFL. Craft unionism versus industrial unionism was at the heart of the controversy, which was at the same time a power struggle for leadership of the AFL. As early as 1936 the CIO, with its crusading industrial unionism, achieved the allegiance of the majority of auto workers.

The various radical political groups in the United States have had at least one thing in common: virtually all of them have vigorously supported the industrial-union principle. Thus, despite the fact that John L. Lewis had ousted the various radical groups from his United Mine Workers Union, he turned to them when seeking organizers for the rapidly growing CIO. Despite his lack of affection for political radicals, he realized that they had a social vision and an enthusiasm that would be useful in building the CIO into an important factor in American life.

Several radical political groups came to play an important role in the CIO's United Automobile Workers Union. The Socialist party, the Communist party, the Independent Labor League of America (Lovestone-ites), and the Socialist Workers party (Trotskyites) participated. Each group was attempting to mold the UAW in terms of its own political image. John L. Lewis, of course, never gave these radical groups a completely free hand. For example, he asserted his will at the UAW's 1936 convention. Because of the opposition of the Socialists, a motion to support Roosevelt's candidacy was initially defeated. Lewis, however, soon let it be known that, if the convention did not get behind Roosevelt, he would withdraw his pledge of $100,000 for a UAW organizational drive. The power of money won out. Just before the convention adjourned, the delegates endorsed President Roosevelt in the coming election by a unanimous vote.

An examination of the backgrounds of the key leaders of the UAW reveals that a strikingly high percentage of them were once members of the Socialist party. During the years 1936–39 the Detroit Socialist party maintained a "union branch" to which the Reuther brothers and most of the other Socialists who were to become prominent in the UAW belonged. Indeed, these trade unionists and Socialists actually held union caucus meetings at the Socialist-party headquarters. The vast majority of UAW members, of course, were never members of the Socialist party, but those who were generally worked as a team within the union. They had some differences among themselves, but on crucial issues they voted as a bloc. In other words, during the early days of the UAW, Socialist-party membership was one of the factors that enabled some of the present-day leaders of the union to acquire official power and to hold on to it. Of course, the fact that most of them were extremely able young men cannot be overlooked. Moreover, it should be noted that the Reuther group did not actually assume major power in the union until 1946 and 1947, which was some time after most of them had left the Socialist party.

Why did Walter Reuther and other UAW officials leave the Socialist party? Specifically, he left it because of a disagreement over the 1938 Michigan gubernatorial race. He was inclined to support the Democratic candidate, Governor Frank Murphy, but the party insisted upon putting up its own candidate. Some party members thought that Reuther should be allowed to stay in the Socialist party; others argued that, if he was determined to support old-party candidates, he did not belong in the Socialist party. Thomas encouraged Michigan Socialists to allow Reuther to remain within the party, which they did. Ultimately, he drifted away.

Irving Howe and B. J. Widick, in their *The UAW and Walter Reuther,* explain well the withdrawal of numbers of union leaders from the Socialist party. They generalize concerning the behavior of Walter Reuther, in particular, but their observations provide insight into the behavior of many other trade unionists in various parts of the country who left the Socialist party during the same period:

As he rose in the UAW, Reuther must for a time have felt —here we can only speculate—that his political opinions and his new role as leader did not conflict. But some time between 1936 and 1938 there seems to have risen in his mind an acute awareness that, since the socialist movement showed no signs of growth and his participation in it might inhibit the free and easy maneuvering he felt union leadership to require, he would soon have to choose between the two. Either the lonely rectitude of radical politics or full participation in the union world, with doctrine straggling as best it could behind power and prestige—that seems to have been his choice.

But to put it so bluntly is to indicate that he never hesitated in making his choice. All the evidence shows that Reuther was by now so deeply immersed in the union world that he did not hesitate a moment to abandon his political ties. He felt that those socialists who wished to exert an immediate, substantial influence on American life would have to abandon their party and its doctrines and join the New Deal parade.[44]

Relationships between the Socialist party and the labor movement were always of a precarious nature, but in the late 1930's they began to worsen markedly. Tension between those Socialists who were actually participating in the labor movement and those who devoted themselves more exclusively to party affairs began to mount. Socialists outside the trade-union movement tended to look upon the union movement as a means to achieving the great end: socialism. Socialist trade-union leaders, for the most part, came ultimately to look upon unionism as an end in itself. Their political comrades frequently dubbed them "labor bureaucrats." When confronted by charges to the effect that they did not behave as Socialists when union affairs were involved, they replied that outsiders did not understand union problems.

The fact that Norman Thomas was somehow always outside the trade-union movement doubtless hindered him in

his attempts to improve relations between the Socialist party
and organized American labor. Thomas was never an insider
in the way that both Debs and Hillquit had been and, therefore, was unable to play an effective role in mediating these
controversies. Moreover, to make matters worse, Thomas did
not seem to adhere to one consistent or clearly defined labor
policy. "The Socialist Party has no clear trade union policy
in the Socialist Party or elsewhere," commented Benjamin
Stolberg in *The Story of the CIO*. "Since the 1936 split between
the so-called militants under Norman Thomas and the right-
wing Socialists under Louis Waldman, in which the Militants
captured the party apparatus, the Socialist Party has been wob-
bling all over the lot." This lack of consistency on Thomas'
part is revealed in his shifting attitude toward the New York
State American Labor party between 1936 and 1938. In a letter
of November, 1936, to Maynard Kreuger, he expressed determined opposition to Socialist-party participation in the Labor
party:

> As for myself, if the party decides that we are forced to
> play the kind of game that some New Yorkers think we
> must play with a very unsatisfactory Labor Party, I shall,
> of course, stay in our party and shall go along in what has
> to be done. But I am through with any attempt at leader-
> ship. I shall speak and write, and support the party rather
> passively. I have no intention whatever myself of playing
> the kind of game that some comrades seem to think must
> be played with Hillman, Lewis, & Company.[45]

Despite these feelings and convictions, Thomas withdrew only
a year later from the 1937 New York mayoralty race. He apparently did so in order to increase the chances of victory for

La Guardia, who had the support of the American Labor party. The Socialist party, however, did not formally endorse La Guardia or the American Labor party.

The 1938 National Convention of the Socialist party was held in April at Kenosha, Wisconsin. The foremost issue at that convention was whether or not the Socialist party should join forces with the various labor parties, specifically, the Farmer-Labor Political Federation in Wisconsin and the American Labor party in New York. The burning issue was whether or not the New York party should be allowed to affiliate with the American Labor party. It was assumed that, in any event, Mayor Daniel Hoan of Milwaukee would not be restrained by a convention decision against uniting with the Wisconsin Farmer-Labor Political Federation.[46] Both Hoan and Thomas argued vigorously that the Socialist party should affiliate itself with labor parties, on local levels, wherever possible. Thomas had apparently been convinced of the wisdom of this point of view by his old friend and co-worker Harry Laidler, the executive director of the League for Industrial Democracy; Jack Altman, secretary of the New York party; and the various members of the trade-union officialdom who still remained within the party. It would appear that President David Dubinsky of the International Ladies' Garment Workers Union was welcoming Socialists into the American Labor party in order to gain aid in his efforts to halt the growing power of the Communist groups within it.

It was widely rumored at the convention and earlier that Thomas would leave the party in the event that his view on the labor-party issue was not adopted. Led by Maynard Kreuger of Chicago, those delegates who opposed affiliation with the labor parties complained that Thomas was trying to bully his party by putting it in a position where it had to choose between accepting his views on the labor-party issue and losing him as a party leader. "The real blackjack for the party trade union burocracy [*sic*] in the party was Norman Thomas," a factional bulletin charged.[47] One delegate, who voted against the Thomas group at the convention, said it was never clearly established that Thomas was actually considering leaving the party. In retrospect, he concluded that the rumor was probably circulated by labor-party partisans without Thomas' knowledge or consent.

The Thomas forces argued for an unqualified entrance of the New York State Socialist party into the American Labor party. Kreuger and his supporters maintained that to affiliate with the American Labor party in order to help fight the Communists therein was a rather negative form of political activity. Moreover, they suggested that they would condone such affiliation only if the Socialists entered as a group rather than as individuals and only if they retained the right to run their own candidates in situations in which they deemed it necessary. Such qualifications ruled out any entrance of the Socialist party into the American Labor party, of course, because it was perfectly obvious that affiliation on this basis would not be acceptable to ALP leadership.

When the debating ceased and the issue was put to a vote, the Kreuger group won by a weighted membership vote of 3,414 to 3,163. Needless to say, Norman Thomas did not resign from the party, as had been predicted. In a real sense, the voting results were testimony to the internal democracy of the Socialist party. The rank and file had determined a major policy contrary to the wishes of Thomas and the other more prominent party leaders.

In the realm of foreign policy the assembled delegates easily came to agreement. They followed Thomas' lead and issued a vigorous antiwar declaration, which included the charge that the administration was on the verge of leading the country into war.

The defeat of the proposal to affiliate with the American Labor party widened the gap between unionists and non-unionists within the Socialist party. During the months that followed the Kenosha convention large numbers of the trade unionists slipped away, usually quietly, from the party. Many of them, such as Walter Reuther, were destined to become major figures in the labor movement. In long-range terms the advantage that the Socialist party was to derive from the fact that so many prominent trade unionists once participated in its activities was practically nil. The most that can be said is that some of these persons retained a vaguely socialistic outlook even after they became involved in the politics of the New Deal. In all probability, the New Deal did significant damage to the Socialist party more by draining away its most valuable personnel than by reducing the number of ballots cast for it.

It was at the 1937 convention that Thomas made one of his greatest concessions to so-called "practical politics." Yet in his *Socialism on the Defensive,* which was completed less than six months after the Kenosha convention, he already seemed to be in the process of recanting his position with regard to the labor-party issue. Although he continued to give praise to the ideal of Socialist participation in a labor party, he was sharply critical of the American Labor party as it was then functioning. "The A.L.P. claims to be," he wrote, "the 'only party in New York loyal to the New Deal,' but it has not yet defined what it means by the New Deal, or what common denominator of conviction and program unites the Republicans, Democrats, Communists, Social Democrats, and pure and simple Labor Party men on its ticket. What the workers are to think of the old parties depends on (1) where they live; (2) what office is involved. This sort of business makes American political confusion worse confounded." [48] Moreover, Thomas was quite specific in his rejection of "joint electoral action" with the American Labor party in the election that was in the offing. "Socialists are unanimous in thinking," he stated, "that in the New York Campaign of 1938 they cannot make the A.L.P. their electoral agency. They must run their own ticket on which may appear some A.L.P. candidates who are neither Communists, Republicans, or Democrats." [49]

Keep America Out of War

For several years following the Kenosha convention Norman Thomas was largely immersed in thought and activities that were designed to keep his country out of the emerging world conflagration. He was to take a position of steadfast opposition to American involvement in the world war that he fully expected to break out. His antiwar view, however, was no longer predicated on an absolute pacifism, as was true of his opposition to World War I. His strong sympathy with the Loyalist government during the Spanish Civil War and his belief that a military victory over Franco was a basic prerequisite to a decent and peaceful world led him to modify his pacifism. Indeed, he strongly urged that the American Socialist party do all within its power to aid the Loyalist government, despite strong protests from pacifist elements within his party.

Thomas' old friend and co-worker for unpopular causes, Reverend John Haynes Holmes, pleaded with him, in December of 1936, to hold fast to his pacifism despite the Spanish Civil War. "You and I, Norman," Holmes wrote, "have been through this business before. We stood fast when Belgians lifted cries as pitiful as those lifted by Spaniards today, and when Paris was beset no less terribly than Madrid. . . . I appeal to you as the successor of Gene Debs, and as yourself an uncompromising pacifist of consistent and heroic record, to save the Party and the nation from this madness before it is too late." [50] Thomas replied, in part:

> . . . I would be a much happier man if I could agree with you.
>
> During the World War I was its opponent on two lines: first Socialist opposition to that particular war and second a Christian position in philosophy. This latter position I was compelled for various reasons—by no means all of them connected with the issue of war—greatly to modify.[51]

Pacifist opposition to the sending of arms to Loyalist Spain was a sentiment that Thomas could understand and respect, but he found no justification for the opposition of President Roosevelt and the Congress to such a move. Indignantly, Thomas pointed out that United States trade with Japan, which was waging an unjustified war against China, had not ceased. Beginning with the Spanish Civil War, he was to subject Roosevelt and his foreign policy to scorching criticism, and as the years went by his attitude became more bitter. In January, 1937, he wrote:

> The whole record shows that with impunity and without rebuke established governments if they are conservative or Fascist have been allowed to buy what they needed in the way of military supplies when not actually at war with another nation. It is only when the Spanish Government fights against Fascism for the peace and freedom of mankind that the President's scruples are suddenly aroused.

What is the explanation? In part, at least this: He sees in the Spanish incident a chance to get discretionary power for the Executive as against Congress over the whole trade in arms. The desire for it in this case is an ominous sign of a drift towards personal government.[52]

Thomas' position on Spain was in keeping, as he saw it, with his strong antiwar convictions. "It is because I believe," he reasoned, "so thoroughly in the horror and futility of war that I think we must do all we can to help our Spanish comrades stop Franco's war and by stopping it greatly increase the world's hope of avoiding the catastrophe of a second world war far worse than the first." [53] Despite his insistence upon the importance of giving aid to Loyalist Spain, he was utterly unwilling to sanction any aspect of American foreign policy that he judged would make more likely the involvement of the United States in another war.

Because of his passionate antiwar conviction, he helped to organize and became a leading member of the Keep America Out of War Congress. In the work of this organization he was joined by other leading Americans who were both staunchly antiwar and anti-Fascist. Among others, its membership included: Charles A. Beard, Alfred Bingham, Bruce Bliven, Paul Brissenden, John Chamberlain, Louis Corey, John Dos Passos, Henry Pratt Fairchild, James T. Farrell, John T. Flynn, John Haynes Holmes, Sidney Hook, Ben W. Huebsch, Edwin C. Johnson, John Paul Jones, Susan La Follette, Harry W. Laidler, Frederick J. Libby, A. J. Muste, David de Sola Pool, and Carlo Tresca. Thomas was to take pains to point out over and over again that his antiwar position did not involve any fondness for fascism. "We who insist that Americans must keep out of war," he declared, "do not do it because we condone

fascism, but because American participation in war will bring
new horrors and sure fascism to America without curing fascism abroad." [54] Even after World War II had begun, in September, 1939, he wrote in a similar vein to Upton Sinclair:
"Much as I hate Nazism, I still believe we can keep America
out of war or else we will see fascism spread." [55]

In the years leading up to Pearl Harbor, Norman Thomas
clearly believed that the most important function of the Socialist party was to help keep the United States out of World
War II. When the 1940 convention of the Socialist party opened
in April at Washington, D.C., it was almost certain that
Norman Thomas would once again be elected as the party's
standard-bearer. Nevertheless, there were some evident signs
of tension and discord among the delegates. There was a defi-
nite cleavage among the assembled Socialists concerning the
advisability of extending aid to the European nations that were
already engaged in war with Hitler. Thomas' position was
that economic assistance to these belligerent nations would
inevitably lead to war. He argued that the Roosevelt program
of extending aid to Britain and France just "short of war"
meant war itself.[56] Indeed, his conviction concerning these
matters was so strong that he let it be known that he would
not accept the nomination unless the convention adopted his
views on foreign policy. Apparently, the majority of the delegates were in substantial agreement with his analysis of the
war situation; yet there was a very vocal, if not large, minority
that argued that aiding the Allies would make Hitler's triumph less likely and, consequently, would make America's
involvement in the war less likely. The crux of this argument
was that most Americans would ultimately choose to go to
war rather than to see a victorious Hitler. Important persons

Candidates Norman Thomas
and Maynard Kreuger salute
fellow party members after
winning the nominations for
president and vice-president,
respectively, at the 1940
Nominating Convention of
the American Socialist
party. (UPI)

Socialist and reformer Norman Thomas is splattered with eggs as he defies Mayor Frank
"Boss" Hague of Jersey City on June 4, 1938, in Military Park, Newark, N.J. (UPI)

Norman Thomas shakes hands with James Farley at testimonial dinner held for the Socialist leader at the Hotel Commodore, New York, on February 4, 1950. James Haynes Holmes, minister of Community Church in New York and Thomas' long-time friend, looks on. (UPI)

Political differences were momentarily forgotten as nine potential presidential candidates and members of the National Press Club gathered for an off-the-record "political rally" in Washington, D.C., on March 1, 1940. Potential candidates are (left to right, seated) Paul V. McNutt, Senator Arthur H. Vandenberg, Jesse Jones, Tom Dewey, (standing) Robert Jackson, Representative Bruce Barton, Senator Burton K. Wheeler, Norman Thomas, and Senator Bennett Champ Clark. (UPI)

in the party supported this position, including Jack Altman, secretary of the New York City party; Alfred Baker Lewis of Massachusetts, perhaps the party's foremost financial angel; and Paul Porter of Wisconsin. The minority report favoring aid to the European democracies was defeated by a vote of 159 to 28. With 210 delegates present at the convention, this vote meant that more than 10 per cent of them refrained altogether from voting on this important issue. Whether these abstainers were motivated by indecision or apathy, their failure to take a stand was rather ominous insofar as the Socialist party's future was concerned.

In his speech accepting the nomination, Mr. Thomas emphasized the theme that America's greatest service to mankind would be to make democracy more effective at home:

> America and American democracy need not fail. And the success of our democracy shall be as a great light whose rays may pierce open the clouds of war and totalitarianism under which our brethren grope in the motherlands of civilization in Europe and Asia.
>
> The magnitude and adequacy of our success lies not wholly in our hands. But if we carry on as this convention has begun, we shall have proved ourselves worthy of our great name and great tradition. We shall be the bearer of hope to mankind. . . .[57]

The foreign-policy plank adopted by the convention echoed Thomas' sentiments and was probably written by him:

> To furnish supplies for other people's war is, to the profit seekers, a welcome alternative to supplying our own people with their daily bread. But the search for war profits and

armament economics leads straight to war. War and frantic preparation for war means the totalitarian state, not Socialist Freedom.

To the whole world let America say:

"We will not share in the collective suicide of your wars. We will, to the best of our ability, aid the victims of war and oppression. We will seek with all neutrals at the first appropriate occasion to mediate in behalf of negotiated peace. And to make that peace effective, we will cooperate in disarmament and in all economic arrangements which will lessen the strain of insecurity and exploitation upon the peoples of the world." [58]

During the campaign of 1940 and afterward, Thomas spoke and acted in strict accordance with his party's platform. He opposed virtually every major foreign-policy measure of the administration in power, including: Selective Service, the destroyer deal with Britain,[59] Lend-Lease, and the convoying of American merchant vessels. At the same time he, rather than Roosevelt or Willkie, advocated the opening of America's doors to the victims of Nazi persecution. Not only did Thomas attack the administration's policies, but he also directed much of his criticism toward Roosevelt as an individual. In the midst of the 1940 presidential campaign he wrote to the President a letter that Roosevelt apparently interpreted as casting aspersions upon his integrity. In July, 1940, Roosevelt replied to Thomas:

. . . I think that knowing me you will want to withdraw the grossly unfair suggestion in your second paragraph, that I am in favor of some form of conscription because of the executive power which it gives me personally. That is unworthy of you.

You and I may perhaps disagree as to the danger to the United States—but we can at least give each other credit for the honesty that lies behind our opinions. Frankly, I am greatly fearful for the safety of this country over a period of years, because I think that the tendency of the present victorious dictatorships is to segregate us and surround us to such an extent that we will become vulnerable to a final attack when they get ready to make it. . . . Incidentally, though you are a student and thinker, I cannot help feeling that my sources of information are just as good and probably better, for the reason that they come from so many more places, than yours.

With a sincerity and an honesty equal to yours, I believe that we ought this Autumn to take some kind of action which will better prepare Americans by selection and training for national defense than we have ever done before.[60]

It would appear that Roosevelt did not succeed in convincing Thomas of the former's integrity on the war question. In March, 1941, months after receiving this note of protest from Mr. Roosevelt, Thomas wrote a letter to Senator Burton K. Wheeler, in which he indicated little trust of the President and considerable bitterness toward him. "I am writing you because it burns me up," Thomas explained to his Senator-friend, "to discover the attitude of so many people who wait with resignation to find out whether the President will put us all the way into war or half way into war or what. Is there nothing at all that you folks in Washington can do to some degree to take the play out of his hands?" [61] In July, 1941, Mr. Thomas wrote to his brother Ralph, "I still think we can and should keep out of belligerent participation in the war, but I have no confidence in Roosevelt." [62]

Even before World War II broke out, the Socialist party had been in a poor state of health. At the Kenosha convention, in 1938, it was reported that the membership had declined to 7,000, which represented a loss of two-thirds from its 1934 high of 21,000. This 1938 figure was even slightly below the party's reported membership for 1928, which had previously been thought of as the year of its greatest weakness. No matter how one evaluates the position that Norman Thomas took on the war question from a moral point of view, there can be no doubt that, practically speaking, it had the effect of furthering the disintegration of the Socialist party. As the war continued, more and more Socialists, especially the more prominent ones, became prowar. Ironically, most of those who had once led the militant caucus, and even persons who had been to the left of it, came to support the war and the New Deal as ardently as had the former old-guard leaders. Considering how lukewarm their radicalism had become by 1940, earlier militant denunciations of the old guard for its refusal to commit itself in advance to revolutionary opposition to any conceivable war seemed almost laughable. Fearing that an open fight on the war question would destroy the Socialist party, Norman Thomas prevailed, with some degree of success, upon those party members who were prowar to leave the party without provoking another factional fight. Consequently, this is usually referred to in Socialist circles as the "silent split."

Of course, after leaving the party, these prowar Socialists did not remain silent. They were, as time went on, increasingly seeing eye to eye with President Roosevelt on a variety of issues rather than with their former party leader. When Thomas testified before a congressional committee in opposition to Lend-Lease in January, 1941, a group of these former Socialists issued a statement expressing their disagreement with his position on the pending bill. They stated that they did not believe that Socialists could remain neutral with respect to a conflict "involving the fate of human values built up over centuries." [63] They referred, with pride, to Socialist opposition to World War I; but World War II, they suggested, was quite a different matter. This statement was signed by Jack Altman, former secretary of the New York City Socialist party; Frank R. Crosswaith, general organizer of the International Ladies' Garment Workers Union; Murray Gross, former chairman of the party's labor committee; Alfred Baker Lewis, former chairman of the Massachusetts Socialist party; Reinhold Niebuhr, of the Union Theological Seminary; and Gus Tyler, former editor of the *Socialist Call*. A few months later many of these same persons helped to found the Union for Democratic Action, which eventually developed into the better-known Americans for Democratic Action.

The noninterventionist position of the Socialist party, under the leadership of Norman Thomas, tended to alienate most of the radical and liberal world. It was, in effect, the final blow to the Socialist party, which was already in a greatly weakened state. Even though the organization mustered up, with the greatest difficulty, enough energy to enter candidates in every presidential campaign through 1956, its existence since the early 1940's has been more akin to death than to life.

CHAPTER VII

From War to Peace?

"PEARL HARBOR meant for me," wrote Thomas in *What Is Our Destiny,* "the defeat of the dearest single ambition of my life: that I might have been of service in keeping my country out of a second world war. I had never forgotten—although I suspect he has—the day when one of my sons, already a veteran in this war but then a little boy just starting school, came home and asked me, 'Daddy will there be another war and must I fight in it? Can't you stop it?' " [1]

"Critical Support"

Once the United States became formally involved in World War II, the Socialist party did not continue its opposition to the war effort, as it had during World War I. Instead, at its 1942 Milwaukee convention it decided upon a position of "critical support." [2] Essentially, this was a compromise position between the absolute pacifists in the party and those members who thought that a democratic Socialist party would be committing political suicide by refusing to support the war in any fashion, and thus indirectly giving aid and comfort to the Fascist dictatorships.

For Thomas it was a choice "between the circles of hell, but to escape the lowest circle of fascist victory was a choice worth making." Norman Thomas, the inveterate crusader who seemed to need to do battle for a good cause in order to sustain himself, "had to accept the kind of world in which decent men could find no immediate alternative to a thing so brutal and self-frustrating as war." He saw "no political chance of trying the alternative either of Gandhi or Trotsky."[3] Over and over again in the course of the hundreds of speeches that he made against American entry into World War II, he promised to do his "best," if the United States did enter the conflict, "to defeat" his "own worst prophecies" concerning the consequences of the country's involvement.[4] He did not give this pledge lightly, and in the years to come he unceasingly devoted his boundless energies to preserving and enlarging democracy at home and to working for the establishment of the kind of peace that he thought would preclude a third world war.

His determination to preserve American democracy was well exemplified by his reaction to the internment of Japanese Americans. No public figure in America reacted so swiftly to the injustice inherent in the situation, nor was any man more involved in the attempt to right this wrong. He spared no effort to make the people of the United States aware of this basic violation of the American tradition of liberty. Early in March, 1942, he wrote:

But by far the worst blot on the good record the American government and people have been making in the preservation of civil liberties is the Presidential order giving to generals in command of wide and ill-defined army areas the power to remove, absolutely, any and all aliens AND CITIZENS from their homes and businesses in those areas. Granting that the Japanese problem on the West Coast is serious, so drastic a provision is a good deal like burning down Chicago to get rid of gangsters. It makes all Americans of Japanese ancestry the scapegoat for possible F.B.I. and army brass hat inefficiency. It invites retaliation by the Japanese against American civilians as well as prisoners of war in the territories they hold.

It sets an enormously dangerous precedent for military dictatorship over our own liberties. It will be taken in other countries as another proof of racial arrogance. The worst feature of the whole bad business is the small volume of protest and the considerable volume of applause from the West Coast for this establishment of military despotism. What a way to defend democracy.[5]

Thomas protested the "relocation" of Japanese Americans from platforms in every corner of the country, not excluding the west coast. He wrote a pamphlet, *Democracy and Japanese Americans,* which was probably the first detailed account of the problem. In short, he did everything in his power to alert his fellow citizens to what many of them came to regard, but only years later, as our worst wartime mistake.

The type of campaign that Thomas waged in the presidential election of 1944 was also consistent with his pledge that, should war come, he would do his best to insure that his own dire predictions concerning its results were not realized. He ran on a platform that argued for a statement of concrete and democratic peace terms rather than insisting upon "unconditional surrender." "Shouting that slogan," it declared, "the Roosevelt Administration is prolonging this war and inviting the next by underwriting with the lives of our sons the restoration and maintenance of the British, Dutch and French Empires in the Far East, and the Balkanization of Europe between Moscow and London." [6]

Thomas' experiences and conclusions with respect to the First World War significantly affected his evaluation and fears regarding the outcome of the Second World War. He had long held that the vengeful Peace of Versailles contributed to the coming of World War II. Thus, he felt determined in his 1944 campaign to persuade his fellow citizens that "There is no hope for peace but forgiveness and reconciliation between the peoples of the world, all of whom have suffered from sins of which none is wholly innocent. No nation, not even if it speaks English, is good enough to play the role of a God of vengeance and wrath to the workers of enemy lands." [7]

In keeping with this position, he lambasted the various theories, especially popular in liberal circles, which seemed to hold Germans responsible, on virtually a racial basis, for the two world wars and for practically all other wars in history. He readily conceded that the Nazi government had perpetrated crimes of such cruelty and barbarity that the whole concept of human civilization was threatened and that large numbers of Germans were personally responsible. Yet he insisted that to condemn a whole people for the behavior of their government, especially a totalitarian government whose acts they could criticize only at the risk of life and limb, was to judge the mass of German people by hero standards, by which few people had ever lived. He pointed to the irony of evaluating our enemy in the context of racism when we were in the midst of a war ostensibly waged to wipe Nazi racism from the face of the earth. White Americans, he observed wryly, even those who believed in full and equal rights for the Negro minority in the United States, were on the whole very timid when it came to fighting segregation and discrimination in their country. The insensitivity of his fellow citizens to the plight of the interned Japanese Americans, Thomas pointed out on every possible occasion, made it even more clear that Americans en masse, as well as Germans, were not of the stuff of which heroes are made.

In a radio address during July, 1944, directed rather specifically to candidate Roosevelt, Thomas lectured, interrogated, and admonished the President. His basic complaint was about the lack of a "peace offensive" to match the "military offensive." "It is terribly clear," he deplored, "that there has been no such statement of the positive aims of the United Nations. The demand for 'unconditional surrender' is no substitute for them. That merely masks the divisions among the United Nations themselves, while it tends to unite to the bitter end the peoples of the enemy countries and their rulers." [8] No aspect of Roosevelt's conduct of the war disturbed Thomas more than the emphasis upon unconditional surrender. He reiterated and elaborated his attack on the phrase in hundreds of speeches and articles. "The war nears its end in an inferno of destruction," Thomas continued in his radio speech, "yet our American boys are left to guess about the kind of peace for which they fight and die. What little information we have had concerns the post-war machinery for enforcing peace, rather than the nature of the peace we are to enforce." [9] In the closing passages of his speech Thomas spoke more directly to the President, and his words became more caustic:

No one doubts, Mr. President, your personal good will to men of all races, yet you almost killed your own Fair Employment Practice Commission, you have countenanced racial discrimination in the armed forces and you have never put your official power behind the drive for anti-lynching and anti–poll tax legislation. What do you now propose to do in this dark field of racial strife?

The political reasons which have silenced you are bound up in a party alignment in America which jeopardizes democracy. Do you believe that a party like your own, which rests organizationally on the Southern Bourbons like Bilbo and the Northern bosses like Hague, both of whom, especially the latter, you have continuously appeased, can ever be the vehicle for plenty, peace, and freedom? [10]

Thomas versus Niebuhr

Perhaps the best way to understand Thomas' reasons for waging the 1944 campaign and his politics as of that time is to read in its entirety an open letter that he sent to former Socialist Reinhold Niebuhr, who was then chairman of the Union for Democratic Action, which in 1947 became the Americans for Democratic Action. Thomas' plea that Niebuhr and his followers return to the Socialist fold provides an excellent summary of the reasons for Thomas' unwillingness—perhaps inability—to accommodate himself to the Democratic party, even under the leadership of Roosevelt. Thomas' letter and Niebuhr's thoughtful and incisive reply lay bare the differences on issues and approaches to politics that separated Thomas then and in years to come from ardent liberals and socialists who had become New Dealers. Thomas wrote to Niebuhr on July 25, 1944:

I write this open letter to you because you stand for—yes, and lead—many men and women of unquestioned sincerity and good-will who, through the Political Action Committee, the Union for Democratic Action or otherwise, are now supporting the Democratic ticket, although by conviction they are democratic socialists. I ask why, this year of all years, you are supporting the Democrats.

I could have understood it far more easily in 1936; I did understand it, despite my own disagreement, in 1940. But NOW! . . .

Is it on the *platform?* That I can hardly believe. The Democratic platform is virtually interchangeable with the Republican. Indeed, the latter is slightly more liberal, for instance, in dealing with the vital matter of action to promote race equality.

However, Roosevelt and Dewey could exchange platforms and the voters would be none the wiser. The Republicans are not more emphatic than the Democrats in asserting their faith in "competitive enterprise." And they will be as little sincere and effective in making such an economic order work after its abysmal failure.

How often have you yourself argued that there can neither be full employment nor abundance without plan and without the social control of the commanding heights of our economic order! You have shared my conviction that such control CAN be democratic and can indeed increase the amount of true freedom in the world. Have you changed your mind now that the undesirability and impossibility of restoring the dominance of the profit system has been proved by depression and war and the miracle of war time production under planning?

I shall not insult you by assuming that you support the Democratic ticket because of its planks, which are virtually identical with the Republican. They contain no application of the ethical principles you have so eloquently preached, and no formula for avoiding that Third World War of whose probability you have warned us. They are based on the fallacy that machinery for the enforcement of peace makes the nature of the peace to be enforced unimportant and that a Quadruple—really a Triple—Alliance masked behind a phoney internationalism will succeed when all similar alliances have failed. That fallacy lies at the heart of the President's Great Design.

If not the platform, is it the man, Roosevelt, whom you are supporting? Granting his real accomplishments, especially in his first term, will you not admit these facts:

Roosevelt has pushed no major progressive legislation since 1937.

Before the war he had not conquered unemployment but had stabilized it and subsidized the unemployment at a level of about 23 per cent of the workers.

Today most of his former progressive associates constitute the New Deal Government-in-exile. His reconverters are the capitalist Bernard Baruch and the cotton broker Will Clayton.

Roosevelt advocated total conscription of human beings in war and gives signs of supporting permanent military conscription of our youth in peace.

He has no program adequate to the conquest of poverty, and his underwriting of white supremacy in the Far East and the Balkanization of Europe between Moscow and London is an invitation to new war.

Finally, on the basis of one of your own favorite quotations, "power corrupts and absolute power corrupts absolutely," there is a very real argument against the fourth term. That agreement may be outweighed by the case against Governor Dewey, but we Socialists offer you an alternative to both. (And that alternative is not support of this New York "Liberal Party," which broke with the Communist-dominated American Labor Party only to support the same candidate as it and the Democrats are supporting!)

There is, or was before the defeat of Mr. Wallace, one more possibility: namely, that your group thought to overcome all these disadvantages by forcing through the Democratic convention the renomination of a genuine, if somewhat erratic, liberal for Vice-President. It would at best have been a poor consolation. BUT EVEN THAT FAILED.

Roosevelt was too sure of you and your liberal and labor colleagues. He had to appease Hague and Bilbo. So the Democrats, with Roosevelt's blessing, gave us as Vice-Presidential candidate and possible future President one of Convict Boss Pendergast's protégés, whose record is not adequately redeemed by the fact that he has been chairman of a useful Senatorial Committee.

Roosevelt told us that Dr. New Deal died. The convention proceeded to jump on his grave.

You left us because of honest differences over an interventionist policy before Pearl Harbor. We got war. It—especially the European war—is almost won. Now, HOW ABOUT WINNING THE PEACE? How about insisting that the demand for unconditional surrender be replaced by terms which may hasten a constructive people's revolution in Germany?

What party but the Socialist Party is demanding that?

You may reply that the kind of peace we want is impossible now. Very likely. But to work for it is the only self-respecting thing to do; the effort may have greater influence than you think: and the struggle need not stop in the postwar years.

The larger the Socialist vote, the greater and more immediate the pressure for a decent peace and for freedom and plenty with which the cause of peace is bound up.

The larger the Socialist vote, the greater the inspiration

toward the kind of political realignment which our friends in Canada are auspiciously achieving.

IN THE LIGHT OF THESE FACTS, I THINK YOU AND THOUSANDS OF MEN AND WOMEN OF LIKE OPINION WILL BE VERY UNHAPPY IF YOU THROW AWAY YOUR VOTE BY VOTING FOR WHAT YOU DON'T WANT, AND GETTING IT—AS YOU WILL IF EITHER ROOSEVELT OR DEWEY WINS.

It is not too late. You will be welcomed with open arms to the company of those who fight under the banner of democratic Socialism—for plenty, peace and freedom.[11]

This was Niebuhr's reply of September 8, 1944:

As chairman of the Union for Democratic Action, allow me to answer your open letter asking the U.D.A. to justify its support of President Roosevelt in the coming presidential election.

Let me say at once the members of the Union for Democratic Action long ago abandoned the "Utopia or bust" position in politics. You suggest that because the foreign policy of the Roosevelt Administration will not lead us at once into a genuine world society, we should renounce the possibility inherent in it of forging a world organization on the basis of continued cooperation of the United Nations. We reject this doctrine. One of the most interesting ironies of this time lies in the spectacle of American Socialists talking of the necessity of "winning the peace"; if America and the democratic world had listened to those Socialists who before Pearl Harbor were telling us that our capitalist society was not pure enough in heart to take up arms against fascist aggression, Hitler would be making the peace today.

You suggest that because the present Administration no longer manifests its earlier New Deal militancy, American progressives should abandon their efforts to make the Democratic Party the liberal party and should cast in their lot with the Socialists. But we believe with Vice-President Wallace that the New Deal must be revived and strengthened. You use the defeat of Wallace as an argument—but you are not seriously concerned with that defeat, nor were you in the battle to win his renomination. If Wallace had won, your position would be the same, and another argument would serve instead.

Indeed, although you profess many progressive ideals and support many progressive measures, there is an exasperating quality of irresponsibility about the whole Socialist position, and it is difficult to take seriously your criticisms. This irresponsibility, which led to the folly of your pre–Pearl Harbor isolationism, stems from your inability to conceive of politics as the act of choosing among possible alternatives. This blindness makes it impossible for you correctly to gauge the political climate of the country.

America, in the years immediately ahead may be the scene of basic political alignments. But Americans will not, in the forseeable future, be called on to make a choice between Socialism and reaction. A sizeable Socialist vote in November will prove nothing and influence no one.

The realistic, actual choice before Americans is that of reverting to the period of Harding-Coolidge normalcy of trying again, under the Dewey-Bricker banner, the laissez faire formula which failed before and ended in depression or of moving militantly forward in the determination to make the last four years of the Roosevelt era a period of

social reconstruction and reform, courageously using whatever resources of government are needed to achieve full
employment and social security. We are convinced that
Americans will not choose another depression.

HAVE NO ILLUSIONS

We do not pretend to be pleased or heartened by many
tendencies which have characterized the Roosevelt Administration in recent years. We are not defenders of the Northern
machine bosses and Southern poll-taxers who still dominate
the Democratic Party. We have no illusions regarding the
difficulty of pushing them from the seats of power. But we
are aware that for the first time in party history, these men
were openly challenged at the Democratic Convention in
Chicago. The lines are drawn.

I remind you once again that the battles ahead will not be
contests between unmitigated evil and absolute good, and
that a true perspective of the struggles of our time cannot
be had from the Olympian heights of Socialist dogma.

If you are contemptuous of the differences between a Roosevelt and a Dewey, between a Congressman who voted
against, and one who voted for, the fortification of Guam,
between a Senator who opposed subsidies and one who supported them, between men who wanted a federal ballot
for soldier vote, between men who, whatever their limitations, have some grasp of the big issues and forces of the
modern world, and men who have no ideas, no plans, only
a longing for "normalcy"; in short, you shun the daily
skirmishes and belittle the modest gains which are the staff
of politics, then you—not we—are "throwing away your
vote" on those decisions affecting the course of the war and
the nature of the peace.

The Union for Democratic Action contends that Americans

cannot afford the luxury of a gesture toward a perfect program, while real issues are being decided on a much more modest level. We refuse to sulk in our tents or to flaunt our ideological superiority in the faces of men and women in all countries who are fighting.

I reiterate that the course we have chosen represents a fighting chance for a sick society. Since the American people, in the years immediately ahead, must not return to the mad Republican cycle of doom and depression, and since they will not advance to a Socialist Commonwealth, the realistic choice is a continuation of the present Administration in office, with a determination to push it forward along the paths of domestic reform and of genuine international organization.[12]

The election returns revealed that Thomas received 80,518 votes, his poorest showing in any presidential race. Just as Reinhold Niebuhr, the American people were apparently inclined to define politics as the art of the possible. Nevertheless, somewhat ironically, Thomas looks back to his 1944 campaign —the least successful by conventional standards—with the greatest amount of pride. He feels that the policies and principles espoused by the Socialist party in this campaign, above all others, were ultimately vindicated by historical events and the opinions of thinking men.

Thomas and Roosevelt

In the campaigns of 1936, 1940, and 1944 Thomas directed most of his critical fire at President Roosevelt rather than at his Republican opponents. On practical grounds his actions were completely understandable, since he knew perfectly well that most persons who were inclined to vote Republican could not possibly be drawn to his Socialist banner. He reasoned correctly that his prospective followers would have to be drawn from persons who were likely to vote Democratic. Therefore, in his attempts to convince such persons to vote Socialist, he dwelled often and at length on the shortcomings of the Democratic party and Roosevelt. Moreover, the fact that Roosevelt was the President made Thomas more sensitive to and more concerned about what he considered presidential mistakes.

Yet such explanations only partially account for Thomas' attitude toward F.D.R. At one time or another, on one ground or another, as Socialist leader, Thomas lambasted most of the leaders of the major parties in recent American history. After all, one of his key political weapons was necessarily criticism of the status quo and its propagators. On the whole, however, his criticism of his political contemporaries was conspicuously free from rancor and bitterness, except in the case of Fascists and Communists. On the other hand, where Roosevelt was concerned, Thomas' criticism was acid and rather consistently merciless. He appeared to regard the leader of the New Deal as bitterly as did rightwing Republicans; both in his writing and in his speaking he would blast away at Roosevelt with gusto. He did admire the President as a public speaker, however, and frequently had words of praise for Mrs. Roosevelt, whom he considered by far the "better half." [13] On the very rare occasions when he found something complimentary to say about F.D.R.'s policies, he did so almost always in a grudging, halfhearted, and highly qualified way. Over and over again Thomas was asked, "Isn't it true that President Roosevelt carried out your socialist program?" His standard reply was, "Yes, on a stretcher." [14]

The correspondence between the Democratic and Socialist leaders reveals a note of warmth and friendliness in the President's letters that was absent from Thomas'. One observer at a meeting between the two men reports that Thomas, atypically, was quite formal, almost cold, whereas Roosevelt was cordiality itself. There is reason to believe that Roosevelt would have been pleased to have Thomas as a supporter of his administration. Supreme Court Justice Felix Frankfurter recalls Roosevelt's evaluation of the Socialist leader: "Norman Thomas is a fine man. I have only one thing against him. . . . I asked him to go on my unemployment commission shortly after I became governor to deal with the unemployment problem in New York when the depression really hit us, and he refused. I thought he should have gone on, but he is a fine man." [15]

Why, then, did Thomas seem to reserve an uncharacteristic bitterness for Roosevelt? It should be noted that, initially, he had little enthusiasm for the prospect of Roosevelt as President. As a close student of and active participant in New York State politics, he was not particularly impressed by Roosevelt's record as Governor of that state. The great emphasis throughout Roosevelt's career upon opportunism and compromise seems to have grated on the nerves of this socialist puritan. Moreover, during the 1930's Thomas watched the New Deal strike a death blow to the Socialist party and felt helpless and frustrated in the face of it. In the late 1930's and early 1940's, the militants were flocking to the Democratic party, just as the old-guard Socialists had done a few years earlier. Thomas would have been less than human had he not regarded negatively the man who appeared to be so directly responsible for the collapse of the Socialist party. Roosevelt's interventionism, as opposed to Thomas' hope of keeping the United States out of the war, and the manner in which the country finally did become involved substantially increased Thomas' antagonism toward the President.

In an article written immediately following Roosevelt's death, Thomas was considerably more charitable in his estimate of the President than had been his custom while the founder of the New Deal still lived. Yet he was by no means willing to retract his rather fundamental criticisms of the man and his conduct of the Presidency. Thomas wrote:

There would have been an element of shock and even tragedy about the sudden death of any man who with the support of millions of people enjoyed such power over the world as President Roosevelt possessed. In his case, the public's sense of loss was more personal because of certain outstanding qualities: his charm, his great courage—witness his gallant struggle against his paralysis—and his sympathy for the underdog.

It is hard to appraise his significance in history in the passions of this hour, but I do not think there will be much dispute that in the crisis of 1933 he magnificently restored confidence, that in his first term he caught America up in the field of social legislation, and that he appreciably revived faith in the ballot among the masses.

After 1937, the picture is more clouded. He came to an end of ideas and plans for ending an unemployment that became chronic. Consciously or unconsciously, he sought relief from it in the boondoggling, first of defense, and then of war. Of course, there were other mighty impulses leading him to war.

Probably it seemed to him a necessary and holy crusade, but his political genius, which became more and more Machiavellian, led him to put us in by processes which he avowed would keep the peace. I do not believe that honest history will justify his course, especially in the Far East, where he helped to arm the enemy for war which his own policies eventually made inevitable.

He was, I think, genuinely interested in establishing the kind of world order that would make for peace, but again he went far to frustrate his own purpose by his costly slogan "unconditional surrender" and his failure to lead his people in working out in time an honest program of inclusive world cooperation instead of a disguised and uneasy triple alliance imperialism.

His very skill in the political game, his opportunism unguided by any deep philosophy, diverted him from paths of true statesmanship. More and more he showed his love of power. This and his essential lack of understanding of the conditions of democracy and peace made him a protagonist of the labor draft and peacetime military conscription. The efficiency and even the integrity of some parts of the bureaucracy Roosevelt set up are yet to be judged. His reputation as a friend of the people actually tended to advance among the masses policies and attitudes which in Europe had contributed to the coming of the totalitarian state.[16]

In the years since 1945 Thomas' view of Roosevelt has mellowed considerably, but he has not been inclined to alter his general assessment. Moreover, he reacts in exasperation to the widespread tendency of so many liberals to engage in nostalgic reminiscence about the glories of the New Deal while developing no new programs to meet the crises of our times.

Hiroshima and Nagasaki

If Thomas was critical of the manner of our entrance into World War II, he was even more concerned about the way in which the conflict ended. He wrote:

The cruelest war in human history is at an end. . . . I can look at my son, home on leave, without being tortured by the thought that it is but a respite from hell.

Yet, as an American, I cannot rejoice over this inestimable boon of the ending of a victorious war without a sense of shame for the horror which the atomic bomb released upon the earth. I shall be told that it was the bomb which ended the war. As things were that is probably true, but I shall always believe that the war might have been ended before the first atomic bomb was dropped on Hiroshima bringing death to at least a hundred thousand men, women and children. . . .

Certainly that bomb should not have been dropped on a crowded city without warning. It is a tragedy which may be an omen of the eventual destruction of our civilization that we human beings, especially we Americans, are so bold in dealing with things and so unimaginative in the realm of ideas.

At the very least it would have been within our power to direct the world's attention to the destructive capacity of an atomic bomb at some designated point, not crowded with human beings. It was wholly inexcusable to drop the second bomb on Nagasaki. Proof of the power of atomic energy did not require the slaughter of hundreds of thousands of human guinea pigs. We shall pay for all this in a horrified hatred of millions of people which goes deeper and farther than we think.[17]

Among prominent Americans Thomas stood virtually alone in regard to his immediate reaction to the dropping of the bomb, but, in the years that followed, a significant number of his fellow citizens concluded that the action was probably unwise and unnecessary. Time and again, during the months after the close of the war, he reiterated his objections to the use of the bomb. His compatriots were frequently displeased by this position, but Thomas felt compelled to remind his audiences of this American crime against mankind. In the postwar era his revulsion of feeling over the fate of Hiroshima and Nagasaki contributed to making the quest for universal disarmament his first passion, indeed, almost an obsession. To those who would argue that to give such great stress to disarmament is idealistic fancy, his reply, in effect, has been that in the nuclear age idealism has become realism. During the postwar years he has never overlooked an opportunity in his writings or his speeches to make a plea for disarmament, to argue that war as a method of settling disputes is obsolete in the age of atomic weapons. It was to the problems of maintaining peace that he addressed himself in *Appeal to the Nations,* his first book following the close of World War II.

End of an Era

During his final presidential campaign, in 1948, Thomas made his usual criticisms of the two major parties and of the party system in the United States. He taunted the Republicans for their charges that the Democrats were leading the country to socialism, when, in fact, both parties had come to accept many measures which had originally been advocated by Socialists. He cited the Social Security program as an outstanding example of such measures.

The leaders of both major parties, he pointed out, paid homage erroneously to free enterprise. This was a national delusion, he argued, because the United States no longer had such a system. Thomas liked to tell his audiences in 1948—and still does—that the only actual practice of free enterprise still extant in the country is small boys playing marbles for keeps, because they play without the benefits of subsidies, tariffs, or other aids. The experience of World War II, he insisted, proved that productive miracles could be wrought through planning. If we could produce for death, why not for life via democratic socialism? he asked.

He charged that the Democrats under the leadership of Roosevelt and Truman had left us a rather unworkable and, in many ways, dangerous legacy in foreign affairs. "The major, but by no means the only threat of war," declared the 1948 Socialist platform, "lies in the aggression of the Soviet empire and the international Communist movement. That aggression has been invited and encouraged by the blunders of American policy from Cairo and Teheran through the Yalta and Potsdam conferences."[18] Thomas came out in favor of the Marshall plan but excoriated the military approach of the Truman doctrine.

The main target for Thomas' scorching criticism in 1948 was Henry Wallace rather than Harry Truman or Thomas Dewey. Had Thomas not felt that the 1948 Progressive party had been completely taken over by the Communists, he might well have favored it, even though, aside from his vigorous objections to its foreign policy, he had some serious reservations about its domestic economic program. He carefully observed the development of the Progressive party in the years following World War II. He attended, in the capacity of a reporter, the convention which nominated Wallace and became absolutely convinced that the party was a Communist-dominated organization, though he readily admitted that most of its members were well-intentioned, but politically unsophisticated, non-Communists. Long before the 1948 election, he had developed some basic reservations about Wallace, on the basis of personal experience. During the 1930's Thomas played a major role in various activities oriented to improving the lot of the impoverished southern sharecroppers. He tried in vain to secure an appointment with Wallace, who was then Secretary of Agriculture, to discuss the situation. Curiously, Thomas was able to see Roosevelt about the sharecropper problem, but Mr. Wallace indicated that he was too busy. Thomas never completely forgave Wallace for what he interpreted as a callousness with regard to America's poorest workers.

In 1948, repeatedly and unsuccessfully, the veteran Socialist campaigner challenged Wallace to meet him in debate. Thomas became especially irate at Wallace's description of the Soviet Union under Stalin as a "directed democracy." Moreover, he charged that the Progressive party

was giving blanket endorsement to the foreign policy of the aggressive Soviet dictatorship, the cruel masters of some ten million slaves, the men primarily responsible for the cold war, the ruthless seekers after universal power. The amazing thing is that Henry Wallace should have persuaded himself and many of his followers that he, propagandist of World War II, ardent supporter of Yalta, Potsdam, and the Morgenthau Plan, apologist for all Stalin's crimes, including the displacement of more millions than Hitler had time to displace, preacher of abject appeasement, should be hailed as an apostle of peace. At best, his program would sacrifice decency in Europe, not to true peace, but to a mere postponement of atomic war. I, who say this, do not believe that war is inevitable.

In behalf of my Party, I have repeatedly presented a program far more likely to lead to peace than the militarism of Harry Truman or the appeasement of Henry Wallace.

But peace can never be achieved or maintained by submission to the mightiest tyranny which has ever appeared on this earth.[19]

The Socialist campaign of 1948 received better publicity and aroused more interest in the country at large than had the campaign of 1944. The probable explanation is that the war was over and the American people were somewhat more willing to give a hearing to dissenting points of view—at least until McCarthyism began to make its inroads. A group of very prominent Americans, including some persons who had been ardent Roosevelt backers, came to Thomas' support. But the greater enthusiasm engendered by the 1948 campaign did not lead to any significant increase in the number of Socialist ballots, for Thomas received 95,908 votes—some 15,000 more than in 1944.

The political campaigns of Norman Thomas never attracted great national attention, but thoughtful people all over America were aware of them. The editorial reaction of the American press to the fact of Mr. Thomas' sixth nomination for the Presidency in 1948 was nothing short of remarkable, especially if one takes into consideration the temper of the times and the conservative reputation of American newspapers. One of America's most influential newspapers, the *New York Times,* commented, ". . . It is good to have Mr. Thomas in the field. . . . We cannot wish Mr. Thomas success in his campaign, but we are not sorry that this sort of campaign is being made by this sort of man." [20] "Norman Thomas is running again and he is worthy of thoughtful attention," declared the *New York Herald Tribune.*[21] ". . . Norman Thomas can be counted upon," remarked the *Washington Post,* "to bring to the campaign, as he has done in the past, caustic yet illuminating

criticism of his major party opponents and a reasoned defense
of the economic doctrines in which he believes. . . . He has
the respect and affection of the American people." [22] The
Cleveland Plain Dealer (Cleveland, Ohio) spoke in a similar
vein: "Norman Thomas is a man who commands respect even
from those who most vehemently disagree with Socialistic
principles. . . . Thomas' decision to be the Socialist candidate
for president again will, on the whole, have a politically
hygienic effect." [23]

Such was the comment of some of America's larger and
more important dailies. Many of America's smaller newspapers, however, were also saying, in effect, that they were
delighted that Mr. Thomas was once again a candidate.
"Thomas is our political and social Paul Revere, riding continuously over the countryside. May his ride continue for years
to come," remarked the *Oregon Journal* (Portland, Oregon). [24]

The *Ithaca Journal* (Ithaca, New York) also heaped extravagant praise upon America's leading Socialist: ". . . Mr.
Thomas . . . will pay the voters the honor of assuming that
they are willing to use their minds rather than their emotions
in determining their political destiny. Would that the old
parties had more men like him in integrity and unselfishness." [25]
"Americans approve of him as a citizen and politician . . . ,"
suggested the *Portland Oregonian*.[26] The *Arkansas Democrat*
(Little Rock, Arkansas) similarly exclaimed, "His devotion to
the public welfare has never been questioned. He is staunch
in his defense of democratic principles." [27]

It is one thing to admire and respect a public figure and
quite another thing actually to give him political support. The
measure of a man is often revealed by the caliber of the men
and women who back him. Norman Thomas never received
the political support of large numbers of his fellow citizens,

but he was backed in one campaign or another by persons who have made truly distinguished contributions to American life. A partial list of the eminent Americans who supported him in one or more of his campaigns would include Franz Boas, Morris R. Cohen, John Dewey, Paul H. Douglas, Irwin Edman, Louis Hacker, Sidney Hook, Robert M. Hutchins, Robert M. Lovett, C. Wright Mills, Broadus Mitchell, Harold Rugg, and Fred M. Shannon in the university world; Franklin P. Adams, Paul Blanshard, Van Wyck Brooks, Heywood Broun, Max Eastman, James T. Farrell, Lewis Gannett, Freda Kirchwey, Max Lerner, Edna St. Vincent Millay, Vincent Sheean, Dorothy Thompson, Oswald Garrison Villard, and Alexander Woolcott in the literary and journalistic world; and Harry Emerson Fosdick, John Haynes Holmes, Francis J. McConnell, Reinhold Niebuhr, and Stephen S. Wise in the religious world. Some of these well-known persons supported him out of socialist or near socialist conviction, but others voted essentially for the man. They were captivated by the personality of Norman Thomas.

The issue of whether or not the Socialist party should largely withdraw from the election field was vigorously debated at the party's 1950 convention in Detroit, Michigan. Thomas had become convinced that it no longer made sense to run candidates in every election, come what may. It was a decision that this veteran Socialist campaigner arrived at not without pain, and with reluctance and sadness.

His experiences in the 1948 campaign, when the leaders of even the most progressive unions put strong pressure on their followers not to support the Socialist ticket, contributed to his growing doubts about the wisdom of carrying on Socialist election activity in the traditional manner. As he looked back, he had some serious doubts about the success of his own campaigns. Moreover, he knew that future Socialist campaigners would face obstacles greater than the ones he had encountered in his long years of electioneering. With its limited resources and personnel the tiny party was finding it impossible to meet the varying and increasingly stringent requirements of state laws that were basically designed to keep minor parties off the ballot. A party that never, even in years of greater strength, spent more than $100,000 to $150,000 on a presidential campaign was in no position, Thomas concluded, to meet the skyrocketing costs of radio, television, and all other forms of publicity. A sense of realism, not egotism, compelled him to face also the tragic fact, for which he was inadvertently partially responsible, that there was no other figure of national prominence in the party. Thus he felt that the campaign of any other Socialist presidential standard-bearer would receive considerably less notice than his own had and, consequently, would prove much less valuable in the task of forwarding Socialist education. Except in special situations, he argued, the Socialist party should abandon the ballot-box approach and reconstitute itself as a Socialist educational and research body which he hoped would serve a function comparable to the historical role of the Fabian Society in Great Britain.

Despite this compelling array of arguments, which was accepted and supported by virtually all of the other prominent leaders of the party, Thomas was not able to convince the rank-and-file Socialists who attended the 1950 convention to abandon election activity. The convention reaffirmed its traditional pattern of electioneering.

In 1952 and 1956 the Socialist party gave its presidential nomination to Darlington Hoopes of Reading, Pennsylvania, a former member of the Pennsylvania State Legislature, and nominated Samuel Friedman of New York, a social worker, as his running mate. It was no secret in Socialist circles that Thomas had no enthusiasm for these campaigns, which he thought unwise, but he maintained cordial relationships with Hoopes and Friedman and on numerous occasions publicly congratulated them for their energetic campaigns. These campaigns were dismal failures, as Thomas had feared. In these elections the Socialist party succeeded in getting on the ballot in only a handful of states. In 1952 Hoopes and Friedman received 20,203 votes; in 1956 they fared even worse with 2,044.

By 1960 the Socialist party, now known as the Socialist party–Social Democratic Federation because the remnants of the Social Democratic Federation had come back to it in 1957, had abandoned its tradition of running presidential candidates. The party was not weaker in 1960 than it had been in the two previous elections; in fact, it was experiencing a mild revival because of the new and younger elements that were being drawn to it. The decision to abandon the election approach stemmed from the facing of hard, practical political facts and a somewhat more optimistic Socialist assessment of the domestic policies of the Democratic party.

"Monday-Morning Quarterbacking"

After 1948 Thomas abandoned his role as perennial Socialist presidential candidate, but by no means did he retire from American politics. He continued to function in American political life as a commentator and critic and has been no more reticent than Harry Truman about interpreting presidential politics for the benefit of his fellow Americans. "I enjoy sitting on the sidelines and Monday-morning quarterbacking other people's performances," he confessed in 1952.[28]

In that year, with vice-presidential prospects Richard Nixon and John Sparkman in mind, he advised that "we should all pray 'God save the President.' " [29] He regarded the presidential candidates with less apprehension but not without serious reservation. "General Eisenhower," Thomas observed, "criticizes Truman's foreign policy in general but approves it in all its important details. He loves General Marshall, whom Senator Joe McCarthy has outrageously denounced, but he'll swallow McCarthy, whatever he thinks of McCarthyism, so long as McCarthy bears the party label. For the same reason Governor Stevenson woos the solid south and plays down differences. Are not principles more important in our democracy than party labels?" [30]

In 1956 Thomas continued in his role as free-swinging critic of both parties and both candidates. Quite obviously, however, he was more sympathetic to the candidacy of Stevenson than to that of Eisenhower; yet, considering the fact that the Socialist party continued to have its own presidential candidates in the field, he felt constrained not to give strong or public emphasis to his rather positive attitudes toward Stevenson. Thomas' private letters reveal that he hoped for Stevenson victories in 1952 and 1956.

By the 1960 election year, the Socialist party's decision to abandon its policy of running presidential candidates allowed Thomas freedom to give a specific endorsement to one major candidate or the other; but he refrained from doing so. Insofar as the leading contenders for the Democratic nomination were concerned, he indicated that he could "restrain his enthusiasm" for any of them. Besides, he quipped, his approval "might be the kiss of death." Nevertheless, he went so far as to say, "Two and one half cheers for Hubert Humphrey." [31]

He was not even willing to go that far concerning the actual nominees in 1960. About Richard Nixon and John F. Kennedy he had this to say:

Their resemblances are far more striking than their differences, although the latter may be developed in the campaign. Kennedy's advantage is mostly in the quality of his advisers —if he'll keep his father, financier Joe Kennedy, out of the picture. Otherwise, we have two young, vigorous, able opportunists. (I use the word opportunists more by way of description than denigration.) Neither is a crusader for any cause. Put them in a room, brainwashed of the words Democrat and Republican and what they stand for, and they would reach agreement on a program at least as easily as did Messrs. Nixon and Rockefeller. But Messrs. Kennedy and Nixon are not fools or principled reactionaries. Either of them may respond to the requirement of events and the pressure of truly enlightened opinion far better than some of his predecessors in the White House. And that's where Socialist agitation and education must come in.[32]

"Both parties have come up with the best platforms in history," Thomas admitted. "The old-timers like Cleveland and McKinley would—if they rose from the dead—find both platforms socialistic."[33] Indeed, Thomas, of all people, found the Democratic platform "in considerable degree Utopian," but he added quickly that he meant in the setting of the free enterprise system which the Democrats spoke of so reverently.[34]

Thomas, in his seventy-sixth year, took to the road during the 1960 election campaign in order to talk about the issues as he saw them. He went across the country, on tour for the Socialist party–Social Democratic Federation, not so much to criticize or take jibes at the candidates as to talk about the interrelated failures of the United States' party system and the cold war. "Despite their noisy conflicts," Thomas argued, as he had so often when he was actually a candidate, "the Democrats and

Republicans do not present us with a meaningful political alignment on fundamental issues. Is this candidate for Congress a Barry Goldwater or Nelson Rockefeller Republican; a James Eastland or Hubert Humphrey Democrat? The differences within both parties are greater than the average between them." [35]

His deep, indeed his searing, concern about the 1960 campaign was that neither party or candidate provided a program adequate for the maintenance of peace. The major parties and their leaders, Thomas contended, were not adequately coming to grips with the relevant facts of life for the 1960's. He felt that they did not recognize the degree to which the United States had become an economy of the "garrison state" and had thus failed to give sufficient consideration to "working out the possibilities of human progress under a planned economy of disarmament." [36] He indicted them for putting greater American military might in first place on their foreign-policy agendas in a hungry world where nations already spend "115 billion annually on the arms race." "Neither party faces fairly," he noted, "the necessity of bringing China into the U.N. if any program of peace and disarmament is to be other than a pious aspiration. . . ." In short, Thomas was appalled that neither party was developing ideas or programs adequate to averting "the wanton suicide of our civilization" via nuclear war.[37]

After the Democrats nominated Kennedy at their 1960 convention, "All sorts of Stevensonians came to me," Thomas reported. "Why aren't you running?" they asked. Thomas' customary reply was, "Where were you the other times I ran? Frequently, I was elected in August, but never in November." Thomas wore nobody's campaign button, but he voted for Kennedy. "I'm rather sorry I can't vote for myself this year," he could not resist telling his audiences during the 1960 campaign.[38]

Thomas' activities during the years following World War II were hardly confined to the role of political commentator. In 1955, at the age of seventy, he resigned from all official posts in the Socialist party in the hope that younger people would fill the various roles that he had played. Yet he continued to function as the major spokesman for his party, to a much larger extent than he had anticipated or than he thought desirable. Moreover, he emphatically did not retire from his various other involvements and activities as social diagnostician and healer. He continued his long record of leadership with the League for Industrial Democracy, the American Civil Liberties Union, the Workers Defense League, and the Post War World Council. The latter organization, primarily a Thomas creation, operates out of his own office, and its major activity seems to be the publication of a bimonthly newsletter written by none other than Norman Thomas himself. "The Council," as stated in its own masthead, "concerns itself with matters of foreign policy and, especially, with a crusade for universal disarmament under effective international control, coupled with a war on the world's poverty, in which lie the seeds of true world government." [39]

During the last decade he has become deeply involved in a host of organizations and activities devoted to peace and civil rights. Age has not dispelled Thomas' addiction to working for the betterment of the world in which he lives, nor has it dampened his crusading zeal. (For a more detailed account of Thomas' recent activities, see Chapter X.)

Respectable Rebel

Almost from the beginning of his political career, Norman Thomas has been regarded as a respectable rebel. As early as 1932 he was awarded an honorary doctorate by Princeton University, his alma mater and an institution far removed from radicalism. By that time he was already in great demand as a speaker in the best university and church lecture series. Although questions were sometimes raised regarding the propriety of inviting a Socialist to speak, the interesting fact remains that great numbers of Americans who rejected his politics were, nevertheless, eager to hear him expound his views.

Since the close of World War II, Thomas' status of respectability and his general reputation have risen enormously. In recent years the platform introductions accorded him have been so glowing and so prone to attribute to him qualities of greatness that, as an antidote, he often responds with the story about "the widow at the funeral, who, on hearing the dear, departed eulogized, sent up Jimmy to see if it was really his father in the coffin that they were talking about." [40] In a more serious vein he told those who gathered to honor him on the occasion of his seventy-fifth birthday: "To any who may be worried lest I acquire an unlovely conceit as a result of the too generous praise bestowed upon me let me say that I am possessed of an inward monitor who takes much satisfaction in reminding me of the many things I would like to have done had I the ability, and those I might have done with more persistence and better use of what capacities I have." [41]

It must be said here that the status of respectability is one which Thomas never sought, which he never anticipated, and about which he never felt entirely comfortable. His great hope was to build a strong Socialist movement and not to win personal esteem. To have been gratifying to him, recognition would have had to stem from the fact that he was a great Socialist leader, and not to have been accorded in spite of that fact.

Thomas has emerged as one of the most unusual figures in American political life, in some ways the most extraordinary. It is astonishing that in the bastion of capitalism a Socialist leader should achieve such exceptional status. A person who observed Thomas closely when the Socialist leader attended the 1948 Republican and Democratic conventions as a reporter comments that the outstanding major-party leaders treated Thomas consistently as a peer and frequently with deference. Thomas' correspondence—including letters to and from most of the major leaders of our time—confirms this interpretation. In letters to Thomas from Republican and Democratic leaders there is almost always a tone of respectful cordiality. Senator Arthur Vandenberg once wrote him that Thomas' communications always had "top priority" in his office. John Foster Dulles informed Thomas, time and again, that he was always happy to have the opportunity to consider Thomas' views on foreign policy. Thomas felt free enough with the Secretary of State to add as a closing note to a letter of May 15, 1953, "How long can the administration stand McCarthy?" [42] After Thomas visited the White House to encourage Truman to adopt a policy of universal disarmament, the President wrote him on August 30, 1950, "It was a pleasure to visit with you the other day and I appreciate it more than I can tell you." [43] The tone of the note sounded almost as if Truman were thanking a president for giving him an audience. Some of the other prominent American political leaders who have treated Thomas as, at least, a peer include: Chester Bowles, Paul Douglas, Hubert Humphrey, William Langer, Wayne Morse, and H. Alexander Smith.

During the post–World War II era, Thomas has tried with some success to enlist the aid of important political figures in the cause of disarmament. Almost invariably, his correspondence reveals that key American decision makers have given his advice—usually unsolicited—serious consideration, even if they did not generally heed it. In short, he has had easy access to those who exercise political power in the United States.

In the history of the United States, perhaps no other radical has been accorded as much general respect and prestige as Thomas has. Even the conservative *Saturday Evening Post* (February 2, 1952) has referred to him as "one of America's most distinguished social philosophers." [44] At a testimonial dinner tendered in his honor in 1950, high tribute was paid to Norman Thomas by renowned American and world citizens. In a statement that he wrote for the occasion, Arthur Hays Sulzberger, then publisher of the *New York Times,* doubtless gave expression to the sentiments of many of the non-Socialists who attended the function:

> Today's political tensions make it a rare pleasure to be able to affirm personal esteem and respect for a man with many of whose political and economic views on vital issues one disagrees.
>
> You [Thomas] have had the great distinction of conferring that pleasure on more people, of more widely varying opinions (excluding, in fact, only the furthest extremes of right and left), than any man in contemporary American life. This you have been able to do because of your personal sincerity and eloquence, and your faith in the methods of democracy. [45]

Even a partial listing of the eminent persons who have lent their names to celebrations in honor of Norman Thomas is impressive. Labor has been represented by David Dubinsky,

William Green, Walter Reuther, and others; from the world of politics, persons such as Clifford Case, James A. Farley, Hubert H. Humphrey, Harold Ickes, Wayne Morse, and Adlai Stevenson have participated; notable university administrators included Harry Woodbourne Chase, Harold W. Dodds, Harry D. Gideonse, Bryn J. Hovde, Robert M. Hutchins, and Robert G. Sproul; other outstanding American scholars were Gordon W. Allport, Adolf Berle, Quincy Howe, Harold Lasswell, Eduard C. Lindeman, Robert M. Maciver, Allan Nevins, Arthur M. Schlesinger, Sr., Arthur M. Schlesinger, Jr., and Louis Wirth; Harry Emerson Fosdick, John Haynes Holmes, and G. Bromley Oxnam have represented the world of American Protestantism. A list of other American notables would include Norman Cousins, Martha Dean, Dorothy Canfield Fisher, H. V. Kaltenborn, Walter Lippmann, Frederick March, and Ezra Stone. Among foreign leaders who have paid tribute to Thomas are Leon Blum, Leon Johaux, and Guy Mollet of France; Harold J. Laski and Morgan Phillips of England; Jawaharlal Nehru of India; Karl Renner of Austria; and Ernst Reuter of Germany.

In 1953, Peter Viereck, historian, poet, and self-avowed conservative, proposed publicly that the voice of Norman Thomas should have a wider hearing. His suggestion was apparently prompted by the fact that the *New York Herald Tribune* had written editorially that Thomas possessed "independence of thought," "candor," and a "deep sense of democratic values" and that he was the "kind of citizen without which any free country would be impoverished." In effect, Viereck issued a challenge to the *New York Herald Tribune* and other conservative newspapers to provide Thomas with a weekly column. The essence of Viereck's argument was that Thomas, as "one of the world's most effective and ardent exposers of Soviet

Russia," should have the opportunity to make his words better known to his fellow Americans and that it was important for Europe to know that communism was being attacked "by a strictly non–Wall Street source." [46] Thomas' anticommunism, suggested Viereck, was appropriately tempered by a healthy respect for the precious American heritage of civil liberties. In closing his letter to the *New York Herald Tribune,* Viereck wrote:

> At a time when demagogy and conformism tarnish the valuable insight of liberalism and the equally necessary insights of conservatism, America needs to hear this sensitive and humane non-conformist, whose paradoxical destiny in history is to be remembered not primarily as a Socialist but as our incorruptible watchdog of our public ethics.[47]

Mr. Thomas has by no means received the wide audience which Mr. Viereck apparently thinks he deserves, but, since the late 1940's, he has been a columnist for the *Denver Post* (Colorado) and other western newspapers. During the Truman administration it was reported by Will Herberg, a scholarly journalist, that Thomas was "mentioned . . . in the best circles as one whose appointment to a high diplomatic post would bring credit to his country." The same source aptly described him as "one of our 'elder statesmen,' a kind of liberal-left Bernard Baruch." [48]

Is Thomas' great respectability testimony to his effectiveness or to his ineffectiveness as a Socialist leader? To Arnold Petersen, a Socialist Labor party leader, who derisively refers to "Parson Thomas" in *Bourgeois Socialism,* there is no doubt that Thomas' respectability is a reflection of his complete ineffectiveness. Concerning a Thomas testimonial dinner in 1950, Petersen remarked, "A most interesting collection of the 'cream' of capitalist society! Mr. Thomas must feel quite at home among them." [49] He characterized Thomas as a "special pet" of the *New York Times* and then quoted that publication as suggesting that Thomas was "about as far removed from the narrow, bitter, and dogmatic spirit of Karl Marx as any man could be. . . ." Petersen took no issue with the statement but merely replied, "Well, we can certainly all agree that Mr. Thomas is far removed from Marx, a fact upon which Marx is to be congratulated." [50]

One need not accept the criticism of a rival minor-party leader to come to the conclusion that Norman Thomas has not frightened many of his fellow Americans, either of the capitalist or noncapitalist varieties. If the proper role of the radical leader is to put fear into the hearts of the majority, Thomas most certainly did not fulfill his obligation. If, on the other hand, it is important for a leader espousing an unpopular cause to make his beliefs more palatable to his fellow citizens, then he has known considerable success. Curtis D. MacDougal, in his *Understanding Public Opinion,* has argued that the word "socialism" has become "less opprobrious" because of Thomas' activities. "Less than a generation ago," he wrote, "it was considered as damaging a label as 'communism.' Among the factors accounting for the change was the personality of the long-time leader of the American Socialist Party, Norman Thomas, a retired minister who used perfect English with outstanding oratorical flourishes and had excellent table manners. As he got around he destroyed the stereotype of the long-haired soapbox crackpot." [51]

The friendly acceptance that large numbers of Americans have accorded Norman Thomas relates to the very aspects of the man to which his critics on the left have vigorously objected. He is accepted because he lives within, rather than outside, the present social order, because his socialism is tempered by liberalism, and because he is willing to assume that even those with whom he has basic disagreements are conceivably behaving in good faith. But it would be a mistake to conclude that Thomas' wide acceptance rests fundamentally upon the fact that he subscribes to a moderate brand of socialism. Americans are not especially adept at distinguishing between one variety of socialism and another, and it would appear that the way in which Thomas is received by his countrymen relates more to his personality than to any quality of mildness in his doctrine. He is an appealing figure because he has never even verged on being a professional crank, which is more than can be said for many participants in radical movements. Only a slight acquaintance with him is enough to convince one that his determination to alter the world does not rise from some deep personal unhappiness. He is the happy reformer who readily admits to enjoying his "role as dissenter": [52]

> It is a great mistake for anyone in America to get the idea that my life has been anything but an extraordinarily happy one. I am blessed as very few men of my acquaintance have been blessed. There isn't an hour of my life, going back to my earliest memories, in which I do not recall affection and friendship and the security that affection and friendship give. And it has always seemed to me that anyone who has been thus blessed is under some obligation to try to make a better country in which the beautiful side, the side of friendship is more apparent.[53]

Thomas' security—in the personality sense—is indicated in many ways, not the least of these being his capacity for not always regarding himself in a serious light. Related to this quality is the fact that—as reformers go—his outlook is con-

spicuously devoid of bitterness. These facets of his personality
are disclosed in an address that he gave to a large group of
Americans who gathered together in order to do him honor
in 1950. He told them:

> When this invitation came out, someone saw me and,
> with a rather cynical smile said, "Well I suppose you know
> that all these people here, you know most of them who signed
> this, never voted for you." I said that I was familiar with the
> facts of political life. I also said that I never voted for them.
> But I did not draw any very cynical lesson from this.
>
> I know what life is like. I am aware that I am talking now
> over the air and otherwise to thousands of people who have
> kept their New Year's resolution, come what may, not to
> vote for Norman Thomas rather better than any other resolu-
> tion that they may have made. I think I am talking to people,
> some of whom take a great deal of pain not to listen to me
> before election because it is a great deal easier to do it after
> election without disturbing the faith that is not too secure.
>
> All this I know and yet very sincerely I say that it is one
> cause for joy in America that we have, in spite of our faults,
> worked out a kind of living here where it is possible for us to
> admire and respect one another and to have confidence in the
> society of which we are part in spite of these differences.[54]

As the years have gone by, a considerable appreciation of
Norman Thomas has matured in America. And it has been a
reciprocal process, for Norman Thomas has developed a deeper
appreciation, indeed a deeper love, of his native land—a fact
which has doubtless been sensed by those non-Socialist Americans who have come to regard him so highly. Thomas' love for
America is well reflected in an article entitled "What's Right
with America" that he wrote in 1947 for *Harper's Magazine.*

"Most of my yesterdays," he began, "have been spent telling what's wrong with America—always, I hope, with suggestions for constructive change. Most of my tomorrows will be similarly employed. Today I am writing about some of the things that are right with America." [55] He pointed to a variety of these items: America's unprecedented generosity in dealing with its allies and its former enemies at the close of World War II, its granting of independence to the Philippines, its relative lack of "snobbery in human relations." [56] "All over our country," he continued, "there is a saving quality of family life, of good humored and good-neighborly responsibility, that someday a modern novelist may discover. For myself, I have even a good word for church suppers and grange fairs." [57] The quality of Thomas' affection for his native land and the fact that even as America's critic he has not lost sight of its virtues are unmistakably and eloquently revealed in his closing words:

> For all this relative freedom and fellowship in America there are various explanations in terms of the hospitality of a new, uncrowded land, its climate, its geographic position, its fertility, and its economic conditions. We are of the same blood as less fortunate Europeans, modesty becomes us, and thankfulness for the extraordinary opportunity that has been ours. But it is not self-righteous for us to be genuinely proud of the great American tradition of liberty, which in the stormy crisis of the present still has strength and validity.
>
> Tomorrow I shall be back to pointing out some of the things wrong with America and to suggesting how they may be made right. I shall do it with more confidence because we have a heritage and a history which justify faith in man's capacity for freedom and fair play.[58]

Chapter VIII

Plenty, Peace, and Freedom

For a variety of reasons the American cultural situation has not given a high valuation to theory. Americans, as a people, have seemingly been too completely involved in the matter of doing to pause to consider why they were doing or what they were doing. It is not surprising that people who have reaped the rich rewards of expending their collective energies toward the eminently practical projects of conquering a continent and building a gigantic machine empire should glorify the practical and disdain the theoretical. Theory has had to fight an uphill battle even in the so-called ivory towers of our universities. It is interesting to note that the most original and significant American philosophical contributions have been related to the development of pragmatism.

This aversion to theory has also manifested itself in American political life. Very few contemporary American political leaders seriously concern themselves with political, social, or economic theory. The philosopher-statesman is not a familiar figure in twentieth-century America. During the earliest period of United States history, the situation was markedly different; John Adams, John Calhoun, Alexander Hamilton, Thomas Jefferson, and James Madison were important political leaders and at the same time important theorists. They were men who held well-formulated social philosophies. Endowed with speculative minds, these men were genuinely interested in ideas; moreover, they had the need and the facility for putting down their ideas on paper. Among the major-party leaders of this century, Woodrow Wilson probably best represents their tradition.

In the present situation most American political leaders adhere to philosophies that are so opportunistic and so loosely formulated that it seems as if they have no social philosophy at all. This characteristic is intimately related to the strange political formula which declares that principles, platforms, and parties are unimportant—and that only the electing of good men to office really counts—which so many Americans equate with political wisdom. American voters have not been especially concerned with the presence or absence of formal statements of political principles—a fact which explains partially why most of their leaders have not been inclined to develop any.

This antitheoretical tendency does not appear so marked in the minor American political parties. Certainly, political groups with a socialist orientation have not disdained theory. Perhaps newer political faiths demand more justification and elaboration. The new in politics is always under attack and must often be justified on theoretical as well as practical grounds. In part, then, the emphasis which minor parties place upon theory may be properly viewed as a defense mechanism, and, no doubt, some of this inclination to espouse theory can be properly ascribed to the need for self-justification of unorthodox views. After all, it is probably quite impossible for the political radical to hold views which are rejected by the majority without having doubts creep into his own thinking now and then.

Whatever the reasons, socialist traditions have required that the policy of Socialist leadership be justified on theoretical as well as on practical grounds. In fact, one of the severest criticisms that all socialist-oriented groups have made of the major parties is that they are not sufficiently concerned with social philosophy or political principles. On the other hand, critics of the socialist movement have charged that this concern with the theoretical has immeasurably weakened radical political organizations in the United States. No matter what evaluation is made of this emphasis upon theory, it is clear that concern with the theoretical constitutes an important distinctive normative pattern among socialist and other "leftist" political groups.

Upon consideration of Norman Thomas' views, in the context of the mainstream of American political life, the unusual fact is revealed that he does have a political and social theory, or perhaps more accurately, that he does have a well-formulated social philosophy. When Mr. Thomas is considered in the light of socialist politics, however, this fact does not seem so surprising.

"You Can't Go Home Again"

A man's philosophy is equivalent to the pattern of assumptions that he makes concerning the world in which he lives and the men who inhabit it. Before attempting to analyze Mr. Thomas' beliefs on specific issues, it is essential to inquire into the mold of thought that guided his activities during an extraordinarily busy life, or what might be called his *Weltanschauung*.

Considering his ministerial background, a good starting point might be his religious orientation. Almost all of his writing and speeches indicate a deep and abiding interest in the kind of ethical problems with which theologians have traditionally concerned themselves, but he seems to find himself apart from organized religion. Writing an essay on American Protestantism some thirty years ago, he declared:

> I speak as one outside the fold of my fathers. No longer do I find adequate, as I once did, the halfway house prepared by modernists who still feel the power of the old traditions as well as the compulsions of the new and confusing day in science, philosophy and social affairs. For good or for evil the religion which was so much and so intimate a part of the life of my boyhood, the religion in which my father's home was founded and nourished, lives for me mostly in memory. To return to it would be an impossible and by no means lovely way of escape from life and its problems.[1]

More recently, he has suggested that, before one can agree to the social necessity of religion, one must agree to some definition of the term. If what is meant by religion, he argues, "is a deep sense of values transcending quantitative measurement," it may then be considered as "necessary to the good life and to the good society."[2] But he rejects religion as being a good influence on the social order if it means an emphasis upon particular creeds or upon the revealed will of God. He contends that "to say that there is no basis for personal and social ethics apart from one or another of the organized religions is untrue to observed fact and immensely derogatory to a God worth respect."[3] He asserts that man is in need of some "unifying loyalty,"[4] but to him religion, which has been as much a divisive force as a unifying one, does not offer much hope as an aid to establishing it. Man must look to the experiences of life itself as the base for broadening his loyalties.

That Thomas wishes he could speak more hopefully of religion cannot be doubted. Moreover, there is nothing in his writing to suggest that he is a foe, or even a bitter critic, of organized religion, as is the case with a large number of individuals in the various sections of the socialist movement. As a matter of fact, Thomas defends American Protestantism against some of the criticisms that have been leveled at it by Harry Elmer Barnes, Sinclair Lewis, H. L. Mencken, and others. He claims that the drab and the harsh qualities of late nineteenth-century Protestantism have been magnified and that much of what was valuable in it has been overlooked by some of its critics. "American Protestantism," he points out, "has been weighed in the balance by our generation and found wanting, if palpably it has failed to meet the needs of a world already caught in the toils of revolution, intellectual as well as social, it did at its best nourish men and women worth loving who faced life and death more bravely for their faith." [5] Calvinist theology, he implies, could not always be taken at face value, and he substantiates his conclusion with references to beliefs that his father held. "He believed in a hell," writes Thomas, "to which all his life I do not think he ever would say that anyone was bound. I do not believe in his hell and yet have been sorely tempted to consign not a few thereto." [6] So far has Thomas moved from the religion of his father that he can no longer accept intellectually the idea of the immortality of the soul or the efficacy of prayer.

The Nature of Human Nature

As a man advocating fundamental changes in our social order, Mr. Thomas has been forced to do some serious thinking about the nature of man, for one of the basic arguments leveled against his socialist creed is that it is not compatible with human nature. Furthermore, his ministerial background would tend to make him deeply interested in the matter. This is not to say that he looks to religious thought for a guide to his view of human nature. In fact, he criticizes religion for making people "think too much of the goodness and badness of men and far too little of the essential nature of the social system which held even the best men in its toils." [7]

Rather than to religion, Thomas turns to "science" for more enlightenment about the nature of human nature. He is conversant with and appears to subscribe to the general conception of human nature which modern anthropology, sociology, and psychology have arrived at, although it is clear that he is perfectly aware of the contradictions and controversies that plague these fields. His own words concerning man's nature coincide rather completely with the assessment made by modern social science:

> If there is a human nature which determines man's conduct and destiny, the process is far more subtle and obscure than in the case of the other animals: ants, bees, wolves, beavers, whose social conduct is instinctively determined. Man is man, separated from the rest of animal creatures by his capacity to use tools, and by his ability to talk and to reflect about the world and himself. Within wide limits set by man's physical and mental equipment, human nature is an amazing variable. It is an attribute of St. Francis of Assisi and Adolph Hitler; Albert Schweitzer and Joseph Stalin; Gandhi and his assassin. It is by definition common to the primitive human beings who lived under the amazingly different cultural patterns so well described and discussed by modern anthropologists. [8]

Paralleling this notion of man's variability is Thomas' assertion that human nature does change and that, therefore, it is possible for men to live under a more rational social and economic order. Thomas alleges that those persons who take the dreary view of human nature not infrequently have something to gain by the preservation of the status quo. "It eases their consciences," he writes, "by giving them a convenient excuse for doing nothing for men except to rail at their follies." [9] Yet he recognizes the fact that many of history's social reformers have been too optimistic about the "perfectibility" of man. "The slavery from which we suffer is, partially at least, within us. Too long has the tree been bent for it suddenly to grow straight; too long have we been in darkness immediately to see clearly. Emancipation at its most hopeful means reeducation." But he immediately qualifies these words by saying:

> To admit this, however, is a very different thing from admitting that we are bound to poverty and war by chains of biological necessity or social inheritance too strong to be broken. Some of the objections to human competency most vociferously urged are extraordinarily lacking in genuine scientific support. Thus the notion that the biological struggle for existence or some instinct of combativeness means eternal war has been pretty well scotched by competent thinkers.[10]

Thomas repudiates another kind of biological theorizing as well. The very notion of racial superiority and inferiority is an anathema to him. As he sees it, the adherence to racist doctrines precludes the possibility of a better world. He points to some of the most significant social-science findings concerning race and expresses some doubt that the word belongs in the vocabulary of science. There is no acceptable evidence, he maintains, to indicate that either culture or intelligence are racially determined. Although he implies that the final verdict of science is not yet in, he clearly does not feel that the situation justifies despair:

The crusaders for a better society can reasonably accept this assurance: most men of every society have more brains and latent abilities than they use. No man is infinitely perfectible, but most men of all races and classes are well enough endowed to be capable of a better education than any they have received and of a higher level of social conduct than they habitually practice.[11]

A Non-Marxist Socialist

Thomas concerns himself, in the course of his writings, not only with the nature of man, but he has written at length about the nature of the historical process and man's relationship to it. His philosophy of history has an important relationship to his evaluation of Marxist theory, as is the case with any professed socialist. Writing of his own intellectual development in *A Socialist's Faith* (1951), Thomas states:

> Certainly I was no anti-Marxist when I joined the Party, but mine, like much of English socialism was non-Marxist. Later I went through various degrees of belief in Marxism. It was, however, when I was closest to that *ism*—in the early nineteen thirties—that I became most aware of a desire that there should be a synthesis such as Marx did not provide between economics, politics, and the knowledge that had been brought to us by the newer schools of psychology.[12]

And when one turns to Thomas' writings of the "early nineteen thirties," which he suggests was the period of his greatest allegiance to Marxist doctrine, it becomes clear beyond question that he was no orthodox Marxist. In the first book in which he stated his fundamental positions on politics and social philosophy, *America's Way Out,* he gave a rather detailed exposition of his position on Marxism. First, he summarized the basic tenets of Marxist thinking, while emphasizing that Marxism is not synonymous with socialism. Moreover, he argued that it is possible to accept an economic interpretation of history without being a socialist. His own stand at the time would appear to have been that economic factors were the most important ones in the historical process. He pointed out, however, that Engels wisely cautioned his followers against oversimplification of the theory of economic determinism. Thomas implied that it was a useful but hardly an infallible tool for social analysis. Also, he indicated that he could not accept any rigid theory of class division and interests.

Marxism, Thomas noted, came into being during a period when the prevalent theories of psychology and philosophy were very different from those of the 1930's. And it was imperative, he maintained, that it be modified in the light of the newer findings in these fields. He emphatically denied that Marxism could be properly viewed as a science. He offered many illustrations of Marxist failures in the fields of social analysis and social prediction, of which some of the most notable were: a revolution in backward Russia was not at all anticipated; the increased vitality which capitalism would derive from the great enlargement of its productive capacities was not realized; the predicted increasing misery for workers did not actually come about; the extremely important role that managers and engineers were to play in the modern productive process was not foreseen; and Marxist theory did not offer adequate insight into the nature of war in the twentieth century. Furthermore, Thomas manifested no surprise at the evidence of shortcomings in Marxist theory: "Can a generation which has had to go far beyond Newtonian physics or atomic chemistry or Darwinian biology be expected to find Marx, who was also the child of his time, infallible?" [13] There is no doubt, however, that Thomas believed at the time of his writing of *America's Way Out* that Marxist theory was of crucial importance in understanding the world about him. Moreover, he was convinced that it would necessarily assume a key position in the kind of "synthesis" of social theory that he hoped would be achieved. He recognized Marxism as a great motive force for altering the world along socialist lines:

> [Marxism] was the philosophy which gave to the workers dignity, cohesion and a sense of place in the cosmic process. It gave them hope while it restrained them from premature and blind revolt. It spoke in the name of science but brought with it most of the emotional satisfactions including the sense of assurance which we associate with religion. In the fourscore years following the appearance of the *Communist Manifesto,* the Gospel, according to Marx, has been preached throughout the world with a firm and persuasive power passing that of the Gospel according to Mark. Socialism has become a religion whose great rival for the supreme allegiance of the common man is not so much the older religion of the church, mosque or synagogue as the religion of nationalism.[14]

His evaluation of Marxism in *As I See It* (1932) was not essentially different from that in *America's Way Out* (1931), but in the later work he is perhaps more insistent that Marxism is analogous to religion rather than to science. Thomas, who had already separated himself from one religious orthodoxy, was in no mood to embrace another. Just as he had done with religious theories, he argued that the various interpretations of Marx would not actually derive their strength from the degree to which they succeeded in correctly appraising the mind of Marx but from the power of the groups which held them.

Thomas also found it necessary to add some qualification to the orthodox Marxist view of the depression:

The Marxian theory of crisis finds immense confirmation in the present depression, and the Marxian prophecy of the destruction of capitalism, when its work was done, by the doom it carried within it, is being fulfilled before our eyes. That doom may have been delayed; when it comes it may be more largely due to the stupid and blind psychology of an acquisitive society and to its nationalistic follies and less to its pure economic weakness than early Marxists thought, but doom it surely will be.[15]

Twenty years later, in *A Socialist's Faith,* his stand on Marxism remains fundamentally the same, although his rejection of it appears to be somewhat more complete and final:

No serious thinker coming with fresh mind to Marxism one hundred years after the *Communist Manifesto* would find in it a completely scientific explanation of life or even of economics and politics. Marxism's importance lies not in its finality as science or religion, but in its record through a century of extraordinary propaganda power over large masses of men. It did not foretell the specific manner of that collapse which it helped to bring about. It is the state religion of the mighty Soviet Union and the international communist movement. It is reverenced by many democratic socialists, who derive from it at vital points conclusions opposite to the communists.

Clearly the world ought to have some more adequate social philosophy. Any new synthesis of our knowledge and aspirations will owe much to Marx, but it will not be Marxist unless by a very loose use of the word.[16]

In conjunction with his refusal to accept Marxism as a philosophy, he has also refused to accept it as his style of language for speaking or writing. Marxist verbiage is conspicuous in its absence from the writings and speech of Norman Thomas. He is convinced that one can be a good socialist without shouting about "class conflict." Indeed, he believes that Marxist terminology has the effect of alienating potential American socialists. It might be added that the language of the ministry and Princeton appear to be so ingrained in Mr. Thomas that, even had he wanted to, it would not have been easy for him to adopt the Marxist jargon.

Call for a New Synthesis

Thus far, several important aspects of Mr. Thomas' thought have been considered: his attitudes toward religion, his estimate of human nature, and his theory of history as exemplified by his appraisal of Marxism. All of these subjects have been discussed explicitly and extensively by him. It is not unusual to find that many of the fundamental elements of a man's thought do not receive specific or lengthy treatment in his writing, and such is the case with Mr. Thomas, who has never laid claim to being a systematic philosopher. Therefore, it is necessary to investigate some aspects of his thinking which are not always completely dealt with by him but which, nevertheless, are crucial to the understanding of his social philosophy.

What are some of these phases of his fundamental philosophy which yet need to be considered? As already indicated above, Thomas believes that we desperately need a "synthesis" of our present knowledge in order to provide a foundation for a more adequate social philosophy. He is of the opinion that economics, philosophy, physical science, psychology, and sociology can somehow be related to each other on a theoretical level, although he does not give the slightest inkling as to how this relationship might be achieved. Furthermore, he suggests that he does not personally feel capable of the task.

It would appear, then, that eclecticism of a not too well-defined variety is characteristic of Thomas' world view. He is convinced that no one field of knowledge has a monopoly on truth concerning man and the universe which he inhabits; yet he seems to weigh economic and social factors more heavily in importance than psychological ones in the historical process. Nevertheless, it is clear that he subscribes, in general, to a theory of multiple causation which is part and parcel of his eclecticism.

Naturally flowing from this eclecticism, or perhaps having caused him to embrace it, is the fact that he rejects orthodoxy in thinking about social phenomena. Having outgrown the religious type, he has not been receptive to any new varieties of orthodoxy. As he sees it, worship at the shrine of Freud is as absurd as worship at the shrine of Marx. Likewise, he is "skeptical" of theories which suggest that there is "a rigid pattern in history, whether they are made by Hegel, Marx, Toynbee or Spengler." [17]

Thus he rejects all varieties of determinism: "If man's end is social tragedy it will not be certain that such tragedy was foredoomed. Disaster may come because man did not wake in time and act in time." [18] Thomas has tenaciously held to this view; even living through the Great Depression and the Second World War has not persuaded him to abandon it. In *A Socialist's Faith* he writes, "There is in human conduct an element of will and choice. Without it freedom and democracy are meaningless, scarcely the substance of a dream." [19]

There appears to be only one absolute among the basic assumptions of the social philosophy of Norman Thomas, namely,

the rejection of absolutes. With some qualifications, he accepts the position of social relativism; yet his conviction that
ethical standards rise from social experience should not be
construed to mean that his world view is devoid of ethics. On
the contrary, he believes that ethics matter profoundly in our
troubled world, and he ascribes much of the world's sickness
to the absence of an ethical orientation. He reasons:

> Acceptance of relativity in social ethics does not require a
> renunciation of ethical standards or methods nor does it re-
> duce them to a mere by-product of economics, a function in
> the struggle of classes. Rather it is true that there is a basic
> morality to which we owe a supreme loyalty, a morality
> derived from our common humanity, a morality greatly
> affected by the conditions under which men work and live,
> but never to be reduced to a mere expression of personal,
> group, class or national interest.[20]

The fundamental ethical principles to which Mr. Thomas
subscribes are two in number. In the first place, "Ends and
means are logically related in the laboratory of life, even if
the relationship cannot be so precisely established as in the
chemical laboratory. Bad means employed for good ends corrupt the ends." In the second place, "In seeking or maintaining
a good society, individual human beings should be treated as
ends, not means." [21] These two principles underlie all of
Thomas' thinking; they constitute the yardstick, so to speak,
with which he takes so many of his measurements concerning
the contemporary world and its citizens. These tenets must
be kept in mind as a background for his analysis of what he
has long believed to be the three most fundamental problems
confronting mankind—those of achieving, to use Thomas'

favorite phrase, "plenty, peace, and freedom." It is to his thought
concerning these three problems that we now turn.

The Conquest of Poverty

The initial assumption that Mr. Thomas makes about "plenty,
peace, and freedom" is that they are interrelated and that they
constitute a triad upon which all hopes for a better world depend. He is convinced that any one of these hoped-for social
conditions can be achieved in any genuine way only if the
other two are also accomplished. When he was writing during
the depression years, however, there is some indication that
he stressed "plenty" as the most fundamental element in the
triad, but in his later works this stress is much less marked.

It must be remembered that Norman Thomas did not in-
herit his socialism. The religious orthodoxy of his middle-class
boyhood home and his education at the rather aristocratic
Princeton University were not conducive to the development
of his socialist philosophy. As has been explained earlier, he
came to detest poverty as a result of personal experiences in
New York slums, when he was engaged in Christian social
work as a young minister.

His early abhorrence of poverty was subsequently strengthened by his conviction that the condition is unnecessary. He
argues that for large numbers of mankind hunger was once
unavoidable, because of the lack of technical means with which
to conquer it, but that this is no longer the situation: "Now, so
far as our physical resources, our mechanical power, and our
means of communication are concerned, there is no excuse for
poverty for any of the children of earth." The pessimism of
"neo-Malthusians" can be answered by "an increase of intelligent birth control." [22] By making starvation unnecessary, he
happily suggests, science and technology have "given us firm

foundations for our utopias. No longer need our great dreamers place their visions in happy islands or fortunate cities or boldly expect the mighty intervention of God to make all things new." [23]

As of 1950, Thomas indicted American capitalism for the fact that, despite the magnificence of American resources and technology, "almost ten million American families . . . received incomes under $2,000," even in the allegedly "prosperous" year of 1948. Thus he concluded that "Roosevelt's famous statement is still approximately true: one-third of our people are ill-fed, ill-clothed and ill-housed." [24] As of 1960, Thomas is inclined to accept, but not without qualifications, John K. Galbraith's thesis that we are living in an "affluent society." He feels obliged to remind us, however, that "America has pockets of unnecessary and disgraceful poverty. And in its wealth even the more fortunate among us have not found inner peace." [25] He admits candidly that the "vitality of a progressive type of capitalism explains the present halt in socialist progress in popular estimation." Yet he emphatically does not view himself as a rebel without a cause. He insists "that the basic problems to which socialism had addressed itself" remain unsolved.[26]

Thomas is especially critical of capitalism for the historical and present waste of precious natural resources, such as coal, forests, natural gas, and oil. What is the reason for this "carnival of waste"? "It is a natural, even a necessary, accompaniment of our American conception of the righteousness of the private ownership of natural resources and their development for private profit." [27] Perhaps Thomas does not take into sufficient consideration, when analyzing the waste of American resources, the fact that a nation endowed with a bountiful supply of natural treasures is likely to use them somewhat prodigally under any economic system.

"Along with waste," he declares, "the great economic crime of private capitalism is that it has given us chronic unemployment." [28] He does not hold with the Marxist theory that it has meant increasing impoverishment for workers, but he does lay modern depressions at the door of capitalism:

It is a simple fact that unemployment as a widespread phenomenon was created by capitalism. It was not characteristic of the old agricultural and handicraft society in which men and women found something to do as long as they had strength, except in times of national disaster. (The idle proletariat of the city of Rome were something of an historical exception to this rule.)

Before cyclical or chronic unemployment could become common, it was necessary that machine production should be able to provide something of a surplus over effective demand, be something different from the total of human wants and needs. Unemployment originates in the fact the whole body of workers with hand and brain receives less than is necessary to buy back the equivalent of what the workers create.[29]

Thomas makes it quite clear that he does not believe that either the New Deal or the Fair Deal, and certainly not the Eisenhower administration, has offered any adequate program for eliminating depressions. He contends that it was basically the Second World War, rather than any program of the Roosevelt administration, which brought prosperity to the United States and that the fact that the economy is once again keyed to war accounts largely for the rather prosperous state at present in the U.S.

What is the way out? How can an economy of abundance be established? Mr. Thomas' answer is, of course, what he likes to call "democratic socialism." To him the concept is more than merely a plan for a new economic system. It is a new way of living, a deep and abiding faith in man's capacity to live in a more co-operative fashion; it involves the development of new loyalties, "because men and societies live by their loyalties." [30] Socialism, he insists, requires an emotional loyalty which is disciplined by the intellect. "Basic to it," he writes, "must be a point of view or a philosophy which wins emotional and intellectual support. The good society of the socialist is something different from and better than an acquisitive society in which material benefits might be made more abundant. It is a society of which men feel themselves actively a part. The conquest of poverty itself requires an active sense of fraternity and a practice of cooperation in which is to be found part of life's joy." [31] The development of this co-operative loyalty, he continues, is even more important than the formulation of specific plans for the better society. "This ethical ideal is a scientific necessity in the successful and peaceful management of our highly interdependent economy." [32] In short, to Mr. Thomas socialism is a moral philosophy as well as an economic doctrine.

The modern world with its economic and social complexities must have planning, he affirms. But he is careful to point out that he is not speaking of rigid blueprints. The planning which he envisions should be more general, laying stress upon "goals" and the means that must be used to achieve them. Moreover, as a democratic socialist, he cautions that planning should not be looked upon "as a good in itself." [33] The amount and kind of planning cannot be determined on any absolute basis but rather will depend upon pragmatic tests. Only with some reluctance does he accept the necessity of planning. "I confess that there are times when I have envied Thomas Jefferson and the men of that period of American history," he admits candidly, "when it was reasonable to believe that the government is best which governs least." [34]

A basic Thomas argument for socialism is that the free enterprise that so many Americans regard reverently simply does not exist in this country. As he sees it, free enterprise is essentially a myth, and a dangerous one at that. It is an absurdly inaccurate label for the American economy, he insists, and does not deserve the name, because there is widespread governmental interference and planning in American economic life, because economic processes are vitally affected by powerful farm and labor organizations, and because private monopolies are still growing in power.

Laissez faire is a dead economic principle in most of the world, Thomas explains, because of two world wars and the present preparations for a third. Patterns of world warfare have necessitated more interference by the state in economic processes, he suggests. It is clear that he does not believe that economic eggs, having once been scrambled, can be unscrambled. He argues that the laissez-faire approach to economics can no longer be justified on the ground that a self-regulating economy is desirable, for in all economic systems contemporary conditions force the state to play a powerful role in economic life.

In his judgment, the question is not whether or not there will be collectivism in American or in world-wide economic life. This situation exists, he suggests, in much of the world and will inevitably develop in those parts of the world where it is not yet established. The extremely important choice that men do have is whether this economic collectivism will be democratic or totalitarian, that is, whether the patterns followed will be the democratic ones established by Great Britain and the Scandinavian countries or the totalitarian ones akin to Soviet Russia and Communist China. Of course, he looks with hope to the former examples, which are more or less in keeping with his dream of democratic socialism, but by no means does he argue that perfection is to be found in these nations.

Norman Thomas wrote very explicitly of the essentials of democratic socialism, as envisioned by him, in *A Socialist's Faith:*

> Sound democratic socialism will seek public ownership under democratic control of the commanding heights of the modern economic order. It is neither necessary nor desirable, so long as there is unity of purpose in the main direction of our economy, that there should be a monolithic type of ownership and control. There is a wholesome stimulus in competition, or emulation, and in diversity of functional apparatus. There is large room for private ownership when the owners are serving a useful function, providing that their ownership does not give them undue control over our social life. Public ownership need not be of one type. Generally speaking, the state should be the agency of ownership, and public corporations or authorities of somewhat various types its administrators. But there will be a large place for cooperatives, especially consumers' cooperatives in the good society.[35]

Generally speaking, these "commanding heights fall in three divisions: (1) natural resources; (2) the system of money, banking, and credit; and (3) the great monopolies or oligopolies." [36]

A major justification for socialization of natural resources, including land (excepting that on which persons live and which they farm), mineral wealth, and forests, would seem to rest on "moral" grounds.[37] These things were neither made nor, in general, discovered nor developed by individual men; therefore, Thomas concludes, they properly belong in the hands

of the whole of society, as all men depend upon them. Moreover, he argues that in mining, for instance, the significance
of the owner is far outweighed by that of the engineer and other
technical experts. It is generally agreed, he implies, that uranium
should be socially owned, because of its importance in the
production of atomic energy. Why then, he asks, should not
other vital resources be publicly owned? Even granting that
the private ownership of them is not quite so fraught with
dangers, it cannot be denied, he declares, that the general welfare is equally dependent upon them.

The socialization of banking and credit is required because
private ownership has led to banking manipulations which
have been detrimental to the whole of society. "Most of the
world's currencies are 'managed,'" he points out, "usually
rather badly managed at that." [38] The banking system is intimately and dynamically related to the whole economic structure, and, consequently, it belongs in public hands, which
would make intelligent social direction possible. Thomas becomes particularly irate when reflecting upon the fact "of the
outrageous system under which generation after generation
pays interest to private banks for no other service than what
ought to be the social function of the creation of money in the
form of credit." [39]

Finally, he develops his arguments for the socialization of the
"great monopolies or oligopolies" along these lines: Since these
industries are characterized by "absentee ownership" and lack
of "effective competition," he asserts that none of the alleged
advantages of private ownership apply here.[40] Furthermore, as
in the case of the mining industry, technical experts and managers have become more important than the owners. He is
not convinced that monopolies are unmitigated evils, although
he recognizes real dangers in bigness per se. The sensible

procedure is not to break up all monopolies, he insists, for this would be in many instances impossible and economically undesirable, but rather to put them under public ownership so that they might function in accord with general welfare. These arguments in respect to monopoly are particularly keyed to the case for the social ownership of public utilities.

There is no rigid answer regarding what should be socially owned, suggests Mr. Thomas:

> Just how far in this industrial field social ownership should go is not a matter which one generation can absolutely determine for the next. . . . Piecemeal nationalization or even socialization won't get very far in a society still dominated by private ownership and the psychological attitude it breeds. . . . On the other hand, wholesale socialization of almost all industry would impose a crushing burden on government and any apparatus it might set up. I suggest, therefore, that when a socialist government has decided what industries should be socialized and what left to private enterprise or cooperatives, the decision, while not immortal, should not be subject to capricious revision.[41]

Despite his insistence that there are no final answers in respect to the extent of socialization, he claims that at least the "major and basic industries" ought to be publicly owned in order to "simplify the conquest of depression." [42] Moreover, he maintains this with an awareness "that automatically social ownership answers fewer problems than we had hoped." [43]

How should these industries be transferred from private ownership to social ownership? Thomas indicates that there is no unanimity of opinion concerning this question among the advocates of democratic socialism. His own position is that it is essential that the transfer be of a nonviolent sort. Therefore, he proposes that "reasonable compensation" to the present owners is the logical way of preventing the socially costly disorder which would accompany uncompensated confiscation.[44] Besides that, he argues, such compensation would only be just in a situation where all industry is not to be socialized. He leaves no doubt, however, that income derived from such compensation would be subject to rigorous taxation, though not on a discriminatory basis.

Concerning the administration of these socialized industries, Thomas looks to TVA as a working model for the public authorities which would be organized. Differing from TVA, however, he advocates the inclusion of workers' and consumers' representation at the decision-making level.

Thomas is deeply concerned with the problems generally associated with the so-called administrative state and admits that democratic socialists have not done enough thinking about these problems. Nevertheless, he maintains that the ills of bureaucracy are not peculiar to socialism. Indeed, he contends that there are more bureaucratic evils inherent in the existing variety of American capitalism than there would be in socialism as he conceives it:

> For effective control over industries still legally owned by private individuals requires a more arbitrary exercise of political power than the state operation of these industries by public authorities under a system of social ownership.
>
> Moreover, the bureaucracy which watches other people work is even more likely than any public authority which actually works to adopt those attitudes and habits which we associate with bureaucracy at its worst. This statement is supported by experience with bureaucratic controls even in wartime when the stimulus of danger was a spur to action.[45]

Furthermore, he stresses the idea of "decentralization," along "functional and geographical" lines, which would tend to mitigate the disadvantages of the administrative state and to promote industrial democracy, which is integral to his version of democratic socialism.[46]

Before passing to another phase of Mr. Thomas' thought, it is important to note that his constant injunction to his followers has, in effect, been: "Let us not be content to rely on the socialist propositions of yesterday, for new times require new thought and perhaps new solutions."[47] Yet he holds fast to the label of socialism for the economy which he envisions, admitting that such a system is one variety of what has been called a "mixed economy." Nevertheless, he prefers "socialism" because with it are associated co-operation and public ownership of important parts of the economic system. In addition, he suggests wryly that "mixed" is a description more appropriate for "our present scrambled economy."[48]

His faith in socialization as a kind of panacea has significantly declined, but his loyalty to the ideals of socialism has remained intact. In general, he is now a much less optimistic socialist than he was, for instance, in the 1920's and 1930's. In an article written in 1952 and addressed primarily to his fellow socialists, he pointed out that

the messianic hope which consciously or unconsciously inspired most of us to become socialists is scarcely tenable in America or elsewhere in the world. . . . History and our better knowledge of our human psychology have destroyed or profoundly altered that particular scheme of earthly salvation. We have learned much about the temptations of power, and we know that there is no messianic working class nor any sort of elite that we can trust automatically to save mankind. . . . There never will be an absolute final victory.[49]

"A World without War"

The history of American social reform is replete with instances in which members of reform groups have attached themselves to more than one cause. For example, it was not uncommon for the same persons who were in the abolitionist movement to be active also in the temperance movement, or in the feminist movement, or in the public education movement, or perhaps in all of them. Similarly, Mr. Thomas thought of himself as both a pacifist and a socialist when he joined the Socialist party during World War I. The party's opposition to the war was a major fact in drawing the young minister to it.

Although in later years he was to abandon pacifism of an absolute sort, his thought concerning war and peace is still to a large extent in the pacifist tradition. He still retains profound respect for Gandhi and his tactics, although Thomas is not convinced that they can be effective with totalitarian powers. "Against a Stalin or a Hitler," he writes, "his method would have been ethically as noble as against the British but certainly it would have led to his early death in some secret dungeon— unless perhaps he had been drugged and tortured into a weird and terrible confession." [50] Thomas does not now consider political pacifism as a practical program for the attainment of peace which is worth the having. Yet he is still inclined to believe that the conscientious objector plays a socially useful role by his protest against the method of war and by his refusal to subordinate the dictates of his conscience to the demands of the state. Moreover, even now he cannot harmonize Christianity and the justification of war:

World War I drove me, at that time an active Christian clergyman, to examine the problem of Christianity and the method of war, whatever the objective. I was constrained to accept Christian pacifism. With due respect to men who are better Christians than I and think otherwise, I am still unable to reconcile Christianity and war on philosophic and ethical grounds. If in the years following the First World War, I, to my sorrow, could no longer accept a Christian absolute of opposition to war, it was because I was constrained to modify my thinking about God, man, and the universe.[51]

It is evident that his uneasy abandonment of pacifism never became total rejection. Indeed, Thomas would clearly be happier and more comfortable if he could still look upon pacifism as the answer to the threatening tragedy of nuclear war. Although he no longer opposes every war, he is still convinced that men do not build better worlds via war. He remains convinced that war, because of the "brutal and irrational nature" of its "method," tends to frustrate the achievement of the end which so many high-minded warriors have made their own."[52] He is highly skeptical of most of the arguments that associate virtue with war and the military life and detests war in virtually all of its manifestations:

Really to tell what war means in material destruction, in the physical agony of its victims, in the lives it warps and twists, in the sexual degradation it breeds, in the juvenile delinquency that it nurtures, in the cruelty it exalts, and in the slavery to the state which it encourages, lies beyond my power—perhaps beyond the power of any man—to put into words.[53]

In the light of what Mr. Thomas has "put into words" concerning the horror of war, it does not come as a surprise that—

even after he was no longer able to accept the pacifist position
—he still opposed America's entrance into the Second World
War. Before examining his actual reasons for taking a noninterventionist stand, it is important to suggest what they were
not, since so many inaccurate statements have been made concerning his position at that time. First, they were not motivated,
by any stretch of the imagination, by sympathy with fascism
of the German, Italian, or American varieties. He opposed
fascism from its inception, with a vigor and consistency not
surpassed by any other American of his time. Second, they
were not based on any orthodox pacifist-socialist analysis of
war. His views concerning pacifism have already been elaborated upon. And just as these underwent modification during
the period between two world wars, so did his attitudes in
respect to traditional socialist interpretations of war. He did
not view World War II simply as conflict between two morally
indistinguishable groups of imperialist powers. Third, and
finally, his position was not predicated upon isolationism, if
this word is given accurate definition; that is, he never maintained that America should have remained aloof from world
affairs or that she should have been unconcerned about the
rest of the world. His point of view was basically internationalist
—though not by the hysterical definitions of the time. He
repeatedly stated his position as: "the maximum possible co-
operation for peace; the maximum possible isolation from
war." [54]

Thomas' noninterventionism was predicated on what he believed to be best for the people of the United States and for
the people of the world. He was convinced, although history
has proved him wrong, that American democracy could not
survive, domestically speaking, if the United States entered
the war. He predicted the establishment of totalitarianism at

home, even though the war would ostensibly be fought against totalitarianism abroad. The resulting situation, he argued, would constitute an American tragedy and a world tragedy.

As Thomas saw it, the greatest contribution that the United States could make to world welfare was to make American democracy work more effectively. Rather than war with foreign powers, he advocated domestic war against poverty and racism, for he believed that "America lacked the wisdom and the power to play God to the world by the devil's method of total war." [55] He proposed that America should remain a beacon of light in a world of darkness, a haven of sanity, an example of peace and democracy.

As he looks back upon his attitude toward the Second World War, he is ready to admit that he overstressed the idea that it was merely a continuation of the First World War and that he overestimated the power of Europe to resist Fascist military might. Thomas never abandoned the view, however, that there was a dangerous element of dishonesty in the foreign policy of the Roosevelt administration. He condemns the late President for assuring the American people that he was following a path leading to peace, while he was, in reality, taking a series of steps that led logically to war. The moral action which Roosevelt should have taken, Thomas insists, would have been to declare forthrightly in behalf of his interventionist position.

Also, Thomas continues to believe that he and the Socialist party were emphatically right in arguing for a concrete statement of peace terms as against "unconditional surrender" and in opposing a peace based on vengeance. He further suggests that history has vindicated the Socialist criticisms of unnecessary appeasement of Stalin at Cairo, Teheran, and Potsdam. [56] "The only positive gain that had come out of the war," he concludes, "was the establishment of an inclusive but imperfect United Nations." [57]

To some extent, in a world in which another great war appears to be a real possibility, Thomas' current foreign-policy views coincide with those he held prior to the outbreak of World War II. There are certain important exceptions, however. Once again he is an ardent opponent of war, but he realizes that the United States would be inextricably involved in any conflicts that might arise. In addition, he is inclined to feel that Soviet Russia is an even greater threat to the peace and security of the world than was Nazi Germany. In 1951, when Stalin still ruled Russia, Thomas suggested that persons devoted to the cause of peace had to do some fresh thinking and face up to some unpleasant realities:

If Russia and America were merely two great national contenders for power, the situation would be dangerous. There would be faults on both sides and accommodation might be possible. But Russia, in the opinion of its communist dictators, is more than a great power; it is the head of an international crusade for universal communism. When noncommunists add to this fact the further fact that the same communist dictators permit absolutely no popular discussion in Russia of the road to peace on the basis of facts accurately stated, we have a situation in which the conventional tactics and programs of peace lovers are gravely inadequate. Our government could be as wise as the serpent and as harmless as the dove (which it is not); its motives could be as pure as the driven snow; its love of peace equal to that of Gandhi; and the communist dictatorship in its present frame of mind would never believe it. It would see only one road to peace and that the road of surrender to communist power. The struggle to avert the third world war is not helped by the failure of so many good people in America to recognize that the primary difficulty is not the usual rivalry for power between great nations, important as that is, but the relentless drive for the supremacy of communism as a secular religion, degraded in practice to a struggle for universal power by the communist elite of the U.S.S.R.[58]

From his extremely pessimistic evaluation of the Soviet dictatorship, it would appear that Thomas virtually accepted the inevitable necessity of war with Stalin's Russia. Indeed, it seems hard to imagine how so logical a mind could escape this conclusion. Nevertheless, this is definitely not the conclusion which he drew. He never ceased to argue that war could and should be averted.

In the Khrushchev era Thomas has become somewhat less pessimistic about the Soviet Union and, perhaps, more convinced that, if the United States pursues a wise foreign policy, peace can be maintained. "Khrushchev's denunciation of Stalin's crimes," Thomas points out in his *The Prerequisites for Peace,* "let loose forces which he has not the power, whatever his desire, entirely to force back into the grim restrictions of Stalinism." [59] Thomas is not "persuaded of any likelihood of revolution in Russia," but he is convinced that "an evolutionary process has begun." [60] Even a Communist society cannot escape social change, he reasons:

> The assertion that "you can't trust Russia" too glibly denies possibilities of evolutionary change from which official communism cannot be exempt, however zealously it may proclaim its unchanging devotion to Marxist Leninism. Neither Marx nor Lenin, nor even Stalin, could foresee what nu-

clear warfare could mean. Certainly it is far more reasonable to assume that Russians, including their dictators, will share our common desire for living than to assume that their talk of coexistence is wholly fraudulent from beginning to end.[61]

Thomas predicts state capitalism for both the United States and the Soviet Union by 1980. "The truth is," he maintains, "that the facts of life are steadily diminishing the economic gulf between capitalism and Communism as both are practiced. Neither is true to the theory or the faith of its fathers." [62]

The crux of his case for peace is that conflict between the United States and the Soviet Union is inevitable and even desirable but that it does not have to be and must not be, for the sake of all mankind, on the level of military warfare. Assuming—or perhaps, more accurately, hoping—that war with Russia is not inevitable, he has formulated a rather detailed program that is calculated to avoid it.

"Our present lifeline to . . . peace," he suggests, "is woven of four strands: disarmament down to a police level for preserving order within states and between states; disengagement at the points of the world's tensions; the strengthening of the U.N. as a guarantor of peace; and a cooperative effort in the holy war against desperate poverty." [63] This program would ideally be accomplished in the setting of a more positive American foreign policy. Instead of putting the stress on negative opposition to what Russia proposes, the emphasis would be on the promotion of democracy both abroad and at home. It would mean the abandonment of racial discrimination at home, which, he points out, does incalculable damage to America's world prestige. It would also involve the termination of the "American application of the adjective *free* to every and any non-Communist nation." [64] Thus, in his judgment, the United States ought to oppose unequivocally dictatorships of the Chiang Kai-shek and Franco varieties.

Among the "four strands" of his agenda for peace, Thomas has probably given disarmament the most detailed and extended analysis in his writings and speeches. The need for disarmament has never been so compelling, suggests Thomas, who speaks as one who has been involved for almost a half-century in one peace cause or another. He is deeply concerned that the United States is not adjusting its foreign policy to the realities of an atomic era, in which war might well mean collective suicide for mankind, and is greatly apprehensive that the balance of terror will lead, perhaps by accident, to a new world war which will have no victor. He insists:

> In this nuclear age peace—at least in the sense of avoidance of a third world war—is the only hope of life for generations yet unborn. The indefinite continuance of the Cold War is at this present time a terribly costly failure in terms of its own avowed purpose. It is not containing, much less overcoming Communism.[65]

Disarmament along the lines which Thomas envisions would include: "the absolute prohibition of the manufacture of weapons of mass destruction"; "the reduction of all armed forces and all armaments within each nation down to a police level"; the demilitarization of . . . narrow waterways . . . as well as . . . island bases"; "the universal abolition of peacetime military conscription"; and "an effective international police force . . . which should be recruited by voluntary enlistment from the smaller nations." [66]

In answer to the assertion that the Soviet government would never consent to such a disarmament program, Thomas points out that Russia has an alleged interest in disarmament, dating

Norman Thomas and former President Harry S. Truman at a luncheon held at the Statler Hilton, New York, in December, 1959, when Truman received the Four Freedoms Award from the United Italian American Labor Council. (The New York Times)

A 1960 peace rally in New York's Madison Square Garden brings together politically diverse Alf Landon, former GOP presidential opponent of F.D.R., Mrs. Eleanor Roosevelt, and Norman Thomas. (Wide World)

Norman Thomas, chairman of Hiroshima Day Observance Committee, speaks to demonstrators in New York on August 6, 1962, the seventeenth anniversary of the atomic attack on the Japanese city. (UPI)

Norman Thomas addresses crowd in Foley Square, New York, on September 22, 1963, during a memorial tribute to four young Negro girls killed a week before in a bomb explosion in a church in Birmingham, Ala. (UPI)

back to the era of the League of Nations; that the rulers of
Russia are realistic enough to be receptive to arguments concerning the mutual destructiveness inherent in the present arms
race; that, because of their assumed role as the great friends
of peace, they will not reject flatly realistic disarmament proposals; and that the more genuine and the more effective
America makes its disarmament proposals, the harder it will
be for Russian leaders to convince their people to make the
sacrifices in their standard of living which are required by huge
armament expenditures. Thomas realizes fully that in the years
since World War II negotiating with the Russians about disarmament has been a tortuous process, but he maintains that
Americans, as well as Russians, must bear a responsibility for
the perpetuation of the arms race. To him, it seems absolutely
imperative, no matter how great and difficult the obstacles,
that the United States continue to work unceasingly and
vigorously toward the goal of achieving universal disarmament.
As of 1960, he had come to feel so strongly about the necessity
of ending the arms race that, personally, he was even inclined
toward Bertrand Russell's advocacy of unilateral disarmament.
Considering his role as a political leader, however, he does not
want to become a public advocate of this position. Also, he
doubtless feels that universal disarmament is the only kind of
disarmament that the American people can possibly be persuaded to accept.

The second element in his program for peace would be "disengagement at the points of the world's tensions." As Thomas
conceives it, disengagement involves: "(1) A phased withdrawal of armed forces from a defined area to create a militarily
neutralized belt or zone. The objective should be the ultimate
recall of all troops (except those in a U.N. police force) to
posts within their national boundaries. At this point disengage-

ment must go hand in hand with disarmament. (2) Withdrawal from, or at least critical clarification of our national
commitments to intervene in other nations' wars." [67]

The successful application of the principle of "demilitarization" in Austria provides real hope, he maintains, that disengagement can be one of the avenues for avoiding a third
world war.[68] Moreover, in *The Prerequisites for Peace,* he presents detailed suggestions as to how disengagement might serve
that end in the Far East, Middle East, and Middle Europe.

In his thinking about the need for a strengthened United
Nations, the third item in his agenda for peace, Thomas relies
heavily on *World Peace through World Law* (1958), by Gren-
ville Clark and Louis Sohn. In line with their reasoning, he
"would abolish the Security Council and substitute for it an
Executive Committee of a strengthened General Assembly." [69]
The number of representatives and voting strength allotted
to each nation in this redesigned General Assembly would be
geared to population rather than having the present arrange-
ment wherein each nation has one vote. This present situation
is absurd, Thomas argues, since it does not take into consideration the tremendous variations in the number of inhabitants of the countries of the world. Among the many
proposals for altering the U.N. that Thomas is inclined to
accept, he seems to regard the creation "of an effective system
of enforceable world law in the limited field of war prevention"
—in the words of Clark and Sohn—as the most necessary
reform.[70] Consequently, he argues for the establishment of an
international court of justice, a world equity tribunal, and a
world conciliation board as "principal organs" of the U.N.[71]

Quite naturally, Thomas views the conquest of world poverty,
the fourth and last of his prerequisites for peace, in a socialist
frame of reference: "In this field, like it or not, we all have

to be socialists." [72] As he sees it, the desperate economic problems of underdeveloped societies cannot be solved as a

consequence of competitive struggle for private profit in a world of fantastically disparate nations all claiming absolute sovereignty over their people. Planning, and what's more international planning, is absolutely essential. The farther we move into a world where only complex scientific processes can supply us with energy and resources essential to a decent life, the more essential correlated planning will be. Its overriding principle must be socialist, that is the dominance of production for use in order that men may be served by things rather than mastered by them.[73]

To implement the conquest of world poverty, he favors the establishment of a world development authority as an agency of the United Nations. In his judgment, co-operation between nations as the guiding ideal of this agency is so important that, in accordance with their ability to pay, all nations—even small and poor ones—should be expected to make contributions to the improvement of the world's standard of living.

"A Fellowship of Free Men"

Through the years, Norman Thomas has done considerable speaking, writing, and thinking about elusive and variously defined—yet vitally important—concepts such as freedom, liberty, and democracy. His thought has consistently revealed a democratic bias, frankly and eloquently attested to in the following passage from *America's Way Out*:

There is still a magnificent challenge in the democratic theory at its best: the theory that the good life is for all men, that there must be equality of opportunity, that the

world in which we must live and work together should be
managed as a fellowship in which free men have the voice
of citizens rather than subjects. . . . What the Hebrew hoped
for the chosen people, and the Greek for the free minority
of his city state, democracy hopes for man. And though
the name, under whose spell so much blood has been spilt,
has lost some of its luster and no longer stirs the heart as
it once did, it still stands for the ideal of government of the
people, by the people, and for the people, which rightly interpreted is our best hope of liberty and peace.[74]

Certainly, these words give expression to a deep, passionate
attachment to the democratic ideal. Yet, during the thirty
years since they were written, his affirmation of the democratic
faith has become even more positive.

For example, in his earlier works, he identifies himself as a
"socialist." In his later works, more often than not, he refers to
himself as a "democratic socialist." It is not so much that he has
become more democratic in his actual thinking; rather it is
that he has become more self-consciously democratic. How
can this fact be explained? It relates basically to the profound
impact that the development of Fascist and Communist totalitarianism—especially the latter—has had upon his social
philosophy. Although, even during the early nineteen thirties,
he was initially extremely critical of many dictatorial and
antidemocratic aspects of the Communist philosophy and Russian society, he still hoped that ultimate good would come
from the Soviet experiment. A series of events shattered all
of his illusions, however. As indicated earlier, the most significant of these were: the famous "purge trials" from 1936 through
1938, his visits to Russia and Spain in 1937, and, finally, the
Nazi-Communist agreements of 1939.

During the Stalin era, Thomas used his powerful pen and

speech to expose and denounce—with the bitterness which characterizes one who has lost a dream—the ugly realities of Russian totalitarianism. "In action," he wrote in 1951, "communism has earned Ignazio Silone's characterization of it as 'Red Fascism.' The dictatorship in the Kremlin pioneered in every crime except racism which fascism and Nazism practiced." [75] While still incessant, his criticisms of the Soviet government became more restrained after Khrushchev became its head.

Nevertheless, the fact of Russian communism, so often equated with socialism, has imposed upon Mr. Thomas the intellectual burden of distinguishing between socialism and communism. To him, of course, socialism represents a fulfillment of democracy; while communism represents the antithesis of democracy. He warns that "modern socialists . . . have to remember that before our eyes total collectivism in Russia" has become "total tyranny." [76] He readily admits that twentieth-century totalitarianism makes it imperative for those who believe in democratic socialism to do some serious thinking about the meaning of democracy.

Democracy as Norman Thomas conceives it is conspicuous by its absence in Russia and is found in much less than perfect form in the United States. He is one socialist who makes it perfectly clear, however, that he prefers American capitalism —with the grave shortcomings that he finds in it—to communism as practiced in Russia. To America he still looks with the hope that it may improve and enrich its democracy, and he adheres to "the American ideal of democracy as government of the people, by the people, and for the people. In modern usage a government may be called democratic in which the ultimate power is in the hands of the people rather than of any one class or any sort of elite." [77]

He objects to attempts to justify democracy on the grounds

that it is sanctioned by the natural order of things or that "the voice of the people is the Voice of God." [78] These contentions are not supported by science or reason, he maintains. He also argues that democracy must be defended on grounds more positive than those which assert that counting noses is better than breaking heads and suggests the following: "(1) It is the way of life that best conforms to what men ought to be and do; what at their best they want to be and do. (2) In practice, with all of its imperfections, it has provided better government than any substitute for it. (3) By its nature it permits its own improvement." [79]

When Norman Thomas surveys America with respect to a cardinal feature of any democratic society, that is, the situation concerning civil liberties, he arrives at the conclusion that there exist here five "outstanding problems of freedom." [80] First, there is the problem which relates to the treatment of minority groups in American society. While recognizing many limitations to legalistic solutions, he, nevertheless, favors the enactment of civil rights legislation, including a federal fair employment practices act. He feels that a government should be ahead of its people on such matters and that the experience of individual states in the use of this approach has been encouraging.

Second, in this age of mass communication, means must be developed for insuring the individual citizen prompt access to accurate knowledge. To be more explicit, American newspapers, magazines, radio stations, and television stations are not presenting many of the basic issues of the day with the fairness and impartiality that is necessary for the health of a democratic society. Concerning the solution to this problem, Thomas argues emphatically against government ownership of major means of communication. His proposals, which are not especially novel, are that the press should establish an organization of its own for the specific purpose of improving its standards and that radio and television stations should be required by the Federal Communications Commission to set aside a specified amount of time for presenting issues, with stress upon a variety of opinions.

Third, the fact that organized labor is now such a powerful factor in contemporary American society poses new problems in the realm of civil liberties. Thomas argues that labor should retain all of the gains that it made under the New Deal. On the other hand, he maintains that it would be to the best interests of society and of the individual members of unions for the government to require each labor organization to grant to its membership a bill of rights. Such a bill would include the right to union membership without respect to race, creed, or nationality, the right to be protected from unreasonable membership fees, the right to clearly defined disciplinary procedures; and the right to accurate statements regarding the union's financial condition.

Fourth, there is the problem of the specific degree of civil liberty to permit to groups, such as the Fascists and Communists, that are dedicated to the destruction of democracy. Thomas suggests that the problem is made more difficult by the fact that the Communists, for instance, do not operate within the American radical traditions. Other radical groups, he points out, have publicly and proudly announced their beliefs and intentions, but the Communists tend to function covertly. With reluctance, he admits that the old formula of punishing people only on the basis of overt acts does not work with covert organizations; therefore, he accepts the necessity of specific legislation designed to protect the nation from those groups which are a real threat to its security. He warns, however, that this legislation must be formulated with extreme care so that it does not endanger American democracy more than the evil with which it attempts to deal. In speeches and in writing, he repeatedly cautioned against "burning down the barn in order to destroy the rats." [81]

To bring home this point, among others, he wrote *The Test of Freedom* during the height of McCarthyism. His general position was to regard "McCarthyism as a bad skin disease rather than a cancer," [82] and subsequent years have tended to justify his conclusion.

Thomas' reactions to the post–World War II crisis were deeply influenced by the thought of his long-term friend Sidney Hook. In *Heresy, Yes—Conspiracy, No,* a book dedicated to Norman Thomas, philosopher Hook carefully distinguished between the heretic and the conspirator. Thomas wholeheartedly accepted Hook's reasoning that the heretic or the dissenter may be a person who embraces and openly advocates points of view which are radically different from those held by his fellow citizens but who accepts the framework of a democratic society and abides by its rules, even as he attempts to persuade others of his philosophy. Therefore, he should be restricted in the exercise of his basic civil liberties no more than his more conventional fellow citizens. On the other hand, conspirators are those persons who are willing to subvert the democratic process to accomplish their ends and thus must be dealt with more rigorously.

Thomas is completely convinced, after long years of first-hand experience, that Communists must be regarded as conspirators. "Within the party and for its supporters," he maintains, "there is but one great commandment, laid down by Lenin himself: Thou shalt believe what the Party tells you and do whatsoever is necessary in the judgment of the Party to advance its interests. Every change of line, every lie or deceit or act of violence thus commanded, is right and holy." [83] Thomas has been bitterly impatient with the inability of many liberals to come to grips with the totalitarian nature of communism. "They may have been finally and reluctantly persuaded of Alger Hiss's guilt, but they cannot forgive Whittaker Chambers," Thomas observes wryly.[84]

Despite his insistence upon the conspiratorial nature of communism, Thomas is opposed to the outlawing of the Communist party and is vigorously critical of the Smith Act of 1940 and the McCarran Internal Security Act of 1950, both of which he regards as repressive and unwise. His own inclination is to say that, insofar as laws are necessary to deal with conspiracy, prohibition should be limited to the following activities:

1. Teaching, by an individual or a group, of methods of espionage or of sabotage of security operations. . . .

2. The advocacy or actual formation of a private, secret or semisecret military body. . . .

3. Advocacy by an individual, or a conspiratorial group, of specific illegal acts of force and violence immediately directed to the overthrow of government on any level. . . .[85]

The fifth central problem of liberty to which Thomas directs his attention is the existence of a powerful church, namely, the Roman Catholic, which attempts to impose its standards of morality not only upon its membership but also upon the rest of society. This problem constitutes another in the realm of civil liberties. Thomas grants the right of a church to prohibit birth control and divorce to its membership but denies its right to pressure for legislation whereby nonmembers will have to conform to its moral views. Similarly, he believes that

Catholics ought to be allowed to educate their children in church schools, if they so desire, but he does not believe that public funds should be used to support this type of segregation in education.

Thomas' advocacy of the democratic faith appears so unequivocal that one is warranted in drawing the conclusion that, if he decided, as others have, that socialism and democracy were incompatible, he would abandon socialism. He writes:

> For the believer in the dignity of the individual, there is only one standard by which to judge a given society and that is the degree to which it approaches the ideal of a fellowship of free men. Unless one can believe in the practicability of some sort of anarchy, or find evidence that there exists a superior and recognizable governing caste to which men should by nature cheerfully submit, there is no approach to a good society save by democracy. The alternative is tyranny.[86]

No final verdict can be passed on the social philosophy of a man who is still actively engaged in the business of living. With the more perfect perspective which only time brings, future historians of the American mind will treat as they see fit the social philosophy of Norman Thomas. Nevertheless, even at this early date, certain generalizations about his thought appear to be valid.

To begin with, Mr. Thomas is not a strikingly original or creative thinker; he is not a Karl Marx or a John Dewey. Yet the quality of his thought and the depth of his learning far surpass those of the average American political leader and compare favorably with the best that is being produced in American universities. While being steadfastly socialistic, his thinking has not been characterized by rigidity. He has consistently been willing to consider new currents in economics, sociology, political science, and psychology.

The social philosophy of Norman Thomas appears to emanate from two important branches of American democratic thought: radicalism and liberalism. In fact, it is not clear whether his thought has developed more along liberal lines or along radical ones, but there is no doubt that his position is distinctly American and decidedly democratic. The key values of American liberalism have been incorporated into the socialist thought of Norman Thomas. The philosophy of America's leading socialist bears testimony, just as do his political activities, to the marginal nature of his role in American political life. In thought and action, he has bridged the worlds of liberalism and radicalism.

Chapter IX

"Successful Failure"

Probably the most significant—and certainly the most glaring
—fact revealed in the course of this study was Norman Thomas'
conspicuous lack of success in holding his party together. How
can this failure be accounted for? Louis Waldman proposed
an answer in his autobiography, *Labor Lawyer:*

> Looking back over the decade of struggle which had taken
> place within the ranks of the Socialist Party, I find that it
> was the character of the Socialist leadership rather than the
> spirit of the times which was responsible for its decline.
> Responsibility for this decline must rest on the shoulders of
> Norman Thomas under whose leadership the party received
> its widest support and under whom it has come to its present
> straits.[1]

Waldman was hardly an objective observer, but it is undoubtedly true that other old-guard partisans shared his view. Virtually no serious and unbiased students of the American socialist movement, however, would accept Waldman's verdict. On
the other hand, few observers of the American radical scene
have evaluated Thomas as a master in the art of practical
politics. Many serious criticisms have been leveled at him as a
party leader.

Criticisms: Just and Unjust

Some of Thomas' alleged shortcomings as a political leader have been explained on a personality basis. In *The Story of the CIO,* Benjamin Stolberg suggested that Thomas was "well-meaning" but that he was "temperamentally" incapable of giving "cohesion to a movement." [2] There is some evidence to support this conclusion in his behavior concerning the labor-party issue during the years following the 1936 convention of the Socialist party. During that period he seemed to waver between opposition to affiliation with a labor party and vigorous support of the idea. Such behavior has been explained on the basis that Thomas is easily influenced by the opinions of those around him. Indeed, in some situations it would appear that he was unable to assert vigorous leadership within his party because of his personality. In the midst of the old guard–militant controversy, the *New York Times* commented that Thomas' position reminded that newspaper's editorial staff of a French political leader who had said: "I must follow them, since I am their chief." [3] One close observer of Thomas' political career suggests that the Socialist leader has been very receptive to the influence of others because he has usually, and frequently mistakenly, assumed that the integrity and honesty of other people equal his own. Thomas' tendency to endow men with his own virtues enabled cynical and unscrupulous party members to manipulate him into unwise positions, this observer argues.

Thomas' impossible dream of an all-inclusive Socialist party can be partly explained in terms of his overabundant faith in his fellow men. One can easily understand his desire to weld America's homeless radicals, including former Communists who had taken various political paths after terminating their affiliation, into one vigorous political organization. But his failure to realize, after years of intimate association with political radicals, that such a move could only lead to bedlam within the Socialist party was indicative of some lack of political shrewdness.

Thomas' vigorous support of the Declaration of Principles appears to have been a major mistake, for the sentiments expressed in and the language of that document could not have had much appeal for the average American, even during the dark days of the depression. They were more likely to alienate him from socialism than to draw him to it. Indeed, the declaration was not in keeping with Thomas' own outlook at the time. He never felt the contempt for American democracy that permeated it. Even at the risk of alienating some of his youthful followers, he should have proposed a compromise resolution, perhaps expressing the basic ideas of the Declaration of Principles in less bellicose language.

Moreover, Thomas erred gravely during this period by overestimating the degree to which the old guard was hamstringing the Socialist party and underestimating the magnitude of the losses that would be involved in the old guard's departure. Had Thomas been more interested in holding the party together and less determined to wrest control from the old guard, he might conceivably have avoided an outright split. In March, 1935, after the controversy had been raging for almost a year, so that its disastrous implications should have been clear to Thomas, some good counsel was extended to him in a letter by Daniel W. Hoan, who was then Socialist mayor of Milwaukee, Wisconsin. Hoan advised:

. . . There is only one way you can help to heal this breach in New York at the present time. It is for you to send word that will be generally spread among the New York comrades . . . that you are washing your hands of the entire controversy; that the leaders of both sides have gone to such extremes in their exaggerations and conduct that they have made the New York local the laughing stock of sincere Socialists all over the nation; and that you are withdrawing entirely from listening to details and tales of woes from either side until New York sees fit to put its house in order. . . .

Your big-heartedness has permitted you to lend advice here and there in the past. It has not helped to prevent this factionalism.[4]

Either Thomas did not see fit to heed these frank words, or he felt that it was already too late for this course. Hoan had the perspective of a successful and practical politician who was functioning in the real political world, a perspective which Thomas did not share or, in all probability, only vaguely understood.

In later years Thomas was to regret his support of the Declaration of Principles in the form in which it was written. In 1961 his political outlook is much more in harmony with old-guard pronouncements of the 1930's than with those issued by the militants. In fact, at the 1948 National Convention of the Socialist party, at Reading, Pennsylvania, an ardent pacifist minority proposed that the party adopt an inflammatory statement, in some ways similar to the Declaration of Principles, of the action it would take in the event of another war. After this proposal had been made, Thomas took the floor and frankly told the delegates that he would not consent to be the party's standard-bearer if such a resolution were adopted by the convention.

Daniel Bell, in his "The Background and Development of

Marxian Socialism in the United States," makes a serious criticism of Thomas as a party leader on the ground that "he strikingly distrusted his own generation and surrounded himself almost entirely with younger men who stood in an admiring and uncritical relation to him." [5] "This need for youthful support," explained Louis Waldman, "appeared to be an emotional necessity for him and he did not have the strength to move against a prevailing current." Waldman added that Thomas apparently needed the "adulation and enthusiasm" of his youthful admirers in order "to sustain him in the hard task of Socialist leadership." [6] Did Thomas cater unduly to the younger people in the party during the 1930's? A leader among the younger Socialists of that period, who later broke with Thomas on the war question, argues that an affirmative answer to this question is not justified. He contends that there was nothing deliberate or devious about Thomas' close relations with the youth in the party. It was Thomas' own natural youthfulness, this young Socialist maintains, that drew the young people in the party to Thomas and him to them. He shared with the party's youth an abundance of enthusiasm for the Socialist cause and a great capacity to become disturbed over injustice. Moreover, this former militant argues that Thomas' relations with persons of his own age group in the party were not characterized by any special difficulty that was related specifically to the matter of age.

Probably the most important criticism that has been made of Thomas as a political leader is that he is lacking in organizational abilities. Numerous former Socialists have also suggested that he is impatient with the slow processes of organization. A famous American crusader, who has never belonged to the Socialist party or voted for Thomas but who has worked with him in connection with various causes "continuously and intimately" since 1917, puts forward this point of view:

As a writer and speaker he has had an influence far outside the Socialist Party. He has figured primarily not as an exponent of socialist principle, but as a critic of the parties in power and of big business. His outlook is essentially a critical one, and his speeches and following reflect rather the opposition to government policies than the supporters of a socialist program. His indignation at injustice rises easily, and it is in his fight for justice that he has won so wide a regard. He has courage, eloquence, and integrity.

But he is not an organization man. He is an evangelist, a crusader, a leader of dissenting opinion, who acts in his own name and right, carrying along those who find him the expression of their hopes and grievances. That he has been the candidate of a party is irrelevant; the party was Thomas. . . . Being that kind of crusader, personal leadership transcended party organization. . . . A man with a stronger sense of organization could have done better with the Socialist Party. Thomas tended to monopolize leadership and to alienate strong characters, surrounding himself with admirers, mostly young.[7]

More specific criticism has been made of Thomas with respect to his organizational abilities. One of the Socialist party's most prominent members during the 1930's and 1940's believes that Thomas has been lacking in two important areas as an organizational leader. He suggests, in the first place, that Thomas was rarely able to discipline his followers effectively. This observer explains that Thomas found the business of giving orders emotionally distasteful, and, as a result, the Socialist party under his leadership seemed almost always to be going in several different directions at the same time. Although Thomas always spoke with "conviction and earnestness," he was more like a "pleading schoolteacher" than a resolute party leader.[8]

Secondly, this Socialist leader maintains that Thomas was never very effective in the important matter of fund-raising. He contends that Thomas was much less than adroit at obtaining donations from the few well-to-do members and friends of the party. This critic suggests that Thomas knew little of the art of high-pressure salesmanship. He does not hold Thomas responsible for the fact that the Socialist party has known an almost perpetual state of financial crisis but implies that a leader with more fund-raising talents might have eased, to some degree, the financial stresses and strains that have plagued the party.

It has been frequently suggested that Thomas was able to establish rapport with university and middle-class church people but not with the majority of American workers. In effect, it has been alleged that Thomas could not communicate with workers because he never spoke their language, in the literal and figurative sense. But this viewpoint has been reiterated much more often than it has been proved. Indeed, Thomas has addressed countless audiences of workers and has been received enthusiastically by them. He also succeeded in establishing good rapport with working people during his minister-social worker days. The type of leader who invariably appeals to workers has not yet been clearly identified, but there is no evidence to indicate that workers always gravitate to leaders with backgrounds and outlooks similar to their own. That workers frequently identify with leaders on a "higher" socioeducational plane cannot be doubted. Certainly, American workers did not find Franklin D. Roosevelt unappealing, and in terms of background he was much farther removed from American workers than Norman Thomas.

Finally, many persons—ironically, even those to the right of him—criticize Thomas for not being sufficiently radical.

They are inclined to subscribe to Trotsky's view that Norman Thomas "called himself a Socialist as a result of misunderstanding." Those who berate Thomas for his lack of radicalism are prone to suggest that he should more properly be thought of as a liberal rather than as a socialist. In reflecting on "Thomas for President?" in the pages of *Politics* (October, 1944), Dwight MacDonald, a former Trotskyite who then considered himself a socialist and militant pacifist, elaborated this type of criticism:

> My objection to Norman Thomas can be put briefly: he is a liberal, not a socialist. A socialist, as I use the term anyway, is one who has taken the first simple step *at least* of breaking with present-day bourgeois society. Despite an undoubtedly sincere personal belief in socialism, Norman Thomas has been unable either intellectually or politically to take this step. His role has always been that of left opposition *within the present society,* the fighting crusader in small matters (like Hagueism and other civil liberty issues) and the timid conformist in big matters (like the present war). His own campaign material describes him accurately as "America's Conscience." It seems a great pity that Norman Thomas did not become the editor of the *Nation* instead of succeeding Debs. Both the *Nation* and the Socialist Party would have gained: the former would have become a more courageous and significant publication, and the latter would have had a better chance to develop into a revolutionary party.[9]

Substantiating his evaluation of Thomas, MacDonald also presented criticisms that were somewhat more specific. He castigated Thomas for his assumption that "Roosevelt and others in power are honest and reasonable men trying just as earnestly as he himself to work out things for the best interest of humanity." [10] From MacDonald's revolutionary pacifist point of view, Thomas' attempt to keep prowar and antiwar Socialists in the same party was deplorable opportunism. In effect, he charged that after Pearl Harbor Thomas straddled the issue of whether to oppose or to support America's participation in World War II. On a less important level, he suggested that Thomas' participation in various human-relations radio programs was unbecoming to him as a socialist leader.

Assuming that all of the criticisms just reviewed concerning Norman Thomas as a political leader were valid, which they are not, do these alleged weaknesses explain fundamentally the almost total disintegration that the American Socialist party has known in recent decades? The answer to this question is, emphatically, no. The ironic fact is that, if Thomas had proved to be a more able negotiator and had somehow or other warded off the departure of the old guard, there is no evidence that the long-term fate of the Socialist party would have been significantly different. By the late 1930's and the early 1940's, the militants and even those Socialists who had accepted the outlook of the ultraradical Revolutionary Policy Committee were flocking to the New Deal, just as the more conservative members of the old guard had done a few years earlier.

An Array of Obstacles

The demise of the Socialist party has to be explained basically in terms of situations that were largely impossible for Thomas to control. For purposes of analysis, they may be designated as external and internal. The most important external situations that accounted for the decline of the Socialist party were dealt with at length in earlier chapters: the rise of fascism and communism, the New Deal, the upsurgence of labor, and the outbreak of World War II. As an individual leader, Norman

Thomas could not have blocked or molded these historical movements so that they would conform more nearly to the needs of his party. Perhaps he could have modified his socialism and in some ways accommodated himself to the New Deal, but from his point of view he would thus have been abdicating as a socialist leader. Indeed, it is highly doubtful that the cause of socialism, as an organized movement, would have been advanced by such action. The Social Democratic Federation followed that course and, until it reunited with the Socialist party in 1957, had less vitality and influence than its parent organization.

There are other external factors that have militated against the development of a strong Socialist party in the United States, including the relatively high standard of living that Americans have known, the marked lack of class consciousness among American workers, the popular misunderstanding about the distinction between socialism and communism, the strong traditional attachment of the American people to the two-party system, and the very great difficulties entailed for a small and poor party in getting on the ballot in fifty states. Finally, the electoral college system for electing presidents has probably deterred many persons from voting minor-party tickets, because of the knowledge that a matter of one vote could conceivably deliver the electoral votes of a whole state to a particular candidate. Again, these were situations that Thomas could hardly have been expected to alter significantly.

Thomas was also confronted by internal situations that were not of his own making and that made his position as Socialist leader frequently difficult, and sometimes impossible. Essentially, these situations stemmed from the culture of American socialism: the shared attitudes and behavior patterns that grew up within the socialist movement and were internalized by most of its participants. Political movements, just as the larger society of which they were a part, may develop cultures. Many of the dominant patterns of the socialist culture have been rather different from those of the larger American society and its politics. A consideration of certain of these patterns is essential to understanding many of Thomas' leadership problems. They were, in effect, situations in terms of which he had to behave.

The orientation of the American socialist culture was always somewhat otherworldly. Socialists have traditionally ridiculed the theologians for emphasizing the life after death to the neglect of life on earth, often arguing that, by thus emphasizing the wonders of the afterlife, churches have encouraged men to put up with evils on earth that should not have been tolerated. Yet socialists have to a large extent thought and acted in terms of a hereafter. Their eyes have been turned away from an "evil capitalism" and toward a "Socialist paradise." The notion that the "system"—as they were wont to call it—would inevitably collapse, because of the contradictions inherent in it, was universally accepted by socialists until very recently. There was no question that socialism would follow in its place. In essence, this was the notion of the inevitability of progress, with socialism naturally being equated with progress. It took the rise of fascism and communism and two world wars to eliminate largely, if not entirely, from socialist thought the conviction that the beautiful socialist world was inevitably on its way.

The otherworldliness of American socialism has manifested itself in a variety of ways. Some socialists argued that the only way to escape the taint of corruption was to found co-operative communities that would be rather isolated from capitalist society. The Socialist Labor party has long prohibited its members from working with the established unions on the ground that these labor organizations are too closely tied to the existing social and economic order. A few persons of socialist conviction, including some with professional training, have taken jobs as factory workers and unskilled laborers in order to be counted among the proletariat.

Traditional socialist voting behavior is also illustrative of this pattern of withdrawing from the world. In terms of traditional socialist mores, voting for a Democrat or a Republican under any circumstance was equated with the worst of sins. Some socialists have even refrained from voting in nonpartisan elections on the ground that they would not vote for people who were not specifically running as Socialists. Many crises in the history of the Socialist party have developed because members of the party accepted positions with non-Socialist political administrations. Individuals who have been thought guilty of co-operating too closely with the capitalist order have been subjected to much verbal abuse and have been derisively called "practical" men. This disdain for the practical is another example of socialist withdrawal from the world.

Yet, despite these tendencies toward withdrawal, the otherworldly orientation of the Socialist movement has never been complete or clear-cut. Indeed, it has always lacked clear definition. As Daniel Bell points out, a crucial fact in the history of the American Socialist party is that the party "could never resolve but only straddle the basic issue of either accepting capitalist society, and seeking to transform it from within as the labor movement did, or becoming the sworn enemy of that society like the communists." [11]

Just as religious movements have been split asunder because of differing notions concerning the surest road to heaven, Socialist parties have broken apart over issues relating to the tactics which should be used to usher in the brave new world—a case in point being the Socialist party during the 1930's. The Declaration of Principles controversy related fundamentally, though not exclusively, to the Socialist party's otherworldly preoccupation. During that decade, the party was attempting to decide to what degree it should live within American society and to what degree apart from it.

The Socialist party's tendency to withdraw from the world lends considerable weight to the viewpoint that the Socialist party and other minor parties are in a basic sense more like interest groups than political parties. Just like its leader Norman Thomas, the American Socialist party has been to a large extent a critic of the American political scene rather than a full-fledged participant. Even before Thomas assumed leadership in them, Socialist political campaigns appeared to be more in the nature of educational rather than political ventures. "A defeated Socialist candidate," wrote Louis Waldman, "didn't have the feeling of impotence, say, of a Republican candidate in Georgia. Socialist candidates and Socialists generally regarded each political campaign as a development in the political maturity in the nation." [12] Such was the rationale behind Socialist election activity throughout the years. Similarly, large numbers of persons who have voted the Socialist ticket have done so to register a protest against the social order or to protest some aspect of the behavior of the major parties. Voting Socialist has often been more akin to an act of conscience than to a political act. In short, the Socialist party has been a bona fide political party only in a very limited sense. It has probably been more of an interest group than a political party; and, in characteristic interest-group fashion, it has been more concerned with the advancing of particular ideas, policies, and programs than with the matter of having its members gain

office. Consequently, ideological differences have probably been
a more important source of factionalism within the Socialist
party than within the major parties. As the anonymous author
of *The Unofficial Observer* has put it, Socialists have "an inherent ability to engage in abstruse, doctrinal controversies until half-past Armageddon." [13]

If the Socialist party has been, in reality, something less
than a political party, it has also been something more. For
many of its members it functioned not only as a political organization but as a fraternal organization as well. Even in
large cities the party membership has generally been so small
that interaction between members has been highly personalized
and intimate. To many members who never abandoned the
Marxist suspicion of religion, socialism was a kind of substitute religion, the source of their deepest values. Because the
socialist ideology was conceived in broad, almost universal,
terms, virtually every issue was deemed to be of party concern.
The consequence was that internal discord frequently resulted
from disagreements over religious, literary, and sexual questions—issues which were not strictly political in nature.

The socialist ideology has always given heavy stress to the
ideal of internationalism. The establishment of a fellowship of
workers throughout the world has been one of its goals. On
the American socialist scene, this tendency was probably rein-
forced by the relatively high percentage of foreign-born within
the party's ranks. In fact, one of the major weaknesses fairly
ascribed to American socialism is that it has tended to view
America through European eyes and that the result was often
a distortion of the realities of life in the United States.

Because of this international orientation, the American socialist movement has always displayed an unusual degree of sensitivity to world events. A critical situation for the European

socialist movement was also likely to produce a crisis within the American Socialist party. It was essential that American socialism be aware of world events, but insofar as its own health was concerned it was probably oversensitive to them. The Stalin-Trotsky feud, the collapse of German and Austrian socialism, and the feuding within the Loyalist camp during the Spanish Civil War had serious repercussions within the American Socialist party. Not infrequently, these events were, in effect, re-enacted with all of the original bitterness by the various party factions.

One of the reasons that European events and other sources of factionalism could wreak such havoc with the American Socialist party is that from its very beginning it was largely undisciplined and loosely organized. Those who founded the Socialist party were bent upon avoiding the highly centralized pattern of the Socialist Labor party, and the end result was that they built a party that was to be almost totally lacking in any kind of discipline. A great amount of local and individual autonomy has been the rule throughout the history of the Socialist party. And these tendencies were never effectively counterbalanced by either Debs or Thomas. It is not that the Socialist party would have been better off with a highly centralized, authoritarian structure, but the organization needed considerably more discipline than it ever possessed in order to survive, in meaningful terms, as a political party.

Controversy is inherent in politics. In every democratic society differences exist not only between political parties but also within them. An obvious and indisputable generalization that can be made concerning the history of American political life is that no party has ever known anything like perfect unity and harmony. The American experience is replete with instances in which the major parties were torn by factionalism brought about by conflicting economic interests, sectionalism, leadership rivalries, and unselfish differences of opinion. Especially in recent times, the major parties have constituted great amalgamations of conflicting and varied interests. In order for them to gain political power, it has been necessary for them to draw to their banners individuals and groups from almost every conceivable stratum of American society. One might well argue that they have known electoral success in proportion to their heterogeneity. In essence, the Democratic and Republican parties have been parties of compromise. It is accurate to say, as Thomas so often has done, that there is more difference within the two parties than there is between them. How have parties so constituted been held together? The anticipation of the tangible rewards of office largely provide the answer. The major parties have almost always known power or reasonable prospects of power on the national level, and even national defeat at the polls has usually been accompanied by some significant state and local successes.

Those individuals who have not been willing to make the compromises that go hand in hand with participation in major-party politics have been drawn to minor parties. These parties have generally taken more clear-cut positions on the issues of the day than have the major political organizations. It does not necessarily follow, however, that they have been more correct ones.

Considering the fact that minor parties have not been parties of compromise to the same degree as the major parties, it would appear to follow that they have probably known more internal unity and cohesion. Nothing could be farther from the truth, however. Factionalism has been a much more prevalent and destructive phenomenon among the minor parties than among the major ones. A basic explanation relates to the fact that the

membership of minor parties has not been held together by the
expectation of office and the fruits that office brings.

The addition of the Socialist party to factionalism and splits
has to be explained along other avenues as well. "It should not
be surprising," wrote Arthur M. Schlesinger, Sr., in *The American as Reformer,* "that isms breed schisms considering the
type of rebellious mentality upon which such movements
draw." [14] In fact, the Socialist party seemed to draw to it persons who had little more than their rebelliousness in common.
"Thus, Agnostic and Christian, Bohemian and Puritan, could
and did join the party and seek to mold it in their own image,"
reports Daniel Bell.[15]

Those persons who have basic disagreements with the status
quo, who envision a society organized along socialist lines, who
condemn the major parties for the compromises they make,
and who argue that adherence to principle is more important
than winning elections are, by and large, not likely to adjust
well within the framework of any political organization. Nonconformists do not abandon their nonconformist behavior patterns upon joining organizations dedicated to social reform. It
would seem that attitudes of discontent and protest become
habitual for large numbers of social reformers. Men who take
upon themselves the role of critics of society at large are not
generally inclined to be passive and uncritical when functioning in political organizations. Their rebelliousness usually continues unabated, and much of it is directed against their political allies and fellow social reformers. The need to criticize
continues to assert itself.

The various aspects of American socialism just delineated
suggest that factionalism was an inherent part of the socialist
culture. Moreover, it is of crucial importance to point out that
the various patterns of behavior and shared attitudes referred
to were integral traits of the socialist culture long before Norman

Thomas became a leading figure in the American socialist movement. Thus he was clearly not responsible for bringing into being these internal dissension-producing traits of the socialist culture. Furthermore, as has already been pointed out, he cannot be held responsible for the existence of the external factors that precipitated dissension within the Socialist ranks. But, of course, it can be argued that a more able leader could have somehow or other overcome these internal and external obstacles.

Comparisons between Norman Thomas and his predecessor, Eugene V. Debs, are inevitable. Both men deserve high rank in the history of American politics. Both men had the courage to turn their backs upon conventional success in the pursuit of principle. Given his leadership qualities, especially his magnificent oratory, either might have secured high public office on a major-party ticket. Indeed, before his conversion to socialism, Debs was elected to the Indiana Legislature. For his socialism Debs abandoned a career rich in promise in the American labor movement; for the same cause Thomas forsook a path that might have led to national leadership in American Protestantism. Both towered above the mass of men, but Thomas' career represents more in the way of discipline and productivity. Life has been kinder to Thomas than it was to Debs. An unsympathetic wife, a childless marriage, incessant financial problems, and sporadic alchoholism were burdens that Debs carried in addition to the difficult tasks of Socialist leadership. Perhaps the trials of his personal life made him more understanding of human frailty than was Thomas, who had an incredibly happy marriage and family life.

Although Debs could relate more personally to human suffering, he did not have Thomas' intellectual grasp of the problems of mankind. While well read, Debs did not complete high school; Thomas, no matter how inadequate he later judged it, received at Princeton about as fine a liberal arts education as was available in the United States at the time. And his graduate training at the Union Theological Seminary significantly broadened his intellectual and social horizons and understanding. Most important, his formal education provided his excellent mind with the foundation and the incentives for continuing and rigorous self-education in the years to come. In the area of public affairs he was always abreast of the best interpretations that modern scholarship had to offer.

If asked about any of the pressing social problems of his day, Debs would offer socialism as the solution to all of society's ills. With his greater intellectual depth and his better understanding of the complexity of modern social problems, Thomas was never content to rely on such a simple answer. He has always been ready with detailed plans short of socialism for improving man's lot in the here and now.

For purposes of this analysis the significant fact to point out is that Debs managed to remain rather aloof from Socialist-party factionalism, whereas Thomas has usually been in the thick of it, perhaps because of his greater interest in ideas. But, just like Thomas, Debs failed to hold his party together. The party that Thomas inherited from Debs was virtually dead when Thomas assumed leadership in it. Under the leadership of Debs the Socialist party succumbed to a powerful combination of factors, which included, among other things, the dissension-producing traits of the socialist culture and of Woodrow Wilson's New Freedom, World War I, and the rise of communism. Some of the factors accounting for the disintegration of the Socialist party under Norman Thomas were the dissension-producing traits of the socialist culture, Roosevelt's New Deal, fascism, communism, and World War II. Thomas has explained the decline of his party more simply: "What cut the ground out pretty completely from under us was this. It was Roosevelt in a word. You don't need anything more." [16]

Neither Debs nor Thomas succeeded in establishing satisfactory relations with the labor movement. Debs was no doubt better known to the working people of the United States than Thomas; yet Debs's relations with Samuel Gompers and the AFL were anything but cordial. Indeed, he was among the founders of the Industrial Workers of the World, which had as a major goal the displacing of the American Federation of Labor.

Could Debs or someone like him have led the Socialist party in recent decades and built it into a significantly stronger or more important organization? The "what might have been" variety of question never has a certain answer, but it can be said that there is little in the way of evidence to indicate that during the recent period a Debs could have done much better with the Socialist party than Thomas did. Considering the array of obstacles that has operated against the development of a strong socialist movement in the United States, it is highly doubtful that any leader—no matter how able—could have succeeded where Thomas has failed. Only those who subscribe to the adolescent theory that individual men are the motive force behind history and that great leaders can overcome any obstacles would be inclined to argue otherwise. If Socialist parties have prospered in other lands, it is not necessarily because of having had more effective leadership than the American Socialist party—a fact which Mr. Thomas pointed out to his Socialist brethren at the Third Congress of the Socialist International in Stockholm, Sweden, on July 15, 1953:

There is something of humiliation in the position of an American socialist, like myself, addressing an international

socialist congress. Our country is so powerful and our organized socialist movement so weak. For this, those of us
who have for decades been identified with the movement
must bear some responsibility. But not, I think, major blame.
Our mistakes have not been worse than yours in countries
where the movement has fared better.[17]

No Heir Apparent

It should be understood that Thomas does not view his failure to build a strong Socialist party with equanimity. Understandably, the present weakness of the movement to which
he has devoted the whole of his life is a source of great pain
and sadness. Yet he realizes, as has been argued here, that the
obstacles to his success were so great that perhaps no man could
have overcome them.

One major aspect of Thomas' failure as a political leader is
not so clearly or completely explained by forces over which he
had no control. To some extent, he must bear responsibility
for the fact that there appears to be no one on the horizon even
vaguely ready to succeed him as the leader of American socialism. Given its recent history of pitiful weakness, the Socialist
party has understandably been no great reservoir of potential
leaders. Nevertheless, by utilizing the appropriate combination
of encouragement, guidance, and incentives, Thomas might
have prepared some person to assume the mantle that he has
carried for so many years.

He made one vain attempt in that direction: For some years
it was Thomas' hope that Maynard Kreuger would assume the
tasks of leadership. In 1944 he urged Kreuger to seek the presidential nomination; but Kreuger refused on the ground that
he wanted to concentrate upon Illinois politics, and soon it
became clear that he was not to follow in the footsteps of Debs

and Thomas. Between 1940 and 1948 Kreuger was second in command of the Socialist party. But he had grave doubts about the wisdom of running a Socialist presidential candidate in 1948, and at the decision to run another in 1952 he left the party. Since Kreuger's departure, no one has emerged who gives even faint promise of becoming an adequate replacement for Thomas in the years to come. Nor has Thomas apparently given much attention to the task of finding a successor.

Thomas' actions do not indicate that he has stood in anybody's way or jealously guarded his leadership status. It may be that he now feels that a democratic leader should not play a large role in determining his successor. In any case, all Socialists must share responsibility with him for the development of a party that has relied so heavily upon the talents and energies of one man.

Ironically, Thomas' enormous capacities as a leader have contributed to the difficulties of finding a successor. Even during their most egotistical moments, few of his fellow Socialists have assumed that they could replace Thomas. Having been awed through the years by his overpowering personality, his intellectual stature and magnificent oratory, his literary craftsmanship, and his tremendous physical vitality, the vast majority of his followers found it utterly absurd to entertain the idea that any one of them could ever fill his shoes. To a great number of his political comrades he has become, quite literally, a father figure. Even thinking about the necessity of one day finding a new leader has been painful and seemed almost disloyal.

It should be noted that during Debs's later years the prospect of finding a new leader of American socialism of comparable stature seemed terribly dim; yet a Norman Thomas did come to the fore. The process whereby Thomas emerged as leader was probably more accidental than inevitable, however. And there is no rule of group life that insures that the tiny Socialist party–Social Democratic Federation will continue to be so fortunate in the character of its leaders. Thomas remains his party's greatest asset; he is the only leader of American socialism who is widely known and influential outside the radical milieu. Public awareness of the existence of a socialist movement in the United States in the period since World War II has largely stemmed from the reputation and character of Norman Thomas.

Writing about "What Happened to American Socialism?" in the pages of *Commentary* (October, 1951), Will Herberg points out that as "Socialism was disappearing from the American political scene as an organized political force, the Socialist program was being translated into law and social practice. . . . Here, if a failure, is surely a successful failure; and the end of the movement's achievements is not yet. Paradoxically, as the Socialist Party lies dying, its 'idea' goes marching on." [18] That Norman Thomas made a tremendous contribution to the survival and propagation of the socialist idea cannot be doubted. As has already been pointed out, most of the immediate demands that Thomas put forth in his 1932 campaign were brought into being under Roosevelt's New Deal. This is not to suggest that there was a direct causal relationship between Thomas' political activities and the New Deal program. But Thomas and his party did initiate important educational spadework in behalf of old-age pensions, unemployment insurance, public-works programs, legalization of collective bargaining, and other measures ultimately incorporated into the New Deal. And some of these programs were undeniably among the most important political, social, and economic innovations of our time.

On the occasion of Mr. Thomas' seventy-fifth birthday, November 20, 1959, the *Washington Post,* in its editorial columns, summarized perceptively his role in American life:

> For most of his 75 years Norman Thomas has been a Socialist in his political affiliation, a radical in economic outlook, a conservative in constitutional principles and a liberal in his friendliness to people and ideas. Above everything else he has been an independent—a man who thought and spoke for himself—with wit and fervor and indignation—an apostle of human freedom, a champion of the defeated, a kind of animated and indomitable conscience of the American people. . . . Yet even as an inveterate loser, he has been among the most influential individuals in 20th Century American politics. His ideas have received from his rivals the supreme compliment of plagiarism and from the American people the accolade of acceptance. . . . We join great numbers of his fellow Americans in congratulating the country on having him as a leader at large.[19]

In short, Norman Thomas, the political leader who never won an election and who did not build a strong party, may be considered, just like his party, a "successful failure."

Chapter X

Epilogue

Despite the infirmities of old age, Norman Thomas has continued his career in a familiar fashion. Like an Old Testament prophet he searchingly examines American public policies and finds much wanting, though he also finds many things of which to be proud. Norman Thomas, in his eighties, gives the impression of having a marvelous mind imprisoned in a very frail and increasingly useless body: his sight is dim; his hearing is impaired; his limbs are wracked by arthritis; his heart is not good. Yet his ideas, his eloquence, his humor, his indignation at every instance of injustice pour forth much as they always have during his more than half a century of social crusading.

The fact that he has not run for office since the presidential campaign of 1948 has not significantly altered his role in American public affairs. As one of the most active and involved octogenarians in the country, he is far more productive than most men half his age. During the last decade he has had three books published, *The Prerequisites for Peace* (1959), *Great Dissenters* (1961), and *Socialism Re-examined* (1963); he has delivered countless speeches, written many articles, and participated at a leadership level in numerous organizations. He has given yeoman service and substantial financial assistance to the National Committee for a Sane Nuclear Policy, Turn Toward Peace (a kind of loose federation of peace organizations), and the Institute for International Labor Research, which has focused upon Latin American affairs; he has also played a leading role in the National Sharecroppers Fund. Under the letterhead of the Post War World Council, he writes a monthly newsletter emphasizing his personal reactions to and assessments of major domestic and international events. In less major ways he has worked in behalf of the Congress of Racial Equality, the American Committee on Africa, Spanish Refugee Aid, Inc., the Committee for World Development and Disarmament, the American Committee for Tibetan Refugees, the American Civil Liberties Union, the American Friends Service Committee. Amazingly, he has also managed to serve in the New York Zoological Society and in Princeton's fund-raising activities.

He remains the leading spokesman of the Socialist party even though he has become less involved in its day-to-day activities. He still writes a regular column for *New America,* the official Socialist publication, and addresses many Socialist conventions and meetings.

Thomas continues to be a prodigious letter writer. His many letters to the President and to members of Congress during the Kennedy and Johnson administrations cover a wide variety of public issues but most often suggest ways and means for constructing a less bellicose and more imaginative American foreign policy. He has also continued his long-term habit of disseminating his political views by sending policy statements to the letter boxes of major newspapers across the country.

His deep interest in the great policy questions confronting America and mankind has not made him lose sight of the needs of individual human beings. True to his ministerial

tradition, Thomas' letters abound with messages of comfort
to the sick, encouragement to the bereaved, and congratula-
tions to those celebrating births, weddings, graduations, and
bar mitzvahs. Habitually he sends greetings to friends and
acquaintances when they have books published or have been
elected to office or have achieved anything of significance.

Public speaking continues to be his great forte. He receives
more speaking invitations than he can accept. During the first
six months of 1965, he spoke at more than forty college cam-
puses throughout the country. His busy schedule also includes
addresses before high school audiences and church groups, as
well as participation in television and radio discussion programs and an assortment of protest marches, rallies, and "teach-
ins."

His physical handicaps have almost become assets in terms
of audience response. As this virtually blind, bent old man
ascends the platform with great difficulty, the audience initially wonders about the wisdom of his appearance. But by
the time he has uttered a few sentences his listeners realize
that they are in the presence of a mind that has triumphed over
a broken body and a fiery eloquence that will not be extin-
guished. His speeches abound with passion, wit, and sparkling phrases. More often than not there are thunderous bursts
of applause and standing ovations. He pokes fun at his physical maladies. "I am a tottering wreck and it's annoying," he
tells his audiences.[1] When asked whether he will run again,
he replies: "Run? I can hardly walk."[2] But he also alludes to
his age in more solemn ways. Addressing a "teach-in" at a
large midwestern university, he exhorted his listeners: "Your
generation has simply got to find other frameworks, other
contexts, in which to work out the relations of men to men
and nations to nations or you won't survive as long as I."[3]

Thomas in his eighties has a special rapport with the young. He stirs university students as do virtually none of their professors. It is the style of university teachers to venture opinions, whereas Norman Thomas exultantly speaks of his convictions. He maintains this continuing rapport with the young because he is sensitive to and concerned about the things that matter most to them. In the 1960's Norman Thomas feels most committed to peace, civil rights, and individual liberty; these are the causes of socially conscious youth in contemporary America.

America and Vietnam

Few recent developments in American foreign policy have so roused Thomas' indignation and deep concern as has the growing American military involvement in Vietnam. From the onset of American participation in the Vietnamese conflict he has condemned it on both moral and political grounds. Ironically, as much as he hates the war itself, it has given the veteran socialist a new burst of vitality and has kindled his crusading passions. The intensity and the depth of his opposition to the war in Vietnam have generated some of the most effective and eloquent addresses of his career. He played a leading role in the November, 1965, March on Washington for peace in Vietnam, which was organized primarily by the National Committee for a Sane Nuclear Policy. He told the 35,000 marchers the kind of things he has been telling audiences all over the country. His indictment of American policy in Vietnam was bitter and incisive:

We are here this afternoon because we are patriots, anxious to recover for our country genuine leadership both for peace and democracy.

We are here because we know that no satisfactory settlement can be imposed in Southeast Asia by military victory of either side. I think I speak for most of our sponsors when I say that we would urge upon our opponents as we most emphatically urge upon our government the necessity of negotiation on honorable terms.

We are here because we believe the war is cruelly immoral and politically stupid.

We fight a war where we count victories by the number of dead. We are shocked, with some reason, by the Vietcong's atrocities, but retaliate by terrible atrocities through bombings and burnings which, regardless of the Administration's intention, indiscriminately destroy civilians not only in North but South Vietnam. The torch on the Statue of Liberty must seem to most Vietnamese civilians as symptomatic not of liberty lighting the world but of the burning by which we hope to win a brutal war. We used to say we were fighting for democracy. We are fighting for a corrupt and inefficient government, the latest in a long series and one which is not secure in any affection of its people. In the name of democracy, we are killing the Vietnamese because it is better for them to be dead than red.

All this we are doing to contain a communism which will not be thus contained. Rather we aid its propaganda around the world. We help it to cover its failure and bridge the chasm between Russian and Chinese versions of communism.

He also addressed some of his words directly to the President of the United States, as he often had done with regard to other issues and other presidents:

Mr. President, you have a chance to live in history as the President of the most powerful nation in the world, who realizes the world cannot be saved by playing the old power-politics game, who knows that we must bring China, for example, into the family of nations. We must have coexistence or ultimately no existence.

Mr. President, you are a man of heart and you cannot rejoice in the suffering of the Vietnamese. Call, then, for an immediate cease-fire; show your good faith by stopping the bombing; ask for UN or neutral supervision of the cease-fire; plead for an immediate convocation of the Geneva nations, including, of course, China, and our principal adversary in the civil war, the National Liberation Front. Tell them again that you want unconditional negotiations, leading to a stabilized peace. Make clear your intention to withdraw the American forces from Southeast Asia. Renew your offer to help rebuild a sorely devasted land.

You have no right to say that such a call for peace and order will be rejected, that this will fail, until you have tried. The heart and conscience of the world will be with you, not in war, but in peace. Not by force but by an exhibition of the excellence of democracy will communism be modified and its excesses contained.[4]

Despite Thomas' bitter opposition to the war in Vietnam he argued against an abrupt withdrawal of American forces, a position which many Socialists had come to advocate. "All, or almost all, of us Socialists," he noted, "have steadily opposed any military intervention in Vietnam and are dedicated to the end of the war." Yet, not too happily, he reminded the members of his own party that "by military intervention the U.S. has incurred some obligations toward its allies in Vietnam. A simple withdrawal of American forces would almost certainly mean a communist military victory with a great toll of bloodshed added to what has already been spilt." He readily granted that "the existence of the Vietcong and the reasons for its existence had to be recognized." But he also emphasized "we are not Communists and we are aware of Vietcong's type of terrorism. We do not want to go out of our way to add strength to a Chinese Imperial Communism (or to a Russian) in Southeast Asia, and that would be the effect of simple withdrawal." He insisted that one should "at least take some account of the fact that not all Vietnamese love the Viet Cong, that about a million migrated to South Vietnam in 1954–55 to escape Communism. Atrocities are atrocities, whether it is Americans burning the villages or Viet Cong's many brutal executions of village leaders." [5]

The Garrison State

Thomas has been deeply concerned about the impact of the Vietnamese war upon American society. He fears the war's inflationary pressures and its "great cost to any war against poverty." He insists that in the process of fighting the war Americans are experiencing a moral erosion. America is tragically indoctrinating "a great many of our youth with a sense of the legitimacy of violence . . . which they will apply not just to the service of the sovereign state but to the service of their racial group or even their gangs at home. There is no question that the legacy of two world wars is at least partly responsible for the growth of crimes of violence, bomb threats and harassments of individuals here at home." [6]

The Socialist leader has long been convinced that the cold war and its hot interludes have had a pernicious effect upon American life. In a debate with Barry Goldwater, at the University of Arizona in November of 1961, he elaborated his misgivings:

What is the effect upon us if we have to go on living forever in terms of a religion of nationalism? Do not misunderstand me, of course I love my country. Of course, I believe in nationalism as against imperialism. And I recognize its contributions in various lands to culture. But I do not believe that we can manage our world in an anarchy of a hundred nations of such diverse size and intent. We've got to do something about that. And I don't think that we can manage—I say it on a Sunday night—to keep any decent moral standards or religion in a world in which our real religion is the religion of the sovereign national state, which is above the moral law and sanctifies to its own use what it conceives will serve its ends. This is the thing that I fear. And this I think we have to attack. We socialists are accused of caring for material things. We care for material things because of their relation to what I care about most which is . . . a fellowship of free men throughout the world. . . .

The real Ten Commandments now have been changed. It is the sovereign national state that says: "I am the Lord, thy God. Thou shalt have no other Gods before me. Thou shalt not take my name in vain for the Senate and House committees will not hold him guiltless that taketh my name in vain. Thou shalt not kill-retail. But thou shalt at my command kill quite indiscriminately as science has enabled us to do. Thou shalt not bear false witness against thy neighbor unless perhaps it is in good cause of fighting Communism somewhere in the world." [7]

Thomas believes that, without quite realizing it, Americans are now living in a garrison state, in which the "religion of nationalism" is the pervasive loyalty.[8] He believes that the cold war has brought this upon the U.S. and frequently quotes from Dwight D. Eisenhower, not usually Thomas' political

mentor, about the grave dangers inherent in this way of life.
"In the councils of government," said Eisenhower in his farewell address, "we must guard against the acquisition of un-
warranted influence, whether sought or unsought, by the
military-industrial complex. The potential for the disastrous
rise of misplaced power will exist and will persist. We must
never let the weight of this combination endanger our liberties
or democratic processes." [9]

Thomas explains much that he finds wrong with America
of the 1960's in terms of the garrison state. In Thomas' judgment, the garrison state leads to a fruitless preoccupation with
military approaches to foreign policy problems and to enormous military expenditures which drain energies and resources
that might otherwise be used to conquer poverty at home and
abroad. This state feeds and encourages phobic reactions to the
forces of communism, as distinct from a rational understanding of the nature of this evil. It has set the stage for the emergence of the radical right, which has a proclivity to stifle dissent and equate every form of political unorthodoxy with
communism. The garrison state also helps to rationalize fantastic corporate profits in the guise of patriotic service. Consciously or unconsciously, in Thomas' view, America's enjoy-
ment of the prosperity it associates with the economy of the
garrison state is one of the factors that makes it reluctant to
bring an end to the arms race. Thomas also takes issue with
the cold war way of life that sanctions military conscription
even during times of peace. He has long regarded compulsory
military service as inimical to individual liberty and democracy and is shocked at how readily and unthinkingly his
fellow citizens have come to accept it.[10]

"Democratic socialists and other lovers of freedom," Thomas
writes, "have not been sufficiently alert in making their fellow

citizens aware that while we have manufactured the arms of the age of overkill in the name of our national freedom, we have been steadily and inevitably reducing the land of the Pilgrim's Pride to the status of a garrison state. We shall thus continue until we come to nuclear war, or turn to lead the nations in the great March toward Peace." [11]

In the age of the garrison state, Thomas has worked vigorously and concretely to preserve and enlarge freedom for the individual. In his own person, he continues to function as a rather active and effective civil liberties bureau. He has been especially sensitive to civil liberties cases with political overtones.

During 1962, Mr. Thomas spent an enormous amount of energy in the attempt to secure the release of Junius Scales, who had been indicted and imprisoned in 1961 under the Smith Act long after he had abandoned communism. Scales severed all connections with the Communist party in 1957 as a consequence of Khrushchev's denunciation of Stalin and the Russian intervention in Hungary. Thomas had long been bitterly opposed to the Smith Act and felt that Scales had been unfairly victimized by it. Hence, he enlisted the support of a large number of prominent Americans in behalf of Scales. A petition requesting commutation was signed by 550 persons, including two federal judges and, amazingly, nine of the twelve jurors who had found Scales guilty. Thomas also barraged persons in high places, not excluding John and Robert Kennedy, with letters of protest. President Kennedy commuted the sentence as of Christmas, 1962, and Scales was released after serving sixteen months of a six-year term. Scales has a unique place in American history as the only person ever jailed specifically for membership in the Communist party.[12] After the commutation, A. H. Raskin of the editorial board of the *New York Times,* who also had been interested in the Scales case, sent a note to Thomas. "I do not delude myself that he would ever have had a commutation," he wrote, "if you and the committee that took its inspiration from you had not worked so devotedly in Scales' behalf. The whole episode was a fresh indication of what your entire life has demonstrated: America will live up to its traditions of freedom if each one of us cares enough." [13]

Thomas also has lent his name and devoted time to the committee that was formed to secure the release of Communist Morton Sobell, who in 1950 was convicted on grounds of espionage and given a thirty-year sentence. In a letter to Norman Cousins, a co-worker for many causes, Thomas outlined his reasons for working for Sobell's release. He explained "that while I am not fully persuaded of his innocence, I think there were irregularities in his trial. Moreover, he has been in prison now for many years and his sentence seems excessive. Our country is not made stronger by injustice." [14]

The plight of William Worthy, a leading American journalist who was indicted under the McCarran Immigration Act for entering the United States from Cuba without a passport, did not escape Thomas' attention. Ironically, the State Department had earlier denied Worthy a passport, apparently on political grounds. Thomas has been opposed to the idea of having the issuance of passports subject to political tests and thus readily became involved in the various efforts to defend Worthy. Thomas issued a statement in behalf of the Workers Defense League in which he declared that "a fundamental human and constitutional right is involved—the right of American citizens to travel throughout the world on their own responsibility without loss of their rights as citizens." [15]

During the 1960's, as in earlier years, Thomas has worked

Norman Thomas gestures characteristically as he addresses a crowd gathered in New York on December 6, 1964, to celebrate his eightieth birthday. (The New York Times)

Norman Thomas shown here with A. Philip Randolph, chairman of the celebration marking Thomas' eightieth birthday. (The New York Times)

Norman Thomas receives Star of Solidarity First Class from Italian Consul Vittorio Montezemolo in May, 1964. (UPI)

Norman Thomas participates in a marathon "teach-in" at the University of Califo at Berkeley in May, 1965, and urged U.S. withdrawal from fighting in Vietnam. (l

zealously for the repeal of the Smith Act (1940) and the McCarran Act (1950), both of which in Thomas' judgment are obstacles to the exercise of political freedom in the United States.

The Negro Revolution

Norman Thomas has not been a major figure in the civil rights revolution. He has not played the kind of towering role that he has in the peace movement. But he has been tremendously sympathetic to the growing aspirations of his Negro fellow Americans and significantly involved in their struggle to achieve full equality of opportunity in American life. During the course of his political career, he has argued and worked for the abolition of every vestige of racism in American life. His *Human Exploitation in the United States* (1934) includes a penetrating and well-documented chapter on the plight of the Negro in the United States.[16]

In the 1960's he gives enthusiastic endorsement to the Negro revolution, wherein so many of his old friends and disciples play key roles. A. Philip Randolph, president of the Brotherhood of Sleeping Car Porters, grand old man of the Negro revolution, and chief inspirer of the March on Washington Movement, has been sharing political causes with Thomas for some forty years. Thomas, in fact, helped Randolph to organize the union that he leads. They traveled to Japan together in 1952.[17] Randolph was chairman of Thomas' eightieth birthday celebration. Thomas has known Bayard Rustin, who is regarded widely as the chief strategist of the Negro revolution, since the latter was a student at the City College of New York.[18] During the many years that Rustin has been a leader in the peace and civil rights movements, he and Thomas have had a close relationship. Thomas also has long been a friend of and worked closely with James Farmer, who founded the Congress of Racial Equality and was its director for many years.[19]

Thomas has not had a close relationship with Martin Luther King, but their social reform paths have crossed often. "We are all enormously in your debt," Thomas wrote to King early in 1961, "for what you have done and are doing and inspiring others to do in the service of the highest ideals of your country and mankind."[20] Dr. King, who has become a warm admirer of Norman Thomas, wrote a highly laudatory article, "The Bravest Man I Ever Met," about Thomas for the June, 1965, issue of *Pageant* magazine.[21]

For Thomas, the Negro revolution has had deep personal meaning. He has extolled it in his writings and speeches and has worked for it in many ways. From its inception, he has regarded it as one of the most encouraging trends of our time and has attempted to explain its meaning and purpose to his fellow Americans. In a letter widely distributed to newspapers across the country and written in March, 1960, to protest a Senate filibuster against proposed civil rights legislation, Thomas made clear his commitment to the Negro revolution:

> What our white fellow citizens forget to their own hurt and their country's is one of the plainest lessons in history. Any race, group or class having made some progress against great odds is bound to come to a time and a strength when it will not tolerate tortuous delay in winning fuller justice. American Negroes have lived through almost a century since emancipation from the horrible bonds of chattel slavery. In city after city, not all in the South, they are still discriminated against in respect to jobs, housing, even the right to equality of courtesy in lunchrooms and stores where

they spend their money. Their patience has been extraordinary. But as was inevitable they are arousing out of apathy or despair and doing what we praise in all our school books: Struggling for their own legitimate rights.[22]

In the company of A. Philip Randolph and James Farmer, Thomas picketed a Woolworth's store in Manhattan in order to protest the firm's segregationist policies in its southern operations. In anticipation of the March on Washington of 1963, Thomas wrote: "I wholeheartedly support this march for jobs and freedom as a democratic expression of support for the constructive Negro Revolution now underway which will at last remove the taint of hypocrisy from American democracy."[23] He participated in the event itself and was greatly stirred by it. "The March on Washington," he exclaimed, "was a most magnificent demonstration, beyond my hopes and my hopes were very high."[24]

Novelist Harvey Swados has perceptively summarized the veteran socialist's place in the peace and civil rights movements:

In each he has played the role not just of elderly well-wisher but of tribune and mentor. No historian will be able to interpret the civil rights battle without assessing the significance of the inspiration Norman Thomas has given to such striking figures as the organizers of the March on Washington, many of whom not only belong to his party but continue to look at him for intellectual moral and practical aid, both in public sessions and in behind-the-scenes activities.[25]

From New Frontier to Great Society

With no great enthusiasm, Thomas voted for Kennedy in 1960 and Johnson in 1964. But he has never thought of himself

as a Democrat and has continued to survey critically the behavior and policies of those in power just as he did during the
years when he was a perennial candidate for high office.

Despite his strong Protestant heritage, Thomas was never
much concerned about Kennedy's Catholicism. During the
midst of the 1960 presidential campaign, Thomas quipped, "I
personally am rather more afraid of the influence of Senator
Kennedy's earthly father and financial supporter than of any
spiritual father of his church." [26] Thomas had some personal
reasons for being favorably disposed toward the young President. His son, Evan Thomas, had edited Kennedy's *Profiles
in Courage* and had often talked very favorably about Kennedy's ability and character. Thomas had "a fascination for
the man" whom he regarded as a "very attractive figure" and
a rather able president.[27] Yet, only rarely did he praise the
policies of the Kennedy administration, and frequently he
criticized them sharply. Thomas had lived through too many
Presidencies to allow the coming of the new administration to
thwart his deeply ingrained, habitual disposition to criticize.
The New Frontier did not sap Thomas of his critical powers,
as it did so many liberals who became intoxicated with the
aura of the Kennedy years.

He did not have very high hopes as Kennedy assumed office.
"The new administration," he wrote in January, 1961, "may in
some ways be an improvement on the old, but the Democratic
Party seems likely, as I write, to insult us and give the lie to
its own sincerity by leaving reactionary southerners in committee chairmanships with power little curbed. We'll get a
little better aid to the aged but not socialized medicine. And
the Pentagon will be asked to help shape disarmament policy
which means that we'll have as much disarmament as we
should have abolition of cigarette smoking for cancer control

if the American Tobacco Company were the chief planner." [28]

A year after Kennedy was elected, Thomas was still not much encouraged and bluntly said:

In national affairs, the record of the President and Congress is only liberal in contrast to the performance of that other President from Massachusetts, Calvin Coolidge. Liberals who argue otherwise are only whistling to keep their courage up. They certainly haven't read the Democratic Platform of 1960 very lately. The President has made some eloquent speeches, advocated somewhat better legislation than he got, and made some good appointments. But he did not try to rouse the people to any lusty liberal program and some of his appointments were very bad.[29]

As Thomas saw it, the Kennedy administration was lacking in a guiding philosophy of social reform that was adequate to the times. He chided Kennedy as "a great believer in the doctrine that politics is the science of the possible" and added "his low estimate of the possible has left him pretty much a captive to the conservatives." [30] Thomas called for more affirmative action with respect to poverty, race relations, social welfare measures, and unemployment. About Kennedy, Thomas liked to say: "The liberals like his rhetoric and the conservatives like his inaction." [31]

Thomas bitterly denounced the Kennedy administration for its part in the Bay of Pigs invasion and was very critical of the developing American policy in Vietnam long before national attention was focused upon that troubled land. On the other hand, he was much pleased by Kennedy's success in negotiating a nuclear test ban with the Russians in October, 1963.

Whatever his day-to-day reservations about the policies of

John F. Kennedy, Thomas saw much promise in the young President and felt "a profound sense of shock" at his death. "We mourn a gallant President," he wrote, "sincerely interested in peace and freedom, who was growing in strength." [32]

Thomas is much less drawn to Johnson, personally, than he was to Johnson's more intellectual predecessor. He credits Johnson with more legislative success than Kennedy, but he points out that the symbol of the "martyred President" significantly aided Johnson in getting Congress to accept the programs. [33] Understandably, he is pleased with the Johnson administration's avowed interest in eradicating poverty in the United States, for the conquest of poverty has loomed large in his own socialist thought and action. Johnson's efforts in behalf of civil rights took Thomas by surprise. He thought Johnson had "an astonishing degree of success in obtaining the comprehensive civil rights legislation . . . on that subject no President ever spoke so forthrightly and effectively as did this Texas Democrat—a convert over whom there must be joy in heaven." [34] But Thomas is hardly an uncritical admirer of the Johnson domestic program. He regards the various poverty and civil rights programs as significant beginning steps, but he believes that they tend to be skimpy and palliative in nature and often poorly administered. He does not see in the Johnson programs any fundamental reconstruction of the American way of life. Johnson has been able to carry through his economic and social programs, Thomas explains, because "he was able in an affluent America to give something to every major group, partly because he avoided attacking any basic injustice in our economic system. Private ownership of natural resources and public utilities, private rights to the rent from land to unearned income from its sale—the whole profit system remained unscathed." [35]

Long an advocate of the welfare state, Thomas, rather ironically, contemplates its emergence in American society with some misgiving. He concedes that capitalism managed along Keynesian lines "can give us an increasingly affluent society, provided it stops the mouths of protest—at least in these days —by grants of bread and a little cake. A prosperous business community has learned to accept that fact cheerfully—especially if it goes along with tax reduction." [36]

He finds it hard to be sanguine about the economic and social trends of the present time. He is not at all sure that America's expanding social welfare programs—which he vigorously favors—are leading the nation toward a democratic socialist conception of a Great Society. "The welfare state," he notes, "does relieve much misery, opens many doors to a fuller life. It may be a stage on the way to a much fairer economic system, with a degree of democracy in industry now lacking; this is the democratic socialist hope. Or the welfare state may become a glorified version of the Roman Government's bread and circuses." [37]

Yet, Thomas' deepest concern is not so much with the specifics of Johnson's domestic policies, about which he has many reservations. He is convinced that Johnson's aspirations for American society are incompatible with his conduct of foreign affairs:

The great trouble is with the President's foreign policy. No Great Society can be founded on an attempt by one mighty power to police the world, by force of arms if necessary. Certainly the revolution of rising expectations cannot be met by emulating some of Communism's bad characteristics in the name of anticommunism. Insofar as President Johnson has won a consensus on his intervention in the

Dominican Republic or on his escalation of the war in Vietnam, it is a consensus based on self-righteousness and faith in violence incompatible with any decent society—in terms even of enlightened self-interest.[38]

At the Hub of Things

Thomas is not merely an elderly socialist commentator on American society and world affairs. He has a way of being at the hub of things. To illustrate, in May of 1966, soon after experiencing and paying little heed to a very severe head injury in an auto accident, he flew to the Dominican Republic. With a group of observers he went, sponsored by the Committee on Free Elections in the Dominican Republic (still another organization in which he plays a leadership role), for the purpose of observing the election of June 1, 1966, and the events leading up to it. It was hoped "that the presence of these observers . . . would serve as a precaution against the eruption of violence and as an expression of support for free elections." [39] Ultimately, the Organization of American States also sent observers, but they only stayed for election day. Indicative of Thomas' wide-ranging influence is the fact that Juan Bosch, who was fearful that bona fide free elections would not materialize and was on the verge of withdrawing from the race, decided to remain a candidate after talking with Thomas. Bosch explained to the Dominican people, over nationwide radio, that the American socialist, Norman Thomas, had persuaded him that his candidacy was necessary if the election was to have any genuine meaning.[40] Thomas had hoped for a victory by Bosch "because it would have symbolized a triumph of democracy over military rule." [41] But Dr. Joaquin Balaguer won decisively. Apart from how one evaluates the election's outcome, it cannot be doubted that Norman Thomas, and the observers whom he led, contributed greatly toward achieving an honest and free election in the Dominican Republic.

In still another way, the unique position of Norman Thomas in American society, and in world society, was demonstrated in the summer of 1966. Early in July, it was reported widely that the North Vietnamese government intended to try as war criminals captured American pilots; execution was said to be their almost certain fate. Americans became especially uneasy because the various U.S. governmental sources did not seem able to get reliable information concerning Hanoi's intentions and did not clearly affirm or deny these ominous reports. In the face of this uncertainty Thomas "took the chance of a direct appeal to Ho Chi Minh." [42] On July 13, he wired the North Vietnamese leader the following message:

> As a worker for peace and strong critic of American bombings I respectfully report that execution of captured American Pilots would have disastrous effect upon American public in our efforts to win it for peace and justice in Vietnam. It would make almost certain great intensification and prolongation of war.[43]

The leader of the North Vietnamese government replied on July 20 as follows:

> Thank you for your message. No doubt you know that policy of Government of Democratic Republic of Vietnam with regard to enemies captured in war is a humanitarian policy. Wish you good health.[44]

This message to Norman Thomas from Ho Chi Minh was virtually the first reassurance that the United States had indicating that the North Vietnamese did not intend to execute the captured American pilots. Thus Norman Thomas, as a respected private citizen and American socialist of world renown, succeeded in acquiring information about North Vietnamese intentions that apparently was not communicated to America's labyrinth of government agencies or its giant news services.

Why does Thomas, with his physical handicaps and at his age, continue to be so completely involved? He candidly says that he wants "to go out with a bang, not a whimper." [45] He also explains that "all my adult life I have found this an interesting, if cockeyed world, in which there are causes outside oneself which richly repay devotion." [46] He is sustained, perhaps more accurately, driven on, by a compulsive humanism. An inextinguishable idealism, somewhat tempered by realism, is characteristically revealed in his speculation about man and his destiny:

> Once socialists of various shades found their utopias a satisfactory substitute for any kind of Kingdom on earth. Privately if not publicly most democratic socialists—and, I suspect, many communists—now acknowledge that they must settle for social changes which, while of immense value, cannot of themselves banish crime or answer all the questions of the human heart caught in this strange, wonderful, beautiful, terrible universe.

> But this lack of a utopia or any sure far-off divine event to which the whole creation moves is no reason for despair or for a let-us-eat-drink-and-be-merry philosophy. Some tomorrow each of us individuals will die. But life will go on, and life can be made better for the whole human family. We are not damned by our gods or our genes. We can find meaning for ourselves and an end to frustration and alienation by joining in a struggle which must be worldwide, a

struggle for a fraternity of mankind dedicated to peace, plenty and freedom. . . . And in man's confused record and present conduct there are elements to give us hope that such a utopia can be attained.[47]

During the last decade the well-established reputation of Norman Thomas has soared. He has become, often to his great discomfort, a kind of living monument, but a very useful and active one. He frets about the fact that he is widely and inaccurately regarded as a kind of benign rebel. Yet he is a realist: "However, uneasy as I am about being spoken of too well by too many men, I don't feel I'm obliged to go out and smash somebody's window to prove that I'm not respectable."[48]

Despite his discomfort, accolades continue to be heaped upon him. In May of 1964, the Italian government awarded its highest decoration, The Star of Solidarity First Class, in appreciation of his aid to Italian anti-Fascist forces during the Mussolini era and for efforts during the World War II years in behalf of a peace with Italy based on justice.[49] *Esquire* has included him in its list of "unknockables," persons of untarnished reputation who represented "the sum of human virtue in 1966."[50] *Life,* in a long and glowing account of his activities, has called him "The Dean of Protest."[51] The Vice-President of the United States, the Chief Justice of the Supreme Court, and many other persons of world fame sent him congratulatory messages on his eightieth birthday.[52] A college journalist, anticipating Thomas' appearance at a midwestern campus, wrote: "The Prophet Cometh."[53]

The much-honored Robert Frost regarded a meeting with Norman Thomas as "one of the great moments of my life" and indicated that he yielded to no one in the depth of his

admiration for Norman Thomas.[54] Barry Goldwater, who debated Thomas at the University of Arizona in 1961, felt "hon-
ored to be on the same platform with him" and lauded him
for "sincerity and very obvious honesty," which he said were
the "hallmarks of Mr. Thomas." [55] Speaking directly to Norman Thomas, Senator Goldwater wryly exclaimed: "Sir, I
hope that when I have reached the point of life that you have
reached that I will hold just a small modicum of the esteem
in which you're held. And I also hope that as many of the
things that I advocate in Government will have been taken by
that time, just as yours have been taken without you getting
the credit for them." [56]

Now in the autumn of his life, Norman Thomas continues
to stand out as one of the towering figures of his time. Charisma, a favorite term in the lexicon of contemporary social
scientists, seems to be especially applicable to America's "Mr.
Socialist." He is a charismatic leader in the sense that he possesses exceptional individuality that sets him apart from other
men. He has an unusual appearance, bearing, and voice. In
contrast to so many others of undistinguished demeanor who
direct the affairs of men, Thomas looks like a leader. He has a
great self-confidence in his own judgment and values, combined with a determination, almost a compulsion, to convince
others of the soundness of his positions. He has the power,
essential to charisma, to impress and to excite attention. To
be with Norman Thomas is to have the feeling that one is in
the presence of greatness. Other persons of fame, as in the case
of Robert Frost and Barry Goldwater, have not been immune
to this feeling.

In 1961, Thomas' *Great Dissenters* was published; in it he
briefly appraised the lives and careers of men who, in his judg-

ment, were among the world's outstanding rebels. Of the dissenters he wrote about, Thomas seemed to be especially drawn
to Wendell Phillips, who was an outstandingly eloquent and
wide-ranging social reformer not unlike himself. Thomas
praises Phillips warmly: "He was a radical pioneer, not only
for the abolition of slavery, but for every good cause; he was
probably the greatest orator that our country has produced." [57]
"I can think of no dissenter with whom it would have been a
greater joy to live and work in close relations." [58] Thomas
reports that Phillips had some interest in winning a seat in
the United States Senate but adds that he did not veer from
his reform path in order to do so. "I question," Thomas concludes, "whether he could have been as happy or as helpful to
his fellow men had he subdued his outspoken voice of conscience to the compromises of politics." [59] Consciously or unconsciously, Thomas seems to be musing not only about
Phillips' career but about his own as well.

Earnest admirers of Norman Thomas often bemoan the fact
that he was never elected to high office. Yet, given the realities
of American politics, if he had been elected, would he have
been able to live by his "voice of conscience"? Would he have
been in a position to champion a host of unpopular causes
from which even liberal officeholders usually have shied away?
The answer to these and similar questions has to be an emphatic "no." Norman Thomas could not have played a comparable role in American political life had he operated, as
doubtless would have been necessary to gain office, in the context of major party politics. He would not have been permitted
his allegiance to socialism, which has been the guiding thread
of his career and which has set him apart from most American
political leaders, whose deepest commitment is to the politics

of expediency and consensus. In short, this vehement, yet strangely respectable, rebel with a clarion voice calling for peace, plenty, and freedom has been able to make his vital contributions to American life precisely because he was never elected to high office.

Chapter References

In the light of other bibliographical information available to the reader in this volume, these footnotes have been basically restricted to documentation of quoted material. Throughout this section certain abbreviations will be used: "N.T." will stand for Norman Thomas. "Autobiography" will refer to Mr. Thomas' unpublished autobiography. "Thomas Reminiscences" will refer to Mr. Thomas' contributions to Columbia University's Oral History Project. Interviews with members of the Thomas family will be cited as "Thomas Family Interview." In order to encourage the most candid responses, Mr. Thomas' past and present political associates who agreed to co-operate with this study were informed in advance that they would be quoted only in anonymous fashion. Unless otherwise cited, letters, memoranda, and other types of correspondence between Mr. Thomas and his relatives are to be found among the Norman Thomas Papers in the Manuscript Division of the New York Public Library.

Chapter I

1. Autobiography, p. 126.
2. N.T., *We Have a Future* (Princeton, N.J.: Princeton University Press, 1941), p. 10.
3. Autobiography, p. 5.
4. *Ibid.*, p. 72.
5. Thomas Reminiscences, Part I, p. 6.
6. *Ibid.*
7. Thomas Family Interview, September, 1960.

8. Thomas Reminiscences, Part I, p. 6.

9. Autobiography, p. 15.

10. *Ibid.,* p. 19.

11. Thomas Family Interview, September, 1960.

12. Autobiography, p. 21.

13. Thomas Family Interview, September, 1960.

14. Autobiography, p. 24.

15. Raymond B. Fosdick, *Chronicle of a Generation* (New York: Harper & Brothers, 1958), p. 56.

16. *Ibid.,* pp. 52–53.

17. Thomas Reminiscences, Part I, p. 20.

18. *Ibid.,* p. 15.

19. *Ibid.,* p. 18.

20. Autobiography, p. 26.

21. *Ibid.,* p. 28.

22. *Socialist Call,* October, 1956, p. 12.

23. Autobiography, p. 32.

24. *Ibid.,* p. 30.

25. Thomas Reminiscences, Part I, p. 17.

26. Autobiography, p. 31.

27. *Ibid.,* p. 43.

28. N.T., *We Have a Future,* p. 11.

29. *Ibid.*

30. Autobiography, p. 48.

31. Lillian Symes and Travers Clement, *Rebel America: The Story of Social Revolt in the United States* (New York: Harper & Brothers, 1934), p. 232.

32. N.T. to Doris R. Sharpe, April 7, 1941, in Doris Robinson Sharpe, *Walter Rauschenbusch* (New York: Macmillan Co., 1941), p. 415.

33. W. E. Woodward, "This Is Norman Thomas," in *The Intelligent Voter's Guide: Official 1928 Campaign Handbook of the Socialist Party* (New York: Socialist National Committee, 1928), p. 27.

34. Interview with N.T., September, 1960.

35. N.T. to Mr. [no first name or initials indicated] Adriance, May 19, 1912.

36. Welling E. Thomas to N.T., August 25, 1914.

37. N.T. to Rev. William P. Shriver, August 25, 1916.

38. N.T. to Rev. Edward Niles, October 21, 1916.

39. N.T. to Harold [no last name indicated], December 6, 1916.

40. N.T., *We Have a Future,* p. 11.

41. N.T. to Howard [no last name indicated], January 31, 1937.

42. N.T. Papers, family box.

43. Ralph Thomas to N.T., February 28, 1918.

44. Emma Thomas to Woodrow Wilson, n.d.

45. N.T. to Dr. [no first name or initials indicated] Laidlaw, January 31, 1917.

46. N.T., "The Church and Industry" (unpublished essay), 1917, p. 9.

47. N.T. to A. T. Carton, August 15, 1917.

48. Morris Hillquit, *Loose Leaves from a Busy Life* (New York: Macmillan Co., 1934), p. 183.

49. N.T. to Morris Hillquit, October 2, 1917.

50. N.T. to Emma Thomas, November 2, 1917.

51. *Ibid.*

52. N.T. to Mrs. Anne T. Brush, September 24, 1918.

53. *Ibid.*

54. N.T. to Alexander Trachtenberg, October 18, 1918.

55. *Ibid.*

56. Thomas Reminiscences, Part I, p. 43.

57. *Ibid.*

58. Autobiography, p. 64.

59. Thomas Reminiscences, Part I, p. 20.

60. *Ibid.*, p. 22.

61. Autobiography, p. 64.

CHAPTER II

1. Symes and Clement, *op. cit.*, p. 191.

2. *Ibid.*, p. 209.

3. Quoted in Thomas H. Greer, *American Social Reform Movements: Their Pattern Since 1865* (New York: Prentice-Hall, Inc., 1949), pp. 57-58.

4. *Ibid.*

5. Quoted in Harry W. Laidler, *Social-Economic Movements: An Historical and Comparative Survey of Socialism, Communism, Cooperation, Utopianism, and Other Systems of Reform and Reconstruction* (New York: Thomas Y. Crowell Company, 1948), p. 581.

6. *Ibid.*, p. 583.

7. Symes and Clement, *op. cit.*, p. 209.

8. Woodrow Wilson, *The New Freedom* (New York: Doubleday, Page & Co., 1913), pp. 28-30.

9. Quoted in Ray Ginger, *The Bending Cross: A Biography of Eugene V. Debs* (New Brunswick, N.J.: Rutgers University Press, 1949), p. 195.

10. Daniel Bell, "The Background and Development of Marxian

Socialism in the United States," in Donald Drew Egbert and Stow Persons (eds.), *Socialism and American Life* (2 vols.; Princeton, N.J.: Princeton University Press, 1952), I, 275.

11. *Ibid.,* p. 267.

12. John Roderigo Dos Passos, "The 42nd Parallel," *U.S.A.* (New York: Modern Library, Inc., 1930), p. 26.

13. Introduction to Eugene Debs, *Writings and Speeches of Eugene V. Debs* (New York: Hermitage Press, 1948), p. ix.

14. Ginger, *op. cit.,* p. 378.

15. *Ibid.,* p. 16.

16. Bell, *op. cit.,* p. 377.

17. Morris Hillquit, *Socialism in Theory and Practice* (New York: Macmillan Co., 1913), p. 168.

18. Quoted in James Oneal and G. D. Werner, *American Communism: A Critical Analysis of Its Origins, Development and Programs* (New York: E. P. Dutton & Co., Inc., 1947), p. 29.

19. N.T., Public Address, April, 1959, Detroit, Michigan.

20. Quoted in Nathan Fine, *Labor and Farmer Parties in the United States, 1828–1928* (New York: Rand School of Social Science, 1928), p. 302.

21. *Ibid.,* p. 315.

22. *Ibid.,* pp. 315–16.

23. *Ibid.,* p. 310.

24. *Ibid.,* pp. 311–12.

25. *Ibid.,* p. 312.

26. *Ibid.*

27. *Ibid.*

28. *Ibid.,* p. 313.

29. *Ibid.*

30. *Ibid.,* p. 314.

31. *Ibid.*

32. *Ibid.,* p. 335.

33. *Ibid.,* p. 332.

34. *Ibid.,* p. 335.

35. *Ibid.,* p. 336.

36. *Ibid.,* p. 334.

37. *Ibid.*

38. *Ibid.*

39. Quoted in Oneal and Werner, *op. cit.,* p. 98.

40. Hillquit, *Loose Leaves from a Busy Life,* p. 300.

41. Nelson M. Blake, *A Short History of American Life* (New York: McGraw-Hill Book Co., Inc., 1952), pp. 604–605.

42. Hillquit, *Loose Leaves from a Busy Life,* p. 306.

43. *Ibid.,* p. 309.

44. Kenneth Campbell MacKay, *The Progressive Movement of 1924* (New York: Columbia University Press, 1947), p. 77.

45. Hillquit, *Loose Leaves from a Busy Life,* pp. 318–19.

46. *Ibid.,* pp. 319, 320.

47. *Ibid.,* p. 321.

48. *Ibid.,* p. 323.

49. David Karsner, "The Passing of the Socialist Party," *Current History,* XX (June, 1924), 402.

CHAPTER III

1. Samuel E. Morison and Henry S. Commager, *The Growth of the American Republic* (2 vols.; New York: Oxford University Press, 1960), II, 557.

2. Interview with N.T., April, 1960.

3. N.T. to Alexander Trochtenberg, October 18, 1918.

4. Woodward, *op. cit.,* p. 33.

5. Autobiography, p. 68.

6. N.T., "The Social Preparation for the Kingdom of God," in Joint Legislative Committee Investigating Seditious Activities, New York State, 1920 (ed.), *Revolutionary Radicalism: Its History, Purpose and Tactics* (4 vols.; New York: J. B. Lyon, 1920), II, 1311.

7. League for Industrial Democracy, *Thirty-five Years of Educational Pioneering* (New York: League for Industrial Democracy, 1941), p. 33.

8. Thomas Reminiscences, Part I, p. 43.

9. National Convention of the Socialist Party "Proceedings," 1928 (typed manuscript, Columbia University Library), p. D64.

10. *Ibid.,* p. D67.

11. *Ibid.,* p. D71.

12. Paul H. Douglas, "An Idealist Masters Realities," *World Tomorrow,* XV (May, 1932), 151.

13. Bell, *op. cit.,* p. 400.

14. Interview with N.T., September, 1960.

15. "If I Were a Politician: The Story of Norman Thomas," *World Tomorrow,* XIII (June, 1930), 259–63.

16. N.T., "The Dissenter's Role in a Totalitarian Age," *New York Times Magazine,* November 20, 1949, p. 13.

17. James Bryce, *The American Commonwealth* (2 vols.; New York: Macmillan Co., 1891), II, 253.

18. F. O. Matthiessen, *1907–1950* (New York: Henry Schuman, 1950), p. 10.

19. Samuel Smilowitz to N.T., February 4, 1935.

20. N.T., Presidential Campaign Address, October, 1948, Detroit, Michigan.

21. *Ibid.*

22. The Unofficial Observer, *American Messiahs* (New York: Simon and Schuster, Inc., 1935), p. 163.

23. Winston Lamont Brembeck and William Smiley Howell, *Persuasion, a Means of Social Control* (Englewood Cliffs, N.J.: Prentice-Hall, Inc., 1952), p. 147.

24. Harry MacArthur, "Thomas Stars in New Role," *Sunday Star* (Washington, D.C.), November 28, 1948, p. C8, 1948.

25. H. L. Mencken, "Mencken Thanks Thomas: Rare Political Hullabaloo by Really Intelligent Man," *Baltimore Sun*, October 18, 1948.

26. *Ibid.*

27. *Ibid.*

28. Letter to the Author, July 23, 1960.

29. Thomas Reminiscences, Part I, p. 36.

30. Letter to the Author, August 3, 1960.

31. Joseph Barnes, *Willkie* (New York: Simon and Schuster, Inc., 1952), p. 195.

32. *Socialist Call,* July 14, 1944, p. 7.

33. *New York Times,* October 27, 1948, p. 18.

34. *Ibid.*

35. Graduate Faculties *Newsletter,* Columbia University, November, 1959, p. 2.

36. Radio Broadcast (October 12, 1948), Arthur Bliss Lane, Max Lerner, O. John Rogge, Norman Thomas, recorded in "How Is Peace with Russia Possible?" *Town Meeting,* 1948, p. 4.

37. N.T., *Mr. Chairman, Ladies, and Gentlemen: Reflections on Public Speaking* (New York: Hermitage House, 1955), p. 16.

38. James Wechsler, *The Age of Suspicion* (New York: Random House, 1953), p. 41.

39. Milton Mayer to the Author, August 2, 1960.

40. Murray Kempton, *Part of Our Time: Some Ruins and Monuments of the Thirties* (New York: Simon and Schuster, Inc., 1955), p. 324.

41. *Ibid.,* p. 323.

42. Question Period Following Public Address by N.T., "The Failure of Our Party System," April, 1959, Detroit, Michigan.

43. *Ibid.*

44. N.T., *Mr. Chairman, Ladies, and Gentlemen,* p. 12.

45. Letter to the Author, July 23, 1960.

46. Thomas Family Interview, September, 1960.

47. *Ibid.,* April, 1960.

48. N.T., *A Socialist's Faith* (New York: W. W. Norton & Co., Inc., 1951), p. x.

49. *Luncheon in Honor of Norman Thomas* (Testimonial Booklet, February 4, 1950, New York), p. 3.

50. Autobiography, p. 21.

51. Francis Sugrue, "Norman Thomas, at 75, Still Has Plenty to Say," *New York Herald Tribune,* November 19, 1959, p. 5.

52. *Ibid.*

53. Letter to the Author, August 8, 1960.

CHAPTER IV

1. Quoted in Bell, *op. cit.,* p. 369.

2. Quoted in David A. Shannon, *The Socialist Party of America: A History* (New York: Macmillan Co., 1955), p. 217.

3. Harold K. Porter and Donald Bruce Johnson, *National Party Platforms, 1840–1956* (Urbana, Ill.: University of Illinois Press, 1956), p. 352.

4. Bell, *op. cit.,* p. 376.

5. *Ibid.*

6. N.T., *The Choice Before Us: Mankind at Crossroads* (New York: Macmillan Co., 1934), p. 64.

7. N.T. to Rhoda E. McCulloch, January 25, 1934.

8. N.T. to Francis G. Cutler, January 27, 1934.

9. N.T., *The Choice Before Us,* p. 124.

10. N.T. to Maury Maverick, December 21, 1933.

11. N.T., *The Choice Before Us,* p. 164.

12. *Ibid.*

13. Arthur M. Schlesinger, Jr., *The Politics of Upheaval* (*The Age of Roosevelt,* Vol. III [Boston: Houghton Mifflin Company, 1959]), pp. 179–80.

14. N.T., *The Choice Before Us,* pp. 80–81.

15. *Ibid.,* p. 81.

16. *Ibid.,* p. 199.

17. *Ibid.,* p. 155.

CHAPTER V

1. N.T., "Fight Fascism," *Eighteenth National Convention Handbook* (Chicago: National Socialist Party Headquarters, 1934), p. 4.

2. *Ibid.*

3. Quoted in Louis Waldman, *Labor Lawyer* (New York: E. P. Dutton & Co., Inc., 1944), p. 259.

4. "Declaration of Principles," *American Socialist Quarterly*, III (July, 1934), 3.

5. *Ibid.*, p. 4.

6. *Ibid.*, pp. 5–6.

7. *Ibid.*, p. 11.

8. *Ibid.*, p. 28.

9. *Ibid.*, p. 33.

10. Interview with N.T., July, 1952.

11. Waldman, *op. cit.*, p. 267.

12. "Declaration of Principles," *op. cit.*, pp. 28–30.

13. *Ibid.*, p. 41.

14. *Ibid.*, p. 60.

15. *Ibid.*, p. 59.

16. Louis Waldman to N.T., June 9, 1934.

17. N.T. to Charney Vladeck, June 13, 1934.

18. Charney Vladeck to N.T., June 14, 1934.

19. N.T. to Charney Vladeck, June 19, 1934.

20. N.T. to Leo Krzycki, June 18, 1934.

21. *New Leader*, June 16, 1934, p. 8.

22. Bell, *op. cit.*, p. 379.

23. *Socialist Voice*, n.d., p. 1.

24. *Ibid.*

25. James Oneal, *Some Pages of Party History* (New York: Published by the Author at 7 E. 15th St., 1935), p. 19.

26. N.T., "What Happened at Detroit," *World Tomorrow*, XVII (June 28, 1934), 321.

27. N.T. to Clarence Senior, July 2, 1934.

28. N.T. to Charles Solomon, July 2, 1934.

29. N.T. to Stevens Point Meeting, September 6, 1934.

30. N.T. to Clarence Senior, October 27, 1934.

31. N.T. to the Members of the New York State Committee of the Socialist Party, November 7, 1934.

32. N.T. to Clarence Senior, December 3, 1934.

33. N.T. to Franz Daniel, December 5, 1934.

34. *Ibid.*

35. N.T. to Alice S. Eddy, December 27, 1934.

36. *Ibid.*

37. N.T. to Samuel Smilowitz, January 31, 1935.

38. N.T. to the New Leader Association, February 25, 1935.

39. See any 1935 Edition of the *Socialist Call*.

40. *New York Times*, March 18, 1935, p. 1.

41. *Ibid.*, July 16, 1935, p. 10.

42. *Ibid.*
43. Press Release by N.T., November 28, 1935.
44. *New York Times,* November 28, 1935, p. 36.
45. *Ibid.,* December 2, 1935, p. 8.
46. *Ibid.,* December 4, 1935, p. 18.
47. Maynard Kreuger to N.T., December 4, 1935.
48. *Ibid.,* December 10, 1935.
49. Memorandum by N.T., December, 1935.
50. N.T. to Charney Vladeck, December 11, 1935.
51. *Socialist Call,* December 14, 1935, p. 12.
52. N.T. to Charles Sands, December 12, 1935.
53. *New York Times,* May 25, 1936, p. 23.
54. *Ibid.,* May 25, 1936, p. 1.
55. *Ibid.*
56. *Ibid.,* May 24, 1936, p. 1.
57. *Ibid.,* May 25, 1936, p. 18.
58. *Ibid.*
59. *Ibid.,* June 4, 1936, p. 6.
60. *Ibid.,* May 26, 1935, p. 1.
61. Letter from N.T., May 11, 1936, quoted in Bell, *op. cit.,* p. 381.
62. Quoted in Bell, *op. cit.,* p. 382.
63. Excerpts from Conversation prior to Formal Interview for Willis Thornton, "Smoking Out the Candidates," *Cleveland Press* (Ohio), June 3, 1936.
64. Formal Interview, *ibid.*

CHAPTER VI

1. *New York Times,* October 31, 1934, p. 6.
2. *Ibid.,* November 3, 1934, p. 6.
3. *Ibid.*
4. See Bell, *op. cit.,* p. 384.
5. James P. Cannon, *The History of American Trotskyism* (New York: Pioneer Publishers, 1944), pp. 224–26, 232.
6. *Socialist Call,* March 6, 1937, p. 12.
7. N.T., "The Party Situation" (unpublished memorandum), June, 1937.
8. *Socialist Call,* August 21, 1937, p. 4.
9. *Ibid.,* p. 3.
10. *Ibid.,* September 4, 1937, p. 4.
11. N.T. to Devere Allen, Jack Altman, and Gus Tyler, October 6, 1937.
12. Cannon, *op. cit.,* pp. 352–53.

13. N.T. to Roy Burt, Maynard Kreuger, and Clarence Senior, January 29, 1937.

14. N.T. to William Rauol, January 10, 1935.

15. *Socialist Call,* December 7, 1935, p. 12.

16. *Ibid.,* August 18, 1936, p. 12.

17. *Ibid.,* August 27, 1936, p. 2.

18. *Ibid.,* February 6, 1937, p. 12.

19. N.T. to the Editor of *World Telegram* (New York), February 8, 1937.

20. *Ibid.,* February 26, 1937.

21. N.T. to Sir Stafford Cripps, March 19, 1937.

22. *Socialist Call,* June 5, 1937, p. 3.

23. *Ibid.*

24. *Ibid.*

25. *Ibid.*

26. *Ibid.*

27. *Ibid.*

28. *Ibid.*

29. *Ibid.,* December 25, 1937, p. 4.

30. *Ibid.,* March 19, 1938, p. 5.

31. N.T. and Joel Seidman, *Russia—Democracy or Dictatorship?* (New York: League for Industrial Democracy, 1939), p. 64.

32. *Ibid.,* p. 65.

33. *Ibid.,* p. 66.

34. *Socialist Call,* September 2, 1939, p. 3.

35. N.T. to Paul Blanshard, September 14, 1933.

36. Press Release by N.T. on Blanshard Resignation, September 14, 1933.

37. Upton Sinclair to N.T., September 27, 1933.

38. N.T. to Upton Sinclair, September 27, 1933.

39. N.T. to Upton Sinclair, May 1, 1934.

40. N.T., *After the New Deal, What?* (New York: Macmillan Co., 1936), pp. 53–54.

41. *Ibid.,* p. 54.

42. *Socialist Call,* October 31, 1936, p. 12.

43. N.T. to Julius Gerber, September 29, 1933.

44. Irving Howe and B. J. Widick, *The UAW and Walter Reuther* (New York: Random House, 1949), pp. 51–52.

45. N.T. to Maynard Kreuger, November 1, 1936.

46. Socialist mayors traditionally acted quite independently of party decisions. Hoan was a rather practical politician who apparently assumed that his political power would be strengthened by such an affiliation.

47. Quoted in Bell, *op. cit.,* p. 389.

48. N.T., *Socialism on the Defensive* (New York and London: Harper & Brothers, 1938), p. 280.

49. *Ibid.,* p. 291.

50. John Haynes Holmes to N.T., December 23, 1936.

51. N.T. to John Haynes Holmes, December 24, 1936.

52. *Socialist Call,* January 2, 1937, p. 7.

53. *Ibid.,* February 13, 1937, p. 7.

54. *Ibid.,* August 27, 1938, p. 3.

55. N.T. to Upton Sinclair, September 16, 1939.

56. *New York Times,* April 8, 1940, p. 1.

57. *Ibid.*

58. *Ibid.,* April 9, 1940, p. 19.

59. In 1940 Roosevelt arrived at an agreement with Great Britain whereby fifty American destroyers were turned over to Britain. In exchange, Britain granted the United States the right to establish military bases in various British territorial possessions.

60. Franklin D. Roosevelt to N.T., July 31, 1940.

61. N.T. to Burton K. Wheeler, March 10, 1941.

62. N.T. to Ralph Thomas, July 28, 1941.

63. *New York Times,* January 23, 1941, p. 20.

CHAPTER VII

1. N.T., *What Is Our Destiny* (Garden City, N.Y.: Doubleday & Company, Inc., 1944), p. 32.

2. *Ibid.,* p. 11.

3. *Ibid.,* pp. 32–33.

4. *Ibid.,* p. 37.

5. The *Call,* March 7, 1942, p. 5.

6. Porter and Johnson, *op. cit.,* p. 414.

7. The *Call,* May 19, 1944, p. 1.

8. *Ibid.,* July 21, 1944, p. 1.

9. *Ibid.,* p. 2.

10. *Ibid.*

11. *Ibid.,* August 4, 1944, pp. 1–2.

12. *Ibid.,* September 8, 1944, p. 5.

13. Interview, October, 1960.

14. *Ibid.,* July, 1960.

15. Harlan B. Phillips (ed.), *Felix Frankfurter Reminisces* (New York: Reynal & Company, Inc., 1960), pp. 240–41.

16. The *Call,* April 23, 1945, p. 1.

17. *Ibid.,* August 20, 1945, p. 8.

18. *National Platform of the Socialist Party Adopted at the May*

7–8–9 *National Convention at Reading, Pa.* (New York: Socialist Campaign Headquarters, 1948), p. 13.

19. *Socialist Call,* September 24, 1948, p. 5.

20. *Ibid.,* May 21, 1948, p. 4.

21. *Ibid.*

22. *Ibid.,* May 28, 1948, p. 2.

23. *Ibid.*

24. *Ibid.,* May 21, 1948, p. 4.

25. *Ibid.,* June 4, 1948, p. 2.

26. *Ibid.*

27. *Ibid.,* June 11, 1948, p. 2.

28. N.T., "I'm Glad I'm Not Running This Time," *American Magazine,* CLIV (October, 1952), 19.

29. *Ibid.,* p. 103.

30. *Ibid.*

31. N.T., Public Address, February, 1960, Detroit, Michigan.

32. *New America,* September 5, 1960, p. 8.

33. N.T., "And If . . . and If . . . ," *Newsweek,* LVI (August 22, 1960), 20.

34. *New America,* September 5, 1960, p. 8.

35. *Ibid.*

36. *Ibid.*

37. *Ibid.*

38. N.T., Public Address, October, 1960, Detroit, Michigan.

39. See any Post War World Council *Newsletter* (New York: Published at 112 E. 19th St.).

40. N.T., Public Address, April, 1959, Detroit, Michigan.

41. N.T., "A World without War" (Public Address, November 18, 1959, New York City), p. 2 (typed manuscript sent to author by Mr. Thomas' secretary).

42. N.T. to John Foster Dulles, May 15, 1953.

43. Harry Truman to N.T., August 30, 1950.

44. See introduction to N.T., "Our One Hope for Peace," *Saturday Evening Post,* CCXXIV (February 2, 1952), 25.

45. *Luncheon in Honor of Norman Thomas* (Testimonial Booklet, February 4, 1950, New York), p. 9.

46. *New York Herald Tribune,* March 7, 1953, p. 10.

47. *Ibid.*

48. Will Herberg, "What Happened to American Socialism?" *Commentary,* XII (October, 1951), 336–44.

49. Arnold Petersen, *Bourgeois Socialism: Its Rise and Collapse in America* (New York: New York Labor News, 1951), p. 107.

50. *Ibid.*, p. 108.

51. Curtis D. MacDougal, *Understanding Public Opinion: A Guide for Newspapermen and Newspaper Readers* (New York: Macmillan Co., 1952), p. 409.

52. N.T., "The Dissenter's Role in a Totalitarian Age," *op. cit.*, p. 13.

53. *Socialist Call*, February 10, 1950, p. 10.

54. *Ibid.*

55. N.T., "What's Right with America," *Harper's Magazine*, CXCIV (March, 1947), p. 237.

56. *Ibid.*, pp. 237–39.

57. *Ibid.*, p. 239.

58. *Ibid.*

Chapter VIII

1. N.T., *As I See It* (New York: Macmillan Co., 1932), p. 154.

2. N.T., *A Socialist's Faith*, p. 122.

3. *Ibid.*

4. *Ibid.*, p. 123.

5. N.T., *As I See It*, p. 154.

6. *Ibid.*, p. 158.

7. *Ibid.*, p. 160.

8. N.T., *A Socialist's Faith*, p. 103.

9. N.T., *America's Way Out: A Program for Democracy* (New York: Macmillan Co., 1931), p. 296.

10. *Ibid.*, p. 298.

11. N.T., *A Socialist's Faith*, p. 109.

12. *Ibid.*, p. 6.

13. N.T., *America's Way Out*, p. 137.

14. *Ibid.*, p. 61.

15. N.T., *As I See It*, p. 16.

16. N.T., *A Socialist's Faith*, p. 8.

17. *Ibid.*, p. 127.

18. N.T., *America's Way Out*, p. 308.

19. N.T., *A Socialist's Faith*, p. 118.

20. *Ibid.*, pp. 303–304.

21. *Ibid.*, p. 304.

22. N.T., *America's Way Out*, p. 4.

23. *Ibid.*, p. 5.

24. N.T., *A Socialist's Faith*, pp. 164–65.

25. N.T., "A World without War," *op. cit.*, p. 2.

26 N.T., "A Socialist Reports on Socialism," *New York Times Magazine*, October 30, 1955, p. 38.

27. N.T., *A Socialist's Faith*, p. 165.

28. *Ibid.*, p. 167.

29. *Ibid.*, p. 168.

30. N.T., *We Have a Future*, p. 11.

31. N.T., *A Socialist's Faith*, p. 183.

32. *Ibid.*, p. 184.

33. *Ibid.*, p. 185.

34. *Ibid.*, pp. 305–306.

35. *Ibid.*, p. 186.

36. *Ibid.*, p. 187.

37. *Ibid.*, p. 183.

38. *Ibid.*, p. 190.

39. *Ibid.*, p. 191.

40. *Ibid.*, p. 187.

41. *Ibid.*, p. 194.

42. *Ibid.*, p. 195.

43. *Socialist Call*, October, 1955, p. 7.

44. N.T., *A Socialist's Faith*, p. 196.

45. *Ibid.*, p. 186.

46. N.T., *What Is Our Destiny*, p. 181.

47. The author has heard Mr. Thomas reiterate such sentiments on many occasions. Here I am quoting from memory.

48. N.T., *A Socialist's Faith*, p. 207.

49. *Socialist Call*, November 14, 1952, p. 8.

50. N.T., *A Socialist's Faith*, p. 309.

51. *Ibid.*, p. 308.

52. N.T., *What Is Our Destiny*, p. 39.

53. *Ibid.*, p. 46.

54. N.T., *We Have a Future*, p. 219.

55. N.T., *A Socialist's Faith*, p. 313.

56. *Ibid.*, p. 278.

57. *Ibid.*, p. 276.

58. *Ibid.*, p. 286.

59. N.T., *The Prerequisites for Peace* (New York: W. W. Norton & Company, Inc., 1959), pp. 38–39.

60. *Ibid.*, p. 39.

61. *Ibid.*

62. *Ibid.*, p. 40.

63. N.T., "Are We as Right as We Think?" *Saturday Review*, XLII (April 18, 1959), 56.

64. *Ibid.*, p. 15.

65. *Ibid.*, pp. 13–14.

66. N.T., *A Socialist's Faith*, pp. 292–93.

67. N.T., *The Prerequisites for Peace*, p. 89.

68. *Ibid.*, p. 143.

69. *Ibid.*, pp. 159–60.

70. *Ibid.*, p. 158.

71. *Ibid.*, p. 161.

72. N.T., "Are We as Right as We Think?" *op. cit.*, p. 56.

73. N.T., "A World without War," *op. cit.*, p. 6.

74. N.T., *America's Way Out*, p. 122.

75. N.T., *A Socialist's Faith*, p. 38.

76. *Ibid.*, p. 178.

77. *Ibid.*, p. 143.

78. *Ibid.*, p. 145.

79. *Ibid.*, p. 146.

80. *Ibid.*, p. 214.

81. N.T., Public Address, September, 1956, Detroit, Michigan.

82. A. H. Raskin, "Norman Thomas Sparkling at 70," *New York Times*, November 20, 1954, p. 20.

83. N.T., *The Test of Freedom* (New York: W. W. Norton & Company, Inc., 1954), p. 49.

84. *Ibid.*, p. 23.

85. *Ibid.*, pp. 112–13.

86. N.T., *A Socialist's Faith*, p. 146.

CHAPTER IX

1. Waldman, *op. cit.*, p. 188.

2. Benjamin Stolberg, *The Story of the CIO* (New York: Viking Press, Inc., 1938), pp. 132–33.

3. *New York Times*, June 5, 1934, p. 24.

4. Daniel W. Hoan to N.T., March 7, 1935.

5. Bell, *op. cit.*, p. 401.

6. Waldman, *op. cit.*, p. 192.

7. Letter to the Author, July 29, 1953.

8. Interview with the Author, December 28, 1953.

9. Dwight MacDonald, "Thomas for President?" *Politics*, I (October, 1944), 278.

10. *Ibid.*

11. Bell, *op. cit.*, p. 217.

12. Waldman, *op. cit.*, p. 180.

13. The Unofficial Observer, *op. cit.*, p. 170.

14. Arthur M. Schlesinger, Sr., *The American as Reformer* (Cambridge, Mass.: Harvard University Press, 1950), p. 31.

15. Bell, *op. cit.,* p. 273.

16. Thomas Reminiscences, Part I, p. 65.

17. *Socialist Call,* July 24, 1953, p. 7.

18. Herberg, *op. cit.,* p. 344.

19. *Washington Post,* November 20, 1959.

CHAPTER X

1. Sylvia Wright, "The Dean of Protest," *Life,* LX (January 14, 1966), 62.

2. Bernard Rosenberg, "The Example of Norman Thomas," *Dissent,* XI (Autumn, 1964), 415.

3. Wayne State University, Detroit, Michigan, May 11, 1966.

4. N.T., "A Message to Johnson," *Sane World,* V (January, 1966), 2.

5. N.T., *New America,* December 18, 1965, p. 3.

6. N.T., Post War World Council *Newsletter,* March, 1966, p. 4.

7. Norman Thomas *v.* Barry Goldwater, "Which Way America?" tape of public debate, November, 1961. (This tape was sold by the Socialist party.)

8. N.T., *Socialism Re-examined* (New York: W. W. Norton & Co., Inc., 1963), pp. 16, 183–92.

9. As quoted in *ibid.,* p. 183.

10. *Ibid.,* pp. 183–92.

11. *Ibid.,* pp. 191–92.

12. Milton R. Konvitz, *Expanding Liberty: Freedom's Gains in Postwar America* (New York: Viking Press, 1966), p. 129.

13. A. H. Raskin to N.T., January 20, 1963.

14. N.T. to Norman Cousins, October 27, 1960.

15. *New York Times,* May 11, 1962, p. 14.

16. See *Human Exploitation in the United States* (New York: Frederic A. Stokes Company, 1934). Chapter XII.

17. Interview with N.T., March 29, 1966.

18. *Ibid.*

19. *Ibid.*

20. N.T. to Martin Luther King, January 25, 1961.

21. See "The Bravest Man I Ever Met," *Pageant,* XX (June, 1965), 22–29.

22. See the *Detroit News,* March 12, 1960, p. 4.

23. *New America,* May 12, 1963, p. 1.

24. *Ibid.,* October 21, 1963, p. 7.

25. Harvey Swados, "New Reasons for an Old Cause," *Saturday Review,* XLVII (February 1, 1964), 43.

26. N.T., *New America,* October 18, 1960, p. 8.
27. Interview with N.T., March 29, 1966.
28. N.T., *New America,* January 15, 1961, p. 8.
29. *Ibid.,* November 10, 1961, p. 2.
30. N.T., *New America,* October 6, 1961, p. 2.
31. Interview with N.T., May 6, 1963.
32. N.T., *New America,* December, 1963, p. 1.
33. Interview with N.T., March 29, 1966.
34. N.T., "President Johnson's Great Society," *Christian Century,* LXXXIII (March 9, 1966), 300.
35. *Ibid.,* p. 301.
36. *Ibid.*
37. *Ibid.*
38. *Ibid.*
39. Memorandum from N.T. to: "Members of the Committee on Free Elections in the Dominican Republic," June 20, 1966, p. 2.
40. *New York Times,* May 20, 1966, p. 16.
41. Memorandum from N.T., *op. cit.,* p. 2.
42. N.T., Post War World Council *Newsletter,* July–August, 1966, p. 1.
43. *Ibid.*
44. *Ibid.*
45. Wright, *op. cit.,* p. 60.
46. N.T. to Bruce L. Sandberg, December 22, 1962.
47. N.T., "President Johnson's Great Society," *op. cit.,* p. 303.
48. "Playboy Interview: Norman Thomas," *Playboy,* XIII (November, 1966), 96.
49. *New America,* May 14, 1964, p. 8.
50. "The Unknockables," *Esquire,* LXV (June, 1966), 84.
51. Wright, *op. cit.,* p. 57.
52. *New America,* November 30, 1964, pp. 8–9.
53. *The Daily Collegian* (Detroit, Michigan), May 10, 1966, p. 1.
54. F. D. Reeve, "Robert Frost Confronts Khrushchev," *The Atlantic,* CCXII (September, 1963), 34.
55. Norman Thomas *v.* Barry Goldwater, "Which Way America?"
56. *Ibid.*
57. N.T., *Great Dissenters* (New York: W. W. Norton & Co., Inc., 1961), p. 129.
58. *Ibid.,* p. 130.
59. *Ibid.,* p. 166.

Sources

Fortunately, in the writing of this book I had access to a great wealth of unpublished, primary material relevant to the political leadership of Norman Thomas. For my purposes the most useful of such materials were the Norman Thomas Papers in the Manuscript Division of the New York Public Library. Mr. Thomas adds periodically to this collection, which includes some materials dating from the first decade of the twentieth century. The collection contains the bulk of Mr. Thomas' voluminous correspondence during the years of his official leadership of the Socialist party and since. Happily, Mr. Thomas was in the habit of making carbon copies of the thousands of letters which he wrote. These papers also include manuscripts of a host of books, pamphlets, articles, speeches, press releases, minutes of Socialist-party meetings, and miscellaneous memoranda. For the most part, these assorted papers and letters are concerned with Mr. Thomas' political activities and relationships; very little in the way of correspondence with members of his family is included.

Also, especially valuable to the development of this book was the opportunity which I had to read Mr. Thomas' unpublished autobiography, which he began at the age of sixty in December of 1944 and completed in March of 1946. Essentially, he regards the manuscript as a document that may be of interest to his children and his friends. Originally, he considered its publication but finally abandoned the idea. In part, his decision was based on his deep suspicion of autobiography as a method of reporting; in the preface to his own he dismisses such writing as being "too often a form of fiction which I have preferred to read rather than to write. . . . I am not driven to public confession or public self defense." This book without a name is much less than a complete record of Thomas' life, but it is also something more. It includes Thomas' assessments and re-evaluations of socialism and religion and his reflections on the sundry problems confronting twentieth-century man.

During the 1950's Thomas was interviewed by the Oral History Project of Columbia University. Next to the unpublished autobiography, "The Reminiscences of Norman Thomas," the transcript of these interviews, is the best source of material on the life and political career of Norman Thomas. There is, in fact, considerable overlapping between his Oral History Project contributions and his autobiography.

The Socialist Party Collection in the Manuscript Division of the Duke University Library is the best source of primary Socialist materials in the country. It is a magnificently organized collection which no serious student of American socialism can afford to miss. The Duke papers include an interesting exchange of letters between Norman Thomas and Clarence Senior, who was then national secretary of the Socialist party, written between 1933 and 1937.

Thomas has been a fantastically prolific writer. Most of his pamphlets, books, and contributions to popular journals are listed in standard periodical guides and catalogs. There are, however, other vitally important and voluminous sources of his writings which should not be overlooked. He was the founder and a long-time contributor to the pacifist and Christian Socialist *World Tomorrow* (1918–34, title varies). The various official newspapers of the Socialist party that appeared through the years provide a rather detailed record of his evolving socialist philosophy and of his reactions to major events. Thomas was the editor of the *New York Leader* in 1923 and a regular contributor to the *New Leader* from 1924 to 1935, when it came under the domination of the old guard. He then became a columnist for the *Call* (1935–60, title and format vary), which had been founded by the militant caucus. In 1960 the *Socialist Call* ceased publication, and, in its place, *New America* became the official newspaper of the Socialist party–Social Democratic Federation. These various Socialist newspapers contain not only vast numbers of articles by Thomas but also the texts of hundreds of speeches, open letters, interviews, and summaries of his campaign activities. It should also be noted that, since the early 1940's, Mr. Thomas has written a flood of articles for the *Progressive*.

The Library of the Tamiment Institute in New York City includes one of the nation's outstanding Socialist and labor collections. It contains the great mass of material gathered under the auspices of the Rand School of Social Science, which from 1906 to 1936 was the Socialist party's most important educational and research center.

The Joseph A. Labadie Collection at the University of Michigan is also a good source of Socialist pamphlets, newspapers, and periodicals. While the collection contains many documents which strongly emphasize anarchism and the Industrial Workers of the World, it also contains a wide variety of materials on almost every phase of American radicalism.

Because of the long-term Socialist affiliations of my parents, much data and insight concerning Norman Thomas and the Socialist party have been acquired by this author through direct observation. In a variety of situations over a twenty-five–year period, beginning in the years of my childhood, I have had numerous opportunities to observe Mr. Thomas and to talk with him informally. He was always apparently willing to give frank answers to frank questions about his thinking, his family life, and his political career. I have heard Thomas and other Socialist leaders deliver countless numbers of public addresses. I have been an observer at three national conventions of the Socialist party and have attended many other official Socialist functions.

I am indebted not only to Norman Thomas but also to members

of his family who graciously agreed to give me their impressions and evaluations of their famous relative. My conversations with various members of the Thomas family were invaluable sources for this book. They included interviews with his brothers, Mr. Ralph Thomas, Dr. Evan W. Thomas, and Mr. Arthur Thomas, with his sister Miss Agnes Thomas, with his son Evan Thomas, with his daughter Mrs. John Gates, and with his daughters-in-law, Mrs. Evan Thomas and Mrs. William Thomas. A number of persons, most of whom were closely associated with Mr. Thomas in one social-reform cause or another, also contributed their impressions of Mr. Thomas via correspondence or interviews. For this valuable co-operation I am grateful to: Roger Baldwin, Paul Blanshard, Henry Hitt Crane, Judah Drob, Max Eastman, Harry Fleischman, Erich Fromm, Donald Harrington, Darlington Hoopes, Harry W. Laidler, Alfred Baker Lewis, Seymour Martin Lipset, Frank Marquart, Milton Mayer, Robert Moses, James Myers, Clarence E. Pickett, Robert Repas, Brendan Sexton, Mulford Q. Sibley, Upton Sinclair, Tucker P. Smith, Mark Starr, Walter H. Uphoff, James P. Warburg, and Frank P. Zeidler. I wish also to thank the Reverend John Haynes Holmes, Professor Reinhold Niebuhr, the Honorable Harry S. Truman, Stephen C. Vladeck, Peter Viereck, and Arthur Hays Sulzberger for permission to quote from privileged materials.

Finally, one secondary work deserves special mention in this bibliographical introduction: the monumental and comprehensive *Socialism and American Life* (2 vols.; Princeton, N.J.: Princeton University Press, 1952). No published work has been more helpful to me than Daniel Bell's brilliant historical and sociological analysis of "The Background and Development of Marxian Socialism in the United States," which appears as Chapter Six of the first volume of *Socialism and American Life*. Its second volume, compiled by T. D. Seymour Bassett and devoted totally to bibliography, was also an indispensable tool. Donald Drew Egbert and Stow Persons, the editors of the two volumes, deserve the gratitude of all students of American radicalism.

These chapter notes indicate sources leaned on most heavily in preparing individual chapters. A bibliography follows, in which all published materials mentioned are cited in full.

CHAPTER I: *A Christian Road to Socialism*

By far the most important sources of material on Thomas' early life are his autobiography and his contributions to the Columbia University Oral History Project. These sources have been supplemented by interviews with Mr. Thomas and his siblings. For gleaning some of the bare facts of his life, the most useful of Mr. Thomas' published books would be *As I See It, We Have a Future, A Socialist's Faith,* and *The Test of Freedom.* Essentially, W. E. Woodward's "This Is Norman Thomas," in *The Intelligent Voter's Guide: Official 1928 Campaign Handbook of the Socialist Party,* drafted as a 1928 campaign document, is also useful for biographical information. The Norman Thomas Papers are crucial to understanding his life and thought as he was moving toward socialism in the era of World War I. See his *The Conscientious Objector in America* for insight into the character and intensity of his early pacifism.

CHAPTER II: *Setting the Stage*

There are two thorough studies of the early years of American socialism: Quint's *The Forging of American Socialism* covers the period from the coming of Marxism to America through the founding of the Socialist party; and Kipnis, in *The American Socialist Movement, 1897–1912,* continues the Socialist story through 1912. Among the more general accounts of American socialism, the very best are Bell's "The Background and Development of Marxian Socialism in the United States" and Shannon's *The Socialist Party of America.* For other useful general works, see Fine's *Labor and Farmer Parties in the United States, 1828–1928,* Greer's *American Social Reform Movements,* Laidler's *Social-Economic Movements,* and Symes's and Clement's *Rebel America.* See Madison's *Critics and Crusaders* for an interesting biographical approach to American radicalism. For a penetrating study of the origins and founding of American communism, see Draper's *The Roots of American Communism*. The Fund for the Republic merits hearty applause for sponsoring this excellent study. Absolutely essential to understanding the Conference for Progressive Political Action and its relation to the Socialist party are MacKay's *The Progressive Movement of 1924* and Hillquit's autobiography, *Loose Leaves from a Busy Life*.

Chapter III: *A Leader Emerges*

To the largest possible extent, this chapter is based upon my own personal observations and impressions of Mr. Thomas. These have been supplemented by conversations with his relatives and by personal interviews and correspondence with other persons who have been closely associated with him in political endeavors over long periods. His autobiography, the Norman Thomas Papers, and the recording "Norman Thomas Reminisces" also proved very helpful. For further insight into Thomas as a public speaker see his chatty *Mr. Chairman, Ladies, and Gentlemen*.

Chapter IV: *The Roots of Factionalism*

Socialist factionalism of the 1930's, analyzed in this chapter and the two that follow, is well described in Bell's "The Background and Development of Marxian Socialism in the United States" and Shannon's *The Socialist Party of America*. Waldman, in his autobiography, *Labor Lawyer*, gives a rather detailed account of this period from a strictly old-guard point of view. Arthur M. Schlesinger, Jr., gives sweeping coverage to the development of this Socialist controversy in his *The Politics of Upheaval*. For Thomas' assessment of fascism and communism as of 1934, see his *The Choice Before Us*.

Chapter V: *Fratricidal Warfare*

The *American Socialist Quarterly* (July, 1934) contains a complete transcript of the Declaration of Principles debate. The *New*

York Times (1934–36) provides a fairly good outline of this intra-party Socialist controversy. The Norman Thomas Papers are an indispensable source for understanding the old-guard–militant controversy in any depth. See Thomas' *After the New Deal, What?* for his own account of Socialist-party factionalism and his evaluations of the New Deal. He also surveys the Socialist split in his autobiography.

CHAPTER VI: *The All-Inclusive Party*

For a detailed statement of Thomas' total rejection of communism, whether of the Trotskyite or the Stalinist variety, see his *Socialism on the Defensive*. For a chronicle of his growing disillusionment with the Soviet Union, see his weekly articles in the *Call* (1936–38). Of course, his correspondence in the Norman Thomas Papers is also useful for understanding his thinking during this period. The two best sources for understanding the role of the Socialists in the labor movement during the 1930's would be Howe's and Widick's *The UAW and Walter Reuther* and Stolberg's *The Story of the CIO*. To comprehend in depth Thomas' reasons for opposing American intervention in World War II, see his and Bertram D. Wolfe's *Keep America Out of War* and Thomas' *We Have a Future*.

CHAPTER VII: *From War to Peace?*

For further insight into the character of Thomas' critical support of World War II, see his *What Is Our Destiny,* in which he is sharply critical of many aspects of the conduct of the war, especially the lack of adequate preparation for the establishment of peace. See his *Appeal to the Nations* for a good summary statement of Thomas' foreign-policy views—with central emphasis upon the need for disarmament—in the post-World War II years. In the preparation of this chapter, the *Call* was the most important source. I also found articles by Mr. Thomas which appeared in the *Progressive* and *New America* extremely useful. I have relied exten-

sively on my own notes and recollections of Mr. Thomas' views
as expressed in public addresses and conversations.

CHAPTER VIII: *Plenty, Peace, and Freedom*

As is apparent from the text of this chapter, I have turned essentially to Mr. Thomas' published writings as a guide to the funda-
mentals of his thought. All of his books have been consulted, with
profit, but some have proved more useful than others. I have relied
very heavily upon *America's Way Out*, which is a basic statement
of his reactions to the Great Depression and a detailed account of
his Socialist proposals for the reconstruction of our crisis-ridden
society. His *As I See It* is a collection of essays, based largely on
earlier articles and speeches and ranging in subject from religion
to Marxism. The most thorough statement of his thinking since
World War II is contained in *A Socialist's Faith*. In *The Test of
Freedom*, written in the midst of the McCarthy era, Thomas out-
lines a program for coping with the civil-liberties crises of our
times.

CHAPTER IX: *"Successful Failure"*

Naturally, almost all of the sources cited earlier are also of rele-
vance to this summary chapter. Here, I have relied heavily upon
assessments of Thomas made by past and present leaders of the
Socialist party and on the viewpoints of other close observers of
American socialism. The work that provides the best insight into
what I have called the culture of American socialism is Bell's "The
Background and Development of Marxian Socialism in the United
States."

CHAPTER X: *Epilogue*

The focus of this chapter is upon the role that Mr. Thomas plays
in contemporary American society, thus the use of recent sources
has been emphasized. Deposits to the Norman Thomas Papers
since 1960 were carefully reviewed. Thomas' two most recent books,
Great Dissenters (1961) and *Socialism Re-examined* (1963), were

also very helpful in the preparation of this chapter. Numerous articles by and about Thomas have appeared during the 1960's and have enlarged my understanding of the subject of this book. *New America,* the official newspaper of the Socialist party, has been an invaluable source for materials pertaining to Mr. Thomas' ideas and activities. Finally, there is no substitute for observing Mr. Thomas in action, which I have had the opportunity to do on many occasions during recent years.

Selected Published Works of Norman Thomas

BOOKS

After the New Deal, What? New York: Macmillan Co., 1936.

America's Way Out: A Program for Democracy. New York: Macmillan Co., 1931.

Appeal to the Nations. New York: Henry Holt & Co., Inc., 1947.

As I See It. New York: Macmillan Co., 1932.

The Choice Before Us: Mankind at Crossroads. New York: Macmillan Co., 1934.

The Conscientious Objector in America. New York: B. W. Huebsch, 1923.

Great Dissenters. New York: W. W. Norton & Company, Inc., 1961.

Human Exploitation in the United States. New York: Frederic A. Stokes, 1934.

and Wolfe, Bertram D. *Keep America Out of War: A Program.* New York: Frederic A. Stokes, 1939.

Mr. Chairman, Ladies, and Gentlemen: Reflections on Public Speaking. New York: Hermitage House, 1955.

The Prerequisites for Peace. New York: W. W. Norton & Company, Inc., 1959.

Socialism on the Defensive. New York and London: Harper & Brothers, 1938.

Socialism Re-examined. New York: W. W. Norton & Company, Inc., 1963.

A Socialist's Faith. New York: W. W. Norton & Company, Inc., 1951.

The Test of Freedom. New York: W. W. Norton & Company, Inc., 1954.

War: No Glory, No Profit, No Need. New York: Frederic A. Stokes, 1935.

We Have a Future. Princeton, N.J.: Princeton University Press, 1941.

What Is Our Destiny. Garden City, N.Y.: Doubleday & Company, Inc., 1944.

and Blanshard, Paul. *What's the Matter with New York: A National Problem.* New York: Macmillan Co., 1932.

PAMPHLETS

The Challenge of War. New York: League for Industrial Democracy, 1924.

Conscription: The Test of Peace. New York: Post War World Council, 1944.

Norman Thomas *v.* Earl Browder. *Debate: Which Road for American Workers, Socialist or Communist?* New York: *Socialist Call,* 1936.

Democracy and Japanese Americans. New York: Post War World Council, 1942.

Democracy versus Dictatorship. New York: League for Industrial Democracy, 1937.

Democratic Socialism: A New Appraisal. New York: League for Industrial Democracy, 1953.

The New Deal: A Socialist Analysis. Chicago: Socialist Party, 1934.

The Plight of the Share-Cropper. New York: League for Industrial Democracy, 1934.

Russia: Promise and Performance. New York: Socialist Party, 1945.

and Seidman, Joel. *Russia—Democracy or Dictatorship?* New York: League for Industrial Democracy, 1939.

The Socialist Cure for a Sick Society. New York: John Day Company, Inc., 1932.

A Socialist Looks at the New Deal. New York: League for Industrial Democracy, 1933.

A Socialist Looks at the United Nations. Syracuse, N.Y.: Syracuse University Press, 1945.

The Truth about Socialism. New York: Socialist Party, 1943.

War as a Socialist Sees It. New York: League for Industrial Democracy, 1936.

What Is Industrial Democracy? New York: League for Industrial Democracy, 1925.

World Federation: What Are the Difficulties? New York: Post War World Council, 1942.

ARTICLES

"American Socialism's Weakest Link," *World Tomorrow,* Vol. XVII (April 12, 1934).

"America's Contribution to an Enduring Peace," *Annals of the American Academy of Political and Social Science,* Vol. CCX (July, 1940).

"And If . . . and If . . . ," *Newsweek,* Vol. LVI (August 22, 1960).

"Are We as Right as We Think?" *Saturday Review,* Vol. XLII (April 18, 1959).

"Armaments and Peace," *Annals of the American Academy of Political and Social Science: Present Day Causes of International Friction and Their Elimination,* Vol. CXLIV (July, 1929).

"Bolshevism, Violence and Expropriation," *World Tomorrow,* Vol. II (March, 1919).

"Can Pacifism Act against Injustice?" *World Tomorrow,* Vol. VII (July, 1924).

"Capitalism Will Not Plan," *New Republic,* Vol. LXVII (August 12, 1931).

"The Christian and the Socialist Revolution," *World Tomorrow,* Vol. II (November, 1919).

"The Church as War Maker," *New Republic,* Vol. XXXII (October 25, 1922).

"Civil Rights, but Not Conspiracy," *New York Times Magazine,* January 7, 1951.

"Collective Security and Socialism," *Socialist Review*, Vol. VI (May–June, 1938).

"The Conscientious Objector: II. Conscience and the Church," *Nation*, Vol. CV (August 23, 1917).

"Conscientious Objector Replies," *New Republic*, Vol. XI (July 7, 1917).

"Credo of an Old-Fashioned Socialist," *American Mercury*, Vol. LVI (April, 1943).

"Dangerous Illusions about the Next War," *Socialist Review*, Vol. VI (March–April, 1939).

"The Dissenter's Role in a Totalitarian Age," *New York Times Magazine*, November 20, 1949.

"European Legislation for Industrial Peace," *Foreign Affairs*, Vol. XVI (October, 1937).

"The Failure of Organized Socialism in America," *Progressive*, Vol. XXIII (January, 1959).

"The Fate of a Gambler's Civilization," *Current History*, Vol. XXXVI (May, 1932).

"The Future of the Socialist Party," *Nation*, Vol. CXXXV (December 14, 1932).

"Great Challenge of the Dissenter," *New York Times Magazine*, November 15, 1959.

"Hastening the Day," *World Tomorrow*, Vol. XVII (March 15, 1934).

"How Can We Escape War? Neutrality Plus Socialism," *Nation*, Vol. CVL (December 25, 1937).

"How Democratic Are Labor Unions?" *Harper's Magazine*, Vol. CLXXXIV (May, 1942).

"How to Fight for Democracy," *Annals of the American Academy of Political and Social Science: Defending America's Future*, Vol. CCXVI (July, 1941).

"If War Is to Be Averted," *World Tomorrow*, Vol. XVI (October 26, 1933).

"I'm Glad I'm Not Running This Time," *American Magazine*, Vol. CLIV (October, 1952).

"Is Peaceful Revolution Possible?" *World Tomorrow*, Vol. XV (September 14, 1932).

"Is the Extension of the Draft Necessary?" *Vital Speeches*, Vol. VI (August 15, 1941).

"Is Violence the Way?" *World Tomorrow*, Vol. II (May, 1919).

"Mr. Wilson's Tragedy and Ours," *World Tomorrow*, Vol. IV (March, 1921).

"A Message to Johnson," *Sane World*, Vol. V (January, 1966).

"New Deal or New Day," *World Tomorrow*, Vol. XVI (August 31, 1933).

"Now I Am Ready for the League," *World Tomorrow*, Vol. XIII (April, 1930).

"Organization or Violence?" *Nation*, Vol. CIX (October 4, 1919).

"Our Immediate Task," *World Tomorrow*, Vol. XVII (February 15, 1934).

"Our One Hope for Peace," *Saturday Evening Post*, Vol. CCXXIV (February 2, 1952).

"Our War with Japan," *Commonwealth*, Vol. XLII (April 20, 1945).

"The Outlawry of War," *World Tomorrow*, Vol. VII (January, 1924).

"The Pacifist's Dilemma," *Nation*, Vol. CXLIV (January 16, 1937).

"Plutocracy in the Saddle: Does Wall Street Rule Us?" *Forum*, Vol. LXXXII (July, 1929).

"President Johnson's Great Society," *Christian Century*, Vol. LXXXIII (March 9, 1966).

"Production for Use or for Profit?" *Rotarian*, Vol. LXVII (October, 1945).

"Proposals for Action at Detroit," *World Tomorrow*, Vol. XVII (April 26, 1934).

"Reflections of an Old Campaigner," *Commonwealth*, Vol. XLI (December 22, 1944).

"Reflections on Russia and Revolution," *World Tomorrow*, Vol. III (September, 1920).

"The Religion of Free Men," *New Republic,* Vol. XI (May 26, 1917).

"Removing Economic Barriers to Peace," *World Tomorrow,* Vol. XIV (November, 1931).

"Socialism's Impact on America," *Modern Review,* Vol. II (January, 1948).

"A Socialist Looks at the Campaign," *Progressive,* Vol. XXIV (November, 1960).

"Socialist Looks at the Constitution," *Annals of the American Academy of Political and Social Science,* Vol. CLXXXV (May, 1936).

"A Socialist Program for Banking," *Nation,* Vol. CXXXVI (March 22, 1933).

"A Socialist Reports on Socialism," *New York Times Magazine,* October 30, 1955.

"Something Better Than Dumbarton Oaks," *Vital Speeches,* Vol. XI (April 15, 1943).

"Spain—a Socialist View," *Nation,* Vol. CXLIV (June 19, 1937).

"Starve and Prosper," *Current History,* Vol. XL (May, 1934).

"The Status of Radicalism in America," *World Tomorrow,* Vol. IV (December, 1921).

"Surveying the New Deal," *World Tomorrow,* Vol. XVII (January 18, 1934).

"The Trouble with ADA," *Progressive,* Vol. XVIII (September, 1954).

"The 'Unholy Union' of Prohibition and Politics," *Current History,* Vol. XXXI (October, 1929).

"We Needn't Go to War," *Harper's Magazine,* Vol. CLXXVII (November, 1938).

"What, Then, Shall We Do?" *World Tomorrow,* Vol. II (October, 1919).

"What about the Use of Violence?" *World Tomorrow,* Vol. XV (April, 1932).

"What Can We Expect from a Third Party," *World Tomorrow,* Vol. VII (June, 1924).

"What Happened at Detroit," *World Tomorrow,* Vol. XVII (June 28, 1934).

"What Has Roosevelt Accomplished?" *Nation,* Vol. CXXXVI (April 12, 1933).

"What of the Church?" *New World* [later entitled *World To-morrow*], Vol. I (February, 1918).

"What's Right with America," *Harper's Magazine,* Vol. CLXLIV (March, 1947).

"Who Are the Liberals?" *American Mercury,* Vol. LXV (November, 1947).

RECORDING

"Norman Thomas Reminisces." New Rochelle, N.Y.: Spoken Arts, Inc., 1959.

OFFICIAL SOCIALIST-PARTY DOCUMENTS AND PUBLICATIONS

Eighteenth National Convention Handbook. Chicago: National Socialist Party Headquarters, 1934.

The Intelligent Voter's Guide: Official 1928 Campaign Handbook of the Socialist Party. New York: Socialist National Committee, 1928.

National Convention of the Socialist Party "Proceedings," 1928–40.

National Platform of the Socialist Party Adopted at the May 7–8–9 National Convention at Reading, Pa. New York: Socialist Campaign Headquarters, 1948.

Shapiro, Theodore; Delson, Robert; and Coleman, McAlister. *Towards a Militant Program for the Socialist Party of America.* New York: Program Committee, 1934.

UNPUBLISHED MANUSCRIPTS

Conaway, Orrin Bryte. "An Investigation of the Organization and Policies of Selected Third Parties in the United States, 1939–1948, with Special Reference to Foreign Policy." Unpublished Ph.D. dissertation, Maxwell Graduate School of Citizenship and Public Affairs, Syracuse University, 1950.

Hall, John Danforth. "The Socialist Party and Its Presidential

Vote, 1904–1936." Unpublished Master's thesis, Maxwell Graduate School of Citizenship and Public Affairs, Syracuse University, 1938.

Seidler, Murray. "The Birth of the CIO." Unpublished Master's thesis, Faculty of Political Science, Columbia University, 1946.

Books and Pamphlets

Allen, Devere. *Adventurous Americans*. New York: Farrar and Rinehart, 1932.

American Labor Year Book, Vols. III–XIII. New York: Rand School of Social Science, 1919–32.

Barck, Oscar T., and Blake, Nelson M. *Since 1900: A History of the United States*. New York: Macmillan Co., 1947.

Barnes, Joseph. *Willkie*. New York: Simon and Schuster, Inc., 1952.

Beard, Charles and Mary. *America in Midpassage*. New York: Macmillan Co., 1939.

———. *The Rise of American Civilization*. New York: Macmillan Co., 1927.

Bingham, Alfred M. *Insurgent America*. New York: Harper & Brothers, 1935.

Blake, Nelson M. *A Short History of American Life*. New York: McGraw-Hill Book Co., Inc., 1952.

Borkenau, Franz. *World Communism: A History of the Communist International*. New York: W. W. Norton & Company, Inc., 1939.

Brembeck, Winston Lamont, and Howell, William Smiley. *Persuasion, a Means of Social Control*. Englewood Cliffs, N.J.: Prentice-Hall, Inc., 1952.

Brissenden, Paul F. *The I.W.W.: A Study of American Syndicalism*. New York: Columbia University Press, 1919.

Brooks, John Graham. *American Syndicalism: The I.W.W.* New York: Macmillan Co., 1913.

Browder, Earl. *Communism in the United States*. New York: International Publishers Co., Inc., 1935.

————. *The People's Front.* New York: International Publishers Co., Inc., 1938.

————. *Victory—and After.* New York: International Publishers Co., Inc., 1942.

Bryce, James. *The American Commonwealth.* 2 vols. New York: Macmillan Co., 1891.

Budenz, Louis Francis. *This Is My Story.* New York: Whittlesey House, McGraw-Hill Book Co., Inc., 1947.

Burns, James MacGregor. *John Kennedy: A Political Profile.* New York: Harcourt, Brace & Company, 1960.

————. *Roosevelt: The Lion and the Fox.* New York: Harcourt, Brace & Company, 1956.

Calverton, V. F. *The Making of Society.* New York: Modern Library, Inc., 1937.

Cannon, James P. *The History of American Trotskyism.* New York: Pioneer Publishers, 1944.

Carroll, Mollie Ray. *Labor and Politics.* Boston: Houghton Mifflin Company, 1923.

Coleman, McAlister. *The Man Unafraid: Eugene V. Debs.* New York: Greenberg, 1931.

Commager, Henry S. *The American Mind.* New Haven, Conn.: Yale University Press, 1950.

Commous, John R., and Associates. *History of Labour in the United States.* 4 vols. New York: Macmillan Co., 1918–35.

Curti, Merle. *The Growth of American Thoughts.* New York: Harper & Brothers, 1951.

Davis, Jerome. *Contemporary Social Movements.* New York: Century House, 1930.

Debs, Eugene. *Writings and Speeches of Eugene V. Debs.* New York: Hermitage Press, 1948.

Dos Passos, John Roderigo. *U.S.A.* New York: Modern Library, Inc., 1930.

Douglas, Paul Howard. *The Coming of a New Party.* New York: Whittlesey House, McGraw-Hill Book Co., Inc., 1932.

Draper, Theodore. *American Communism and Soviet Russia.* New York: Viking Press, Inc., 1960.

––––––. *The Roots of American Communism*. New York: Viking Press, Inc., 1957.

Dumond, Dwight L. *Roosevelt to Roosevelt: The United States in the Twentieth Century*. New York: Henry Holt & Co., Inc., 1937.

Egbert, Donald Drew, and Persons, Stow (eds.). *Socialism and American Life*. 2 vols. Princeton, N.J.: Princeton University Press, 1952.

Fine, Nathan. *Labor and Farmer Parties in the United States, 1828–1928*. New York: Rand School of Social Science, 1928.

Fosdick, Raymond B. *Chronicle of a Generation*. New York: Harper & Brothers, 1958.

Ginger, Ray. *The Bending Cross: A Biography of Eugene V. Debs*. New Brunswick, N.J.: Rutgers University Press, 1949.

Gosnell, Harold F. *Boss Platt and His New York State Machine*. Chicago: University of Chicago Press, 1924.

Gouldner, Alvin W. (ed.). *Studies in Leadership: Leadership and Democratic Action*. New York: Harper & Brothers, 1950.

Greer, Thomas H. *American Social Reform Movements: Their Pattern Since 1865*. New York: Prentice-Hall, Inc., 1949.

Hacker, Louis M., and Zahler, Helen S. *The United States in the Twentieth Century*. New York: Appleton-Century-Crofts, Inc., 1952.

Harris, Herbert. *Labor's Civil War*. New York: Alfred A. Knopf, Inc., 1940.

Haynes, Frederick Emory. *Social Politics in the United States*. New York: Houghton Mifflin Company, 1924.

Heberle, Rudolph. *Social Movements: An Introduction to Political Sociology*. New York: Appleton-Century-Crofts, Inc., 1951.

Hillquit, Morris. *History of Socialism in the United States*. New York: Funk & Wagnalls Co., 1910.

––––––. *Loose Leaves from a Busy Life*. New York: Macmillan Co., 1934.

––––––. *Socialism in Theory and Practice*. New York: Macmillan Co., 1913.

Holmes, John Haynes. *I Speak for Myself*. New York: Harper & Brothers, 1959.

Hook, Sidney. *Heresy, Yes—Conspiracy, No.* New York: John Day, 1953.

———. *Towards the Understanding of Karl Marx.* New York: John Day Company, Inc., 1933.

Hopkins, Charles. *The Rise of the Social Gospel in American Protestantism, 1865–1915.* New Haven, Conn.: Yale University Press, 1940.

Howe, Irving, and Coser, Lewis. *The American Communist Party: A Critical History, 1919–1951.* Boston: Beacon Press, 1957.

——— and Widick, B. J. *The UAW and Walter Reuther.* New York: Random House, 1949.

Joint Legislative Committee Investigating Seditious Activities, New York State, 1920 (ed.). *Revolutionary Radicalism: Its History, Purpose and Tactics.* 4 vols. New York: J. B. Lyon, 1920.

Kempton, Murray. *Part of Our Time: Some Ruins and Monuments of the Thirties.* New York: Simon and Schuster, Inc., 1955.

Key, V. O., Jr. *Politics, Parties, and Pressure Groups.* New York: Thomas Y. Crowell Company, 1948.

Kipnis, Ira. *The American Socialist Movement, 1897–1912.* New York: Columbia University Press, 1952.

Konvitz, Milton R. *Expanding Liberty: Freedom's Gains in Post-war America.* New York: Viking Press, 1966.

La Follette, Belle Case and Fola. *Robert M. La Follette, 1855–1925.* 2 vols. New York: Macmillan Co., 1953.

Laidler, Harry W. *Social-Economic Movements: An Historical and Comparative Survey of Socialism, Communism, Co-operation, Utopianism, and Other Systems of Reform and Reconstruction.* New York: Thomas Y. Crowell Company, 1948.

———. *Socialism in the United States: A Brief History.* New York: League for Industrial Democracy, 1952.

Lasswell, Harold D., and Blumenstock, Dorothy. *World Revolutionary Propaganda.* New York: Alfred A. Knopf, Inc., 1939.

Lavine, Harold, and Wechsler, James. *War Propaganda and the United States*. New Haven, Conn.: Yale University Press, 1940.

League for Industrial Democracy. *Thirty-five Years of Educational Pioneering*. New York: League for Industrial Democracy, 1941.

Levinson, Edward. *Labor on the March*. New York: Harper & Brothers, 1938.

Lyons, Eugene. *Assignment in Utopia*. New York: Harcourt, Brace & Company, 1937.

————. *The Red Decade*. New York: Bobbs-Merrill Company, Inc., 1941.

MacDougal, Curtis D. *Understanding Public Opinion: A Guide for Newspapermen and Newspaper Readers*. New York: Macmillan Co., 1952.

MacKay, Kenneth Campbell. *The Progressive Movement of 1924*. New York: Columbia University Press, 1947.

Madison, Charles A. *American Labor Leaders: Personalities and Forces in the Labor Movement*. New York: Harper & Brothers, 1950.

————. *Critics and Crusaders: A Century of American Protest*. New York: Henry Holt & Co., Inc., 1947.

Matthiessen, F. O. *1907–1950*. New York: Henry Schuman, 1950.

May, Henry F. *Protestant Churches and Industrial America*. New York: Harper & Brothers, 1949.

Merriam, Charles E., and Gosnell, Harold F. *The American Party System: An Introduction to the Study of Political Parties in the United States*. 4th edition. New York: Macmillan Co., 1949.

Morison, Samuel E., and Commager, Henry S. *The Growth of the American Republic*. 2 vols. New York: Oxford University Press, 1960.

Murray, Robert K. *The Red Scare*. Minneapolis, Minn.: University of Minnesota Press, 1955.

Nash, Howard P. *Third Parties in American Politics*. Washington, D.C.: Public Affairs Press, 1959.

"Norman Thomas," *Current Biography, 1944: Who's News and Why,* ed. Anna Rothe. New York: H. W. Wilson Co., 1944.

Oneal, James. *Some Pages of Party History.* New York: Published by the Author at 7 E. 15th St., 1935.

———— and Werner, G. D. *American Communism: A Critical Analysis of Its Origins, Development and Programs.* New York: E. P. Dutton & Co., Inc., 1947.

Parrington, Vernon L. *Main Currents in American Thought.* New York: Harcourt, Brace & Company, 1927.

Petersen, Arnold. *Bourgeois Socialism: Its Rise and Collapse in America.* New York: New York Labor News, 1951.

Phillips, Harlan B. (ed.). *Felix Frankfurter Reminisces.* New York: Reynal & Company, Inc., 1960.

Porter, Harold K., and Johnson, Donald Bruce. *National Party Platforms, 1840–1956.* Urbana, Ill.: University of Illinois Press, 1956.

Quint, Howard H. *The Forging of American Socialism: Origins of the Modern Movement.* Columbia, S.C.: University of South Carolina Press, 1953.

Rauch, Basil. *The History of the New Deal.* New York: Creative Age, 1944.

Sait, Edward M. *American Parties and Elections.* New York: D. Appleton-Century Company, Inc., 1939.

Salter, John T. *The American Politician.* Chapel Hill, N.C.: University of North Carolina Press, 1938.

Schlesinger, Arthur M., Sr. *The American as Reformer.* Cambridge, Mass., Harvard University Press, 1950.

Schlesinger, Arthur M., Jr. *The Coming of the New Deal.* (*The Age of Roosevelt,* Vol. II.) Boston: Houghton Mifflin Company, 1959.

————. *The Crisis of the Old Order, 1919–1933.* (*The Age of Roosevelt,* Vol. I.) Boston: Houghton Mifflin Company, 1957.

————. *The Politics of Upheaval.* (*The Age of Roosevelt,* Vol. III.) Boston: Houghton Mifflin Company, 1959.

Schriftgresser, Karl. *This Was Normalcy.* Boston: Little, Brown & Co., 1940.

Shannon, David A. *The Socialist Party of America: A History.* New York: Macmillan Co., 1955.

Sharpe, Doris Robinson. *Walter Rauschenbusch.* New York: Macmillan Co., 1941.

Stolberg, Benjamin. *The Story of the CIO.* New York: Viking Press, Inc., 1938.

Symes, Lillian, and Clement, Travers. *Rebel America: The Story of Social Revolt in the United States.* New York: Harper & Brothers, 1934.

Truman, David B. *The Governmental Process: Political Interests and Public Opinion.* New York: Alfred A. Knopf, Inc., 1951.

The Unofficial Observer. *American Messiahs.* New York: Simon and Schuster, Inc., 1935.

Viereck, Peter. *Shame and Glory of the Intellectuals: Babbitt Jr. vs. the Rediscovery of Values.* Boston: Beacon Press, 1953.

Waldman, Louis. *Labor Lawyer.* New York: E. P. Dutton & Co., Inc., 1944.

Wechsler, James. *The Age of Suspicion.* New York: Random House, 1953.

———. *Revolt on Campus.* New York: Covich, Friede, Inc., 1935.

Wecter, Dixon. *The Age of the Great Depression, 1929–1941.* New York: Macmillan Co., 1948.

Wilson, Woodrow. *The New Freedom.* New York: Doubleday, Page & Co., 1913.

Magazine and Newspaper Articles of Special Interest

Baldwin, Roger. "In Search of Peace, Freedom, Plenty," *New York Herald Tribune Book Review,* April 8, 1951.

Bercowitz, Anna. "The Milwaukee Convention," *American Socialist Quarterly,* Vol. I (Summer, 1932).

Chaffee, Edmund B. "Norman Thomas Leaves the Ministry," *Christian Century,* Vol. XLVIII (October 28, 1931).

Coleman, McAlister. "Norman Thomas," *Nation,* Vol. CXXVII (August 8, 1928).

Douglas, Paul H. "An Idealist Masters Realities," *World Tomorrow,* Vol. XV (May, 1932).

———. "Why I Am for Thomas," *New Republic,* Vol. LVI (October 24, 1928).

Fuess, Claude M. "Norman Thomas: Socialist Crusader," *Current History,* Vol. XXXVII (October, 1932).

Ghent, W. J. "Collapse of Socialism in the United States," *Current History,* Vol. XXIV (May, 1926).

Graduate Faculties *Newsletter,* Columbia University, November, 1959.

Herberg, Will. "What Happened to American Socialism?" *Commentary,* Vol. XII (October, 1951).

Hillquit, Morris. "Problems Before the National Convention," *American Socialist Quarterly,* Vol. I (April, 1932).

"If I Were a Politician: The Story of Norman Thomas," *World Tomorrow,* Vol. XIII (June, 1930).

Josephson, Matthew. "Norman Thomas: The Enraptured Socialist," *New Republic,* Vol. LXXI (August 10, 1932).

Kantorovitch, Haim. "Notes on the United Front Problem," *American Socialist Monthly,* Vol. V (May, 1936).

Karsner, David. "The Passing of the Socialist Party," *Current History,* Vol. XX (June, 1924).

King, Martin Luther. "The Bravest Man I Ever Met," *Pageant,* Vol. XX (June, 1965).

Kreuger, Maynard C. "Is Socialism Dead in America?" *Progressive,* Vol. XVI (August, 1952).

Lane, Arthur Bliss; Lerner, Max; Rogge, O. John; and Thomas, Norman. "How Is Peace with Russia Possible?" *Town Meeting,* 1948.

MacArthur, Harry. "Thomas Stars in New Role," *Sunday Star* (Washington, D.C.), November 28, 1948.

MacDonald, Dwight. "Thomas for President?" *Politics,* Vol. I (October, 1944).

Mencken, H. L. "Mencken Thanks Thomas: Rare Political Hullabaloo by Really Intelligent Man," *Baltimore Sun,* October 18, 1948.

"Norman Thomas Re-examines U.S. Capitalism," *Fortune,* Vol. XLII (September, 1950).

Oneal, James. "The American Trade Union Movement," *American Socialist Quarterly,* Vol. II (Winter, 1933).

——. "Changing Fortunes of American Socialism," *Current History,* Vol. XX (April, 1924).

"Playboy Interview: Norman Thomas," *Playboy,* XIII (November, 1966).

Raskin, A. H. "Norman Thomas Sparkling at 70," *New York Times,* November 20, 1954.

Reeve, F. D. "Robert Frost Confronts Khrushchev," *The Atlantic,* Vol. CCXII (September, 1963).

Rosenberg, Bernard. "The Example of Norman Thomas," *Dissent,* Vol. XI (Autumn, 1964).

Shapiro, Theodore. "The Militant Point of View," *American Socialist Quarterly,* Vol. I (April, 1932).

Shils, Edward A. "Socialism in America," *University Observer,* Vol. I (Spring–Summer, 1947).

Sorokin, P. A. "Leaders of Labor and Radical Movements in the United States and Foreign Countries," *American Journal of Sociology,* Vol. XXXIII (1927).

Sugrue, Francis. "Norman Thomas, at 75, Still Has Plenty to Say," *New York Herald Tribune,* November 19, 1959.

Swados, Harvey. "New Reasons for an Old Cause," *Saturday Review,* Vol. XLVII (February 1, 1964).

Thornton, Willis. "Smoking Out the Candidates," *Cleveland Press* (Ohio), June 3, 1936.

"The Unknockables," *Esquire,* Vol. LXV (June, 1966).

Woolf, S. J. "Thomas, 'If I Were Elected President,'" *New York Times Magazine,* June 7, 1936.

Wright, Sylvia. "The Dean of Protest," *Life,* Vol. LX (January 14, 1966).

Index

Addams, Jane, 72
Agricultural Adjustment Act, 2.
  See also New Deal
Agricultural Workers' Union, 85
Allen, Devere, 127, 132–134
Altman, Jack, 173, 176, 200, 207, 211
Amalgamated Clothing Workers' Union, 142, 162, 190–192
Amalgamated Meat Cutters, 59
American Civil Liberties Union, 74, 80, 84, 241, 319
American Committee for Cultural Freedom, 241
American Committee for Tibetan Refugees, 319
American Committee on Africa, 241, 319
American Committee on Conditions in Ireland, 72
American Federation of Labor, 34, 43, 63, 65, 66, 194, 195, 313
American Federation of Teachers, 190
American Friends Service Committee, 319
American Labor party, 173, 178, 190, 191, 199–202, 219
"American Plan," The, 59
American Railway Union, 38
Americans for Democratic Action, 211, 217, 221, 223

American Socialist party, 37–40, 75
American Socialist Quarterly, 193
American Tobacco Company, 333
American Workingmen's Alliance, 31
Appeal group. See Socialist party: Appeal group
Austrian Social Democracy, 114, 135

Baker, Ray Stannard, 36
Bakunin, Michael, 31
Balaguer, Joaquin, 336
Baldwin, Roger, 27, 80
Barnes, Harry Elmer, 73, 255
Baruch, Bernard, 219, 246
Bauer, Otto, 114
Beard, Charles A., 70, 205
Bebel, August, 113
Bellamy, Edward, 36
Benson, Allan, 49
Berger, Victor L., 38, 43, 45, 46, 52, 74
Berle, Adolf, 245
Biemiller, Andrew J., 107, 132
Bilbo, Theodore, 217, 220
Blanshard, Paul, 73, 105, 113, 188, 189, 235
Bliven, Bruce, 73, 205
Blum, Leon, 245
Boas, Franz, 235
"Bolshevo," 182

385

Bosch, Juan, 336
British Labor party, 58, 135
Brookhart, Smith W., and the CPPA, 62
Brotherhood of Painters, 60
Brotherhood of Sleeping Car Porters, 190, 329
Browder, Earl, 82, 155, 156, 185
Bryce, James, 84, 85
Bureau for the Fourth International, 176
Burleson, Albert S., 71

Cairo Conference, 278
Camp Tamiment, 113
Cannon, James P., 174, 177
Case, Clifford, 245
Chamberlain, John, 205
Chase, Stuart, 73
Chiang Kai-shek, 282
CIO, 193, 195, 196
City Central Committee of the Party, 176
Clarity group. *See* Socialist party: Clarity group
Coleman, McAlister, 105
Committee for Industrial Organization, 195
Committee for the Defense of Trotsky, 180, 181
Committee for World Development and Disarmament, 319
Committee on Free Elections in the Dominican Republic, 336–337
Committee on War and Militarism, 50–52
Communist International, 55, 56
Communist Labor party, 57
Communist Manifesto, 260, 261
Communist party, 57, 171, 196. *See also* Socialist party and Communism

"Comrade Sharts," 133
Conference for Progressive Political Action, 60–68
Congress of Racial Equality, 319, 330
Coolidge, Calvin, 59, 66, 333
Cousins, Norman, 1, 245, 328
Cripps, Sir Stafford, 181
Crosswaith, Frank, 211

Daniel, Franz, 107, 158
Darrow, Clarence, 73
Davis, Jerome, 190
Davis, John W., 63, 66
Debs, Eugene V., 38, 39, 43–45, 46, 49, 52, 53, 56, 57, 67, 70, 71, 74, 87, 88, 199, 301, 308, 311–313
Declaration of Principles, 127–150, 154
de Leon, Daniel, 33, 34, 35, 36, 39, 43. *See also* Socialist Labor party
"Democratic Socialism," 268–270, 286, 287
Denver Post, 246
Depression, 75, 76, 107
de Sola Pool, David. *See* Pool, David de Sola
Detroit Convention of 1934, 125–150, 154. *See also* Socialist party; Declaration of Principles
Dewey, John, 73, 105, 106, 235
Dewey, Thomas E., 92, 93, 218, 219, 223, 231
Dodds, Harold W., 245
Dollfuss, Engelbert, 114
Dominican Republic, 336–337
Dos Passos, John, 95, 205
Douglas, Paul H., 73, 79, 105, 235, 243
Dubinsky, David, 162, 190, 191, 200, 244
DuBois, W. E. B., 105
Dulles, John Foster, 243

Edman, Irwin, 235
Eisenhower, Dwight D., 238, 325–326
End Poverty in California Plan, 189
Engels, Friedrich, 31, 36, 259
Era of normalcy, 58, 75
Ernst, Morris L., 105
Esquire, 339

Fabian Society, 236
Fairchild, Henry Pratt, 205
Fair Deal, 267
Fair Employment Practices Commission, 216
Farmer, James, 330, 331
Farmer Labor party, 60, 61
Farmer-Labor Political Federation, 200
"Farmers' and Workers' Rights Amendment," 169
Farmers' National Council, 61
Federal Communications Commission, 289
Fellowship of Reconciliation, 18, 20
First International, 31, 32
Flynn, John T., 205
Foreign Language Federation, 41, 56
Fosdick, Harry Emerson, 235, 245
Fosdick, Raymond B., 8, 9
Foster, William Z., 57, 172
Franco, Francisco, 203, 205, 282
Frankfurter, Felix, 226
Frazier-Lunden Bill, 168
Frazier, Lynn, and the CPPA, 62
Friedman, Samuel, 236, 237
Frost, Robert, 339–340

Gandhi, Mahatma, 213, 275, 279
General German Workingmen's Union, 31

George, Henry, 36
Gerber, Julius, 157, 192
German Socialist party, 58
Gideonse, Harry D., 245
Gitlow, Benjamin, 71, 172
Goldwater, Barry, 324, 340
Gompers, Samuel, 43, 62, 71
Grangers, 36
Great Society, 334–336
Green, William, 245
Gross, Murray, 211

Hacker, Louis, 235
Hague, Frank, 85, 95, 217, 220
Hapgood, Powers, 133–158
Harding, Warren G., 3, 4
Harriman, Job, 39
Hayes, Max, 39
Herberg, Will, 246, 316
Herron, George D., 52
Hillman, Sidney, 162, 191, 192, 199
Hillquit, Morris, 43–67 *passim,* 74, 105–113 *passim,* 135, 169, 199
Hillquit Report, 50–52
Hiroshima and Nagasaki, 228–230
Hiss, Alger, 291
Hitler, Adolph, 113, 166, 184, 187, 206, 222, 232, 256, 275
Hoan, Daniel W., 61, 110, 126, 154, 161, 163, 200, 296, 297
Ho Chi Minh, 337
Hochman, Julius, 190
Holmes, John Haynes, 70, 144, 203, 205, 235, 265
Hook, Sidney, 205, 235
Hoopes, Darlington, 236, 237
Hoover, Herbert, 92, 116
Hosiery Workers' Union, 162
Hovde, Bryn J., 245
Howe, Quincy, 245
Humphrey, Hubert, 238, 243, 260, 265

Hunter, Robert, 53
Hutchins, Robert M., 235, 245

Ickes, Harold, 245
Independent Labor League of America, 196
Industrial Workers of the World, 313
Institute for International Labor Research, 319
Inter-Collegiate Socialist Society, 42, 73
International Ladies' Garment Workers Union, 162, 190, 191, 200, 211

Japanese Americans, Internment of, 213, 214, 215
Jewish Daily Forward, 42, 106, 110, 113, 132, 141, 153, 159, 165
Johaux, Leon, 265
Johnson, Lyndon B., 319, 322–323, 331, 334–336
Johnston, William H., 61, 64
Jones, Rufus H., 70

Kaltenborn, H. V., 245
Kautsky, Karl, 55, 113, 143
Keep America Out of War Congress, 205
Kempton, Murray, 95
Kennedy, John F., 238, 239, 319, 331–334
Kennedy, Joseph, 239
Kennedy, Robert, 327
Khrushchev, Nikita, 280, 287, 327
King, Martin Luther, 330
Kirkpatrick, George R., 49, 132
Knights of Labor, 34, 36
Kreuger, Maynard, 107, 157, 158, 199, 201, 214, 215
Krzycki, Leo, 158, 162, 192

Labor, 190–203
Labor Unions. *See* individual groups
La Follette, Robert M., 62–67
La Follette, Susan, 205
La Guardia, Fiorello, 188, 189, 200
Laidler, Harry W., 73, 163, 200, 205
Langer, William, 243
Laski, Harold J., 245
Lasswell, Harold, 245
League for Independent Political Action, 105, 106
League for Industrial Democracy, 73, 77, 78, 105, 145, 163, 184, 185, 200, 241
League of Nations, 283
Lee, Algernon, 132, 133, 144, 157
Lenin, Nikolai, 143, 173, 183, 280, 290
Lerner, Max, 235
Levinson, Edward, 105
Lewis, Alfred Baker, 207, 211
Lewis, John L., 195, 196, 199
Lewis, Sinclair, 255
Libby, Frederick J., 205
Life, 339
Lindeman, Eduard, 245
Lippmann, Walter, 245
Lloyd, Henry D., 36
Lochner, Louis P., 70
London, Jack, 42, 52, 73
Lovestone, Jay, 71, 171, 172
Lovett, Robert M., 73, 235

McAdoo, William, 63
MacArthur, Harry, 89
McCarran Internal Security Act (1950), 291, 329
McCarthyism, 233, 238, 290
McConnell, Francis, 73
MacDonald, Ramsay, 55, 93

MacDougal, Curtis D., 247
Machinists' Union, 61
Maciver, Robert M., 245
McLevy, Jasper, 144, 163
Marshall, George, 238
Marx, Karl, 31, 143, 173, 247, 258–261 *passim,* 280
Matthiessen, F. O., 86
Mattoon, Emma. *See* Thomas, Emma
Mattoon, Reverend Stephen (maternal grandfather of NT), 5, 6
Maurer, James H., 75, 144
Maverick, Maury, 117
Mayer, Milton, 96
Mazey, Emil, 98
Mazzini, Guiseppe, 31
Mechanics Educational Society, 195
Meiklejohn, Alexander, 73
Mencken, H. L., 90, 255
Militant Group. *See* Socialist party: Militant Group
Militants. *See* Old guard-militant controversy
Mills, C. Wright, 235
Mitchell, Broadus, 235
Mollet, Guy, 245
Morgenthau Plan, 232
Morse, Wayne, 243, 245
Moscow-Berlin Pact (1939), 187
Muckrakers, 36
Mussolini, Benito, 113
Muste, A. J., 205

Nagasaki. *See* Hiroshima and Nagasaki
Nation, 71, 73, 74, 301
National Catholic Welfare Council, 61
National Committee for a Sane

Nuclear Policy, 241, 318–319, 321
National Conventions of the Socialist party. *See* Socialist party: National Conventions
National Executive Committee of the Socialist party, 137, 142, 152–160 *passim,* 172, 176, 192
National Industrial Recovery Act, 116, 194, 195
National Methodist Federations of Social Services, 61
National Sharecroppers Fund, 319
Nearing, Scott, 70
Nehru, Jawaharlal, 245
Neue Beginnen Group, 135
Nevins, Allan, 245
New America, 319
New Deal, 2, 19, 85, 111–120 *passim,* 188, 189, 198, 202, 210, 222, 267, 289, 302, 303, 316
New Freedom, 37, 50, 53
New Frontier, 331–334
New Leader, 113, 142, 145, 153, 159
New Voice, 153
New York City Central Committee, 157
New York City Socialist party, 211
New York Zoological Society, 319
Niebuhr, Reinhold, 74, 105, 113, 165, 211, 217, 221–224, 234
Nixon, Richard, 237–239
Nonpartisan League, 60, 61
Norris, George W., 62, 72, 106
North American Federation of the International Workingmen's Association, 32

Old guard-militant controversy, 60–65, 105–114, 124–159, 295, 296

Oneal, James, 61, 145, 146, 193
Organization of American States, 336
Overstreet, Harry, 70
Oxnam, G. Bromley, 245

Pageant magazine, 330
Palmer, A. Mitchell, 57, 70
Panken, Jacob, 132
Pearl Harbor, 206, 212, 220, 221
People's party, 36
Petersen, Arnold, 246, 247
Phillips, Morgan, 245
Phillips, Wendell, 341
Pool, David de Sola, 205
Porter, Paul, 105, 173, 207
Post War World Council, 241, 319
Potsdam Conference, 278
Progressive party (1924), 60–68; (1948), 173, 232
Progressives, 106–108, 113
Pullman Strike of 1894, 38

Railway Workers, 59
Randolph, A. Philip, 190, 329, 331
Rand School of Social Science, 42, 113, 165, 337
Raskin, A. H., 327–328
Rauschenbusch, Dr. Walter, 14
"Red scare," 59, 69–71, 132
Renner, Karl, 245
Reuter, Ernst, 245
Reuther, Victor, 98, 196
Reuther, Walter, 98, 197, 198, 202, 245
Revolutionary Policy Committee, 115, 173, 302
Rieve, Emil, 162, 190
Roosevelt, Eleanor, 1, 225
Roosevelt, Franklin Delano, 2, 85, 88, 93, 117, 190–192, 196, 204–232 *passim*, 267, 278, 316

Roosevelt, Theodore, 66, 118
Rugg, Harold, 235
Russell, Bertrand, 283
Russian Revolution of 1917, 54
Rustin, Bayard, 329

St. Louis Declaration, 54, 133, 135
St. Louis Resolution. *See* Hillquit Report
Sayre, John Nevin, 71
Scales, Junius, 327–328
Schlesinger, Arthur M., Jr., 245
Schlesinger, Arthur M., Sr., 245
Schlossberg, Joseph, 190
Seamen's Union, 59
Second International, 48, 49
Seidman, Joel, 186
Senior, Clarence, 149, 150, 151
Shannon, Fred M., 235
Shapiro, Theodore, 107
Sheean, Vincent, 235
Shipstead, Hendrik, and the CPPA, 62
"Silent split," 210
Silone, Ignazio, 287
Simons, A. M., 52
Sinclair, Upton, 42, 53, 73, 189, 190, 206
Smith Act of 1940, 291, 327, 329
Smith, Alfred E., 66
Smith, H. Alexander, 243
Sobell, Morton, 328
Social Democracy, 38
Social Democratic Federation, 163, 190, 237, 303
Social Democratic Workingmen's Party of North America, 32
Socialist Appeal, 175
Socialist Call, 153, 155
Socialist Labor party, 32–61 *passim,* 304, 308
Socialist party: birth of, 36–47;

founding convention, 40; membership, 41, 42, 53, 57, 58, 76, 164, 210; and capitalism, 46–48, 305; "golden age," 43, 46–48; and government harassment, 53; and World War I, 22–24, 47–53, 211, 212, 312; and labor, 42, 43, 47, 60–68, 105, 128, 171–178, 190–203; under Debs' leadership, 43–45, 57–67; and Marxism, 46, 106, 107, 113–115, 126, 127, 131, 143, 307; presidential campaign 1916, 49; National Convention 1917, 50; and Communism, 54–57, 105, 114, 120–124, 144, 145, 154–156, 165, 166, 171, 172, 178, 181, 187, 188, 200, 201, 302–304, 312; and CPPA, 60–68; and LID, 73; under Thomas, 74–78, 104–241, 294–316; and League for Independent Political Action, 105–106; and the Progressives, 106–108, 113; and the old guard-militant controversy, 104–114, 124–165; and the Depression, 75, 107, 128; National Convention 1932, 109; presidential campaign 1932, 112; and the New Deal, 105, 111, 116–120, 162, 171, 188–191, 202, 210, 302, 312; and fascism, 105, 112–114, 130, 131, 142, 149; National Convention 1934, 125–150, 154, 306; National Convention 1936, 161, 164, 165; presidential campaign 1936, 224; militants (after 1936), 173, 174; Clarity group, 173; Appeal group or Trotskyites, 174–178; and Spanish Civil War, 175, 177, 203–205, 308; National Convention 1938, 200–203; National Convention 1940, 206, 207; presidential campaign 1940, 224; attitude toward war, 129, 131, 149, 202–211; and World War II, 105, 205–230; National Convention 1942, 212; National Convention 1948, 297; presidential campaign 1948, 230, 233; and socialist elections activities, 235, 236; presidential campaign 1952 and 1956, 236, 237; becomes "Socialist Party–Social Democratic Federation" 1957, 237, 316; cancels Socialist presidential campaign, 237; and theory, 252, 253; reasons for decline, 67, 68, 127, 165, 211; assessment as party, 302–310, 312–316

Socialist Trade and Labor Alliance. *See* Socialist Labor party, 34, 35

Socialist Unionists, 193. *See also* Socialist party: and labor

Socialist Voice, 143, 144, 146

Socialist Workers party, 196

Solomon, Charles, 144

Sorge, F. A., 31

Southern Tenant Farmers' Union. *See* Agricultural Workers' Union

Soviet Union, 179–187, 259, 261, 279–283, 286, 287

Spanish Civil War, 175, 203–205, 308

Spanish Refugee Aid, Inc., 241, 319

Spargo Report, 50

Sparkman, John, 237

Spring Street Settlement House, 12

Sproul, Robert G., 245

Stalin, Joseph, 172, 177–187 *passim*, 256, 275, 278, 279, 280, 286, 308

"Statement for the Majority in Defense of the Declaration of Principles," 137

"Statement for the Minority in Opposition to the Declaration of Principles," 138

Steffens, Lincoln, 36

Stevenson, Adlai, 238, 265

Stewart, Frances Violet. *See* Thomas, Frances Violet

Stewart, John A. (grandfather of Mrs. NT), 13

Stokes, J. C. Phelps, 53

Stolberg, Benjamin, 199

Stone, Ezra, 245

Swados, Harvey, 331

Tarbell, Ida M., 36

Teheran Conference, 278

Ten Commandments, 325

Third International, 54, 55, 57, 74, 124

Third party–CPPA, 62–67

"Thirty Reasons Why the Declaration Should be Defeated," 144

Thomas, Arthur (brother of NT), 19

Thomas, Becky (daughter of NT), 101

Thomas-Browder Debate, 155, 156

Thomas, Emma (mother of NT), 6, 7, 13, 19, 20

Thomas, Evan (brother of NT), 7, 19, 71, 101

Thomas, Evan (son of NT), 101, 332

Thomas, Frances (daughter of NT), 101

Thomas, Frances Violet (wife of NT), 100

Thomas-Goldwater Debate, 324–325

Thomas, Norman (son of NT), 101

Thomas, Norman: personality and appeal, 1–3, 9, 77, 79–84, 88–97, 102, 103, 235, 245, 248, 249, 300, 319–321, 339–342; ancestry and family, 3–8, 13, 16, 19, 20, 71, 101, 209; childhood, 3, 4; education, 3, 7–14, 312; and religion, 3, 4, 12–21 *passim*, 25, 26, 71, 72, 77, 245, 253–256, 275, 276, 291, 292, 300, 325; adolescence, 7, 8; and socialism, 10, 12, 15, 16, 22–29, 184, 185, 259, 260, 265–275 *passim*, 278, 284–287 *passim*, 292; as minister, 12–15 *passim*, 27; trip around the world, 13; and capitalism, 12, 166–169 *passim*, 266, 267, 273, 281, 287; marriage and children, 13, 14, 70, 100–102, 311; and World War I, 16–22 *passim*, 48, 215, 275–278; and democracy, 17, 84, 207, 213, 214, 257, 263, 269, 275–278 *passim*, 281, 286–288, 292, 293; and war, 22, 23, 136, 147, 163, 166, 202–207, 212, 213, 240, 275–277; and Socialist party, 22–28, 69, 74–82, 90, 104–241 *passim*, 295–316; and organizational activities, 26, 27, 84, 115; and the "Red scare," 69–71; and Senate Committee Investigation, 70; and the Soviet Union, 71, 85, 178–187, 279–287; and Irish Freedom, 72; and Communism, 75, 82, 122–125, 155, 156, 166, 178–181, 186, 225,

231, 246, 261, 279–282, 286, 287, 289–291, 295, 322–323, 326; and League for Industrial Democracy, 73–78 *passim,* 87, 105; and National Conventions of Socialist party, 75 (1928), 109, 110 (1932), 125–139 (1934), 161, 164, 165 (1936), 200–202, (1938), 206, 207 (1940), 297 (1948), 235, 236 (1950), 212 (1942); and presidential campaigns, 75, 76 (1928), 109, 111, 112 (1932), 163–166 (1936), 207, 208 (1940), 214–224 (1944), 230–234 (1948); and labor, 77, 85, 97–100, 172, 190–193, 198–203, 244, 245, 289, 300, 313; civil liberties and freedom, 84–85, 179–181 *passim,* 187, 213–214, 246, 263, 285–293, 326–329; and the New Deal, 85, 116–120 *passim,* 188–189, 202, 217, 226, 228, 267; and W W II, 85, 205–216, 220, 228–231, 263, 267, 277–279; and Truman, 90, 93, 231–232, 238; and Franklin D. Roosevelt, 93, 117, 118–120, 163, 204–209, 214, 216–222, 224–228, 231, 232, 267, 278, 313; and Thomas Dewey, 90–93 *passim,* 231; attitude toward Democrats and Republicans, 97, 218–220 *passim,* 225, 226, 230, 231, 238–240, 331–336; and the old guard-militant controversy, 104, 105, 109–114, 124, 125, 134–165, 295, 296; and Marxism, 113, 134, 136, 147, 148, 258–262, 267; and fascism, 125, 147, 155, 163, 173, 179–187 *passim,* 204, 205, 206, 212, 225, 277, 278, 286, 289; and the Declaration of Principles, 132–136 *pas-*

sim, 139–151, 296–297; and the farmer-labor movement, 151, 167, 170; the 1936 campaign interview, 165–170; and the "all-inclusive party," 171–178, 211, 295; and the Appeal group or Trotskyites, 175–178; and the Spanish Civil War, 203, 204, 205, 308; and the Japanese American problem, 213–215; and Niebuhr, 217–224; and Mrs. Roosevelt, 225; and disarmament, 230, 241, 244, 279–285; reaction to presidential campaigns 1952–1960, 237–240; and McCarthyism, 243, 290; and American political thought, 251–257, 262–264, 292, 293; and the Depression, 261–263; and the Fair Deal, 267; and "democratic socialism," 268–274, 286, 287; and the United Nations, 281–285; the "four strands" of his agenda for peace, 281–285; "outstanding problems of freedom," 288–293; compared to Eugene V. Debs, 311–313; assessment as party leader, 294–302, 311–317; "America's Conscience," 301; reactions to war in Vietnam, 321–324; Thomas-Goldwater Debate, 324, 340; evaluation of garrison state, 325–327; civil rights, 329–331; appraisal of Kennedy administration, 331–334; analysis of Great Society, 334–336; evaluation of welfare state, 335

Thomas, Polly (daughter of NT), 101

Thomas, Ralph (brother of NT), 19, 20, 209

Thomas, Thomas (paternal grandfather of NT), 5
Thomas, Welling E. (father of NT), 3, 5, 6, 16, 18
Thomas, William (son of NT), 101
Thompson, Dorothy, 235
Thornton, Willis, 165–170
Townley, Arthur C., 60
Tresca, Carlo, 205
Trotsky, Leon, 172–181 *passim,* 213, 301
Trotskyites. *See* Socialist party: Appeal group
Truman, Harry, 90, 93, 231, 232, 237, 243
Turn Toward Peace, 319
Twenty-one Points, 54–56
Tyler, August, 173, 211

Union for Democratic Action. *See* Americans for Democratic Action
United Automobile Workers, 98, 99, 100, 193, 196, 197
United Communist party, 57
"United front," 122–124
United Mine Workers Union of America, 60, 195
United Nations, 216, 221, 281, 284–285

Vandenberg, Arthur, 243
Viereck, Peter, 245, 246
Vietnamese War, 321–324, 337–338
Villard, Oswald Garrison, 70, 73, 105, 235

Vladeck, Charney, 110, 132, 140, 141, 142, 159

Wagner Act, 194
Waldman, Louis, 132, 135, 139–141, 156, 157, 161, 190, 199
Walker, James, 93
Wallace, Henry A., 9, 220, 222, 231, 232
Ward, Dr. Harry, 14
War Resisters League, 19
Wechsler, James, 94
WEVD radio station, N.Y., 165
Wheeler, Burton K., 62, 209
Willkie, Wendell, 92, 208
Wilson, Woodrow, 11, 20, 37, 49, 50, 53, 70, 71, 88, 166, 252
Wirth, Louis, 245
Women's Trade Union League, 61
Workers Defense League, 241, 328
Workers' party, 57
Workingmen's International Association, 31
Workingmen's Party of the United States, 32
Workmen's Circle, 165
World War I, 15–24 *passim,* 47–53, 211, 212, 275–278, 312
World War II, 105, 205–230, 232, 250, 302
Worthy, William, 328

Yalta and Potsdam conferences, 231, 232
Young People's Socialist League, 154–160

Zam, Herbert, 173